Children and the Church

CHILDREN AND THE CHURCH

"Do Not Hinder Them"

Edited by

William den Hollander
Gerhard H. Visscher

CHILDREN AND THE CHURCH: "DO NOT HINDER THEM"

Copyright © 2019 by Publication Foundation of the Canadian Reformed Theological Seminary. All rights reserved. Except for brief quotations in critical publications or reviews, no part of this book may be reproduced in any manner without prior written permission from the Publication Foundation of the Canadian Reformed Theological Seminary.

Website: www.canadianreformedseminary.ca.

Lucerna CRTS Publications
110 West 27th Street
Hamilton, ON, Canada
L9C 2A1

ISBN 13: 978-0-9950659-5-6

Ebook: 978-0-9950659-6-3

Library and Archives Canada Cataloguing in Publication

Title: Children and the church : "do not hinder them" / edited by William den Hollander, Gerhard H. Visscher.
Names: Den Hollander, William, editor. | Visscher, Gerhard H., 1953- editor.
Identifiers: Canadiana (print) 2020015219X | Canadiana (ebook) 20200152203 | ISBN 9780995065956 (softcover) | ISBN 9780995065963 (PDF)
Subjects: LCSH: Church work with children.
Classification: LCC BV639.C4 C55 2019 | DDC 259/.22–dc23

Contents

Contributors	vii
Acknowledgments	ix
Preface	xi
"Do Not Hinder Them": Children in the Gospels *Gerhard H. Visscher*	1
Reading with Ancient Eyes: Children, Households, and Baptism in the First-Century World *William den Hollander*	11
Peter, Paul, and the Promises of God to the Children of Believers *Gerhard H. Visscher*	31
Growing Up into Christ: Renewing the Pathway to Maturity in the Church *Bill DeJong*	45
Children, Passover, and Lord's Supper *Cornelis Van Dam*	73
Let the Children Receive the Sign of the Covenant *Jason Van Vliet*	103
Pearls, Gifts, and Beggars: Infant Baptism in the Early Church *Tyler J. Vandergaag*	137
"Whoever Is of God Has the Spirit of God": Children in the Reformation Documents, with Particular Reference to Heinrich Bullinger and Guido de Brès *Theodore G. Van Raalte*	153
"Sanctified in Christ" *Arjen Vreugdenhil*	181
Mature in Christ: The Practice of Covenant Nurture in American Presbyterianism *Eric B. Watkins*	201

Contributors

Dr. Bill DeJong is Minister of the Word at Blessings Christian Church in Hamilton, Ontario, Canada

Dr. William den Hollander is presently Minister of the Word at Langley Canadian Reformed Church in Langley, British Columbia, Canada, and has been appointed Professor of New Testament at the Canadian Reformed Theological Seminary in Hamilton, Ontario, Canada

Dr. Cornelis Van Dam is Professor Emeritus of Old Testament at the Canadian Reformed Theological Seminary in Hamilton, Ontario, Canada

Rev. Tyler J. Vandergaag is Minister of the Word at Taber Canadian Reformed Church in Taber, Alberta, Canada

Dr. Theodore G. Van Raalte is Professor of Ecclesiology at the Canadian Reformed Theological Seminary in Hamilton, Ontario, Canada

Dr. Jason Van Vliet is Professor of Dogmatology at the Canadian Reformed Theological Seminary in Hamilton, Ontario, Canada

Dr. Gerhard H. Visscher is Professor of New Testament at the Canadian Reformed Theological Seminary in Hamilton, Ontario, Canada

Rev. Arjen Vreugdenhil is Minister of the Word at Eben-Ezer Canadian Reformed Church in Chatham, Ontario, Canada

Dr. Eric B. Watkins is Minister of the Word at Covenant Presbyterian Church in St. Augustine, Florida, U.S.A.

Acknowledgments

This book has its origins in conferences organized by the Canadian Reformed Theological Seminary and held on January 17-19, 2019, in Burlington, Ontario, and January 24-26, 2019, in Langley, British Columbia. The conferences, like this volume, had as their main focus the topic "Children and the Church" and welcomed engaged audiences in both locations.

The editors wish to acknowledge all those who were involved in the organization and running of the conferences. We would like to highlight the efforts of Mrs. Leanne Kuizenga, the Faculty Administrative Assistant at CRTS, whose tireless labours make these regular conferences run smoothly and efficiently. We would also like to thank those who presented at the conference, served on the panels, and contributed to the discussions as participants or audience members.

We are grateful to Dr. William Helder for his meticulous work in editing the papers included in this volume and assisting throughout the publication process. We also thank Rev. Ryan J. Kampen for his expert efforts in preparing the book for publication. Credit for the attractive cover layout and design belongs to Mrs. Lynn VanEerden.

May this volume serve to sharpen our understanding of the place of children in the church and deepen our joy and delight in the abounding grace of our covenant God.

Preface

It has become popular in Christian circles, as any Google search will show, to play with the terms *believe, behave, belong* and, in particular, to consider their proper order. While these words are used for varied purposes, we can also use them to reflect on the question of children and the church. If we survey the broader landscape, the approach often seems to follow along the lines of *behave, believe, belong*—at least in practice, if not in principle. As you parent the children God gives, the first objective is to see to it that they *behave*. You want them to do only good things: to show respect, to treat others kindly. You dread the possibility that the children might embarrass you and show patterns that are far from Christian. So, *behave* is then first. You tell them in the morning to please act in such a manner and investigate in the evening whether it has been done approximately so. As you journey through the years with them, you sincerely hope that they will also *believe* and profess their faith. You have prayed for it earnestly, your hearts have yearned for it, and it has been the goal of so much of your instruction. When they finally do so, you breathe a sigh of relief with the assurance that they also *belong*. You become convinced now that they belong not just to you, but to God. A highpoint of your life is when you see that visibly as you sit together with your children, and maybe grandchildren, not only at the family table but, even better, at the table of our Lord, eating his broken body and drinking his shed blood.

While at first glance this may look to be an acceptable approach, one of the objectives of this book, with all its varied essays, is to show you that it fails to account for the privileged place God has given children in the (old and new) covenant community. A Reformed and—we are convinced—truly scriptural approach tells us that we ought to see children of believers as *belonging* already from birth, and even conception. The old and new covenant Scriptures tell us that the promise is theirs (Gen 17:7; Acts 2:39). The Psalms never approach children as if they are outside of the covenant circle (cf. Pss 8, 78, 127, 128). They also attest to our experience that little children on the laps of parents seldom if ever express doubt as they hear "the glorious deeds of the Lord, and his might, and the wonders he has done" (Ps 78:4). The opening Lord's Day of the Heidelberg Catechism was written for the benefit of the children first of all, so that they might grow up professing, "I *belong* with body and soul, both in life and in death, to my faithful Saviour Jesus Christ." In this way the words of our Lord Jesus echo through the confessions into Reformed homes: "to such *belongs* the kingdom of God" (Mark 10:14).

Of course, this does not mean that they do not need to *believe*. Children as well as adults need to embrace the promises of God. The whole church needs to reflect on the truth that our Lord spoke to a rabbi of Israel: "Unless one is born of water and the Spirit, he cannot enter the kingdom of God" (John 3:5). This reality sinks into the hearts of Christian parents already in the second sentence of the classic Reformed Form for the Baptism of Infants, which teaches that our children are "by nature children of wrath, so that we cannot enter the kingdom of God unless we are born again" (*Book of Praise*, 597). But the strength of Christian child-rearing rests and builds upon the promises of God to these same children.

As for *behaving*, hopefully it will happen frequently. But while general rules of morality and human expectation might be of some benefit here, new behaviour patterns develop all the more powerfully through grafting into the vine that is Jesus Christ (John 15:5; Rom 8:3, cf. Heidelberg Catechism, Q&A 64, 86). Right behaviour is then a demonstration of the transforming power of the gospel. It is above all by faith and by the indwelling Spirit that they will bear fruit and *behave* as great sons and daughters of a glorious and gracious Father.

The overarching argument of this book is, therefore, that it should not be *behave, believe, belong*. Instead, recognizing that our children *belong* already, we need to give them a sense of belonging. We need to bring them up in the grace and security of the covenant promises of God. We need to cultivate *faith* and *belief* in that gracious context and, under God's care and blessing, God-pleasing *behaviour* will be there in abundance.

In this volume we offer you a selection of papers addressing this theme in various ways. Most of these contributions first made an appearance as presentations at back-to-back conferences in Burlington, Ontario, and Langley, British Columbia, in January 2019.

Gerhard H. Visscher offers us two essays, the first on the perspective of our Lord Jesus on the position of children, and the second on the view of the apostles Peter and Paul in the same regard. In both contributions he makes the point that the children of believing parents belong. They belong in the loving embrace of Jesus, under his blessing hands, and they belong in the new covenant community.

William den Hollander takes a close look at the Book of Acts and how baptism was administered in apostolic times, particularly in the context of households. He places the household baptisms of the early church firmly in their Graeco-Roman world to argue that the first-century reader would have assumed the inclusion of infants on these occasions.

Bill DeJong provides a biblical and historical survey of how Christian maturity has been viewed, how it ought to be regarded in our day, and how that ought to shape the way we disciple youth in the church.

Cornelis Van Dam examines the biblical data for children's participation in the Passover of the old covenant, as well as for the precise relationship between that old covenant meal and the Lord's Supper of the new covenant, and explores the ramifications for our understanding of who may participate.

Jason Van Vliet investigates the biblical evidence for the way in which signs and sacraments are to be regarded and considers how our Reformed confessions conform to that. Along the way he makes the important argument that the sacrament of baptism is a sign of the promises of God and a seal of their reliability, and thus should not be denied to the children of the covenant, who have indeed received these very promises.

Tyler J. Vandergaag considers the apostolic age of the church in his contribution to this volume, investigating in particular the writings of Tertullian, Gregory of Nazianzus, and Augustine. He demonstrates the diversity of viewpoints in the early church regarding baptism and the challenge this presents as we continue to strive to realize the unity of the faith.

Theodore G. Van Raalte takes a close look at the Reformation period with a view to the question how children of believers were regarded at that time. He explores the writings of Guido de Brès and Heinrich Bullinger, focusing on the ways in which they used Scripture to make their case.

Arjen Vreugdenhil examines carefully the history and significance of the expression in the previously mentioned Form for the Baptism of Infants that children are "sanctified in Christ." He makes it clear that the truth of this phrase is both a comfort for Christian parents and a call for them to take seriously their responsibility to nurture their children in the Christian faith.

Lastly, Eric B. Watkins gives us insight into how confessional Presbyterians seek to develop maturity in Christian youth. He presents the results of a survey he conducted within the OPC and PCA regarding their practice of catechesis and the communicant membership vows they require and provides pastoral reflections on the strengths and weaknesses of these approaches.

This volume, as were the above-mentioned conferences, is motivated by the desire to demonstrate that the scriptural truth that the children of believers belong to God and thus ought to be baptized and treated accordingly is not a doctrine to be sacrificed or neglected but cherished as foundational for Christian churches and families everywhere. The book is therefore dedicated to all the children of believers around the world, but especially to those born to and loved by its contributors.

William den Hollander
Gerhard H. Visscher
editors

"Do Not Hinder Them": Children in the Gospels

Gerhard H. Visscher

There is little doubt that our culture is very dismissive of children. As adults, we seldom gauge their opinions, appreciate their attitudes, or engage them in conversation in any serious way. They are of no or little account in today's world—little people who are there, but aren't, and will count only some time later.[1]

Among the many surprising things about the ministry of our Lord Jesus, there is this clear fact: his positive, appreciative approach toward children. He fails to make our mistakes, even here. In every possible way, the Old Testament affirmative approach to children resonates in the Gospels and in the life of our Lord.

Two Special Children

Before observing our Lord interacting with children, though, we would be remiss if we overlooked the obvious fact that according to the Gospels, Jesus came into the world not as an adult, but as a child himself. Two of the Gospels go to great lengths to tell us about the birth and infancy of both Jesus and John the Baptizer. We are even told that Jesus, like all other Jewish boys of his day, was circumcised on the eighth day (Luke 2:21; Gal. 4:4-5). Noting the Old Testament background, in which marriage and children were valued highly (e.g., Psalm 127), Charles A. Gieschen suggests:

> The genealogies and birth narratives concerning Jesus in the Gospels of Matthew and Luke provide additional testimony to the value of the created order of marriage blessed with children. These genealogies testify to the

---

1. For a very interesting discussion on this, see Postman, *The Disappearance of Childhood*, 150. He complains that today's culture has "adultified" childhood and "childified" adulthood. "American adults want to be parents of children less than they want to be children themselves."

pattern of children as the means by which God fulfills his promise to multiply Abraham's offspring and to bless all nations (e.g., Gen 12:2-3; 17:6).[2]

Similarly, the narratives about the birth of Jesus and John provide a testimony to the value and the miracle of life in the birth of children. Even life in the womb is highlighted as the pre-born John greets his Saviour (Luke 1:43). In the context of the birth of the son of Abraham and David, the son of God, the reader of Matthew's Gospel is horrified as this precious birth takes place in the very area where the innocent boys of Bethlehem were slaughtered (Matt 2:16-18). And one of the most profound testimonies to the value of children and the Child resonates from John's Gospel as he describes the wonder with one powerful sentence: "The Word became flesh."[3]

The Kingdom Belongs to the Children

As for the rest of the Gospels, when we take note of the words and actions of our Lord Jesus at face value, there are very strong indications that children are included in the Kingdom.

Of course, most famous of these passages are the synoptic accounts of Jesus welcoming the children, contrary to the expectation of the disciples (Mark 10:13-16; Matt 19:13-15; Luke 18:15-17). As Judith Gundry puts it, "This text is particularly significant in that it combines Jesus' *teaching about* little children and the kingdom of God and Jesus' *ministry to* children and shows the relationship between them."[4]

Before we get into this, it is worthwhile to notice whose children these are. Notice that according to all three Gospels this event happens in Judea, in the very heart of the Jewish world. So surely, in all likelihood, these are covenant kids. Jewish boys and girls. Luke even frames the passage between the Parable of the Pharisee and the Tax Collector and the Parable of the Rich Young Ruler,[5] who is also Jewish (Luke 18:21). In

---

2. Gieschen, "The Value of Children According to the Gospels," 195-211.

3. On all this, see also Gieschen, 198-201.

4. Gundry, "Children in the Gospel of Mark, with Special Attention to Jesus' Blessing of the Children (Mark 10:13-16) and the Purpose of Mark," 149.

5. "Ruler" does not necessarily refer to a person with civic authority. BDAG suggests that the reference is to one of the Jewish leaders, perhaps a member of the Sanhedrin, who had a leading role in Israel.

the context of the high and mighty of Israel, we are told about lowly children.

What motivates the adults who are bringing the children? Here, too, we have a Jewish motive.

According to Jewish sources it was the custom of Jewish parents to bring their children to the scribes on the eve of the Day of Atonement. We read there that parents would bring them to the scribes in order that they might lay their hands on them in blessing and prayer so that the children might one day "attain to the knowledge of the Law and good works."[6]

So perhaps the parents are acknowledging something of the authority and the greatness of Jesus. But clearly, they are in one line with the Jewish belief which considered the children to be part of the covenant community. Strikingly, Luke refers to them bringing not just "children" (*paidia*, Matt 19:13; Mark 10:13) but "infants" (*brefh*, Luke 18:15); this is in keeping, no doubt, with Luke's theme of including those who would otherwise be marginalized.

What's the reaction of our Lord? He rebukes the disciples for their rebuke and orders the children to be brought to him. Mark even references Jesus' anger here (Mark 10:14).

And then notice several surprising things about how our Lord relates to these children. Notice that he gives to children the things they need the most, also today.

First of all, he gives them *time*. Children are not marginal to Jesus. He takes out time for them. As all three Gospels point out, he even emphasizes it with a double command: *"Let the children come to me."* "*Do not hinder them*" from being here with me.

Second, he assures them that they belong. What do children need more than assurance that they belong and are loved? Jesus assures them by saying something he never says to any adult: *"for it is to such as these that the kingdom of God belongs."*

Third, he also gives them his *touch*. Both Mark and Luke mention this (Mark 10:13; Luke 18:15), and Mark even has Jesus taking the children in his arms (Mark 10:16). Also in that ancient culture, appropriate touch was a way of making it clear that the little ones mattered.

---

6. *Soferim* 18.5 is one of the smaller "non-canonical" treatises of the Talmud; s.v. "Soferim," *Encyclopedia Judaica*, 12:82.

Fourth, in obvious Jewish fashion, Matthew even frames the story with references to the fact that Jesus "laid his hands on them" (Matt 19: 13, 15). Clearly, this is a special touching—it is the touch of *blessing*, as Mark also makes clear (10:16): he "blessed them, laying his hands on them."[7] Say Davies and Allison, "The hands are not for the healing of disease or defect but for the transmission of blessing."[8] Surely it is noteworthy that precisely this sign of inclusion among God's people is given to the little ones. One needs to ask the question: are blessings usually given to those who are not among the people of God?

And then there's a fifth. Matthew adds one more verb to the actions of our Lord Jesus. The children are brought to Jesus, according to verse 13, in order that he might lay his hands on them "*and pray*." The parents live under the Mishnaic understanding that their little ones are included among the people of God and that respectable rabbis will both bless and pray for their little ones.[9]

In any case, a first conclusion here certainly is *that covenant children do belong to the community of God's people, and any position which fails to fully recognize this disagrees with both the words and the example of our Lord Jesus.*

Calvin says it appropriately for us:

> This narrative is highly useful; for it shows that Christ receives not only those who, moved by holy desire and faith, freely approach to him, but those who are not yet of age to know how much they need his grace. Those little children have not yet any understanding to desire his blessings; but when they are presented to him, he gently and kindly receives them . . . . We must observe the intention of those who present the children; for if there had not been a deep-rooted conviction in their minds, that the power of the Spirit was at his disposal, that he might pour it out on the people of God, it would have been unreasonable to present their children.[10]

---

7. The participle following the main verb should be understood as indicating an accompanying circumstance. France, *The Gospel According to Mark*, 398: "Jesus . . . gave the children a *thorough* blessing."

8. Davies and Allison, *A Critical and Exegetical Commentary on the Gospel According to Saint Matthew*, 3:33. They also reference Gen 48:14, Deut 34:9, and Acts 8:17.

9. There is a very interesting suggestion by Derrett that seventeenth- and eighteenth-century scholars already regarded Jesus' blessing of the children as analogous to Jacob's blessing Joseph through the blessing he gives to Ephraim and Manasseh. The gesture suggests, as it were, that Ephraim and Manasseh were sons to Jacob. "Jesus' hug, therefore, can be seen as an adoptive embrace, an assumption of a parental role," comments Gundry. See Derrett, "Why Jesus Blessed the Children (Mk 10:13–16 par.)." Cf. Gundry, "Children in the Gospel of Mark," 154–56.

10. Calvin, *Commentary on a Harmony of the Evangelists, Matthew, Mark, and Luke*, 389.

Or in the words of the classic commentator C. E. B. Cranfield:

> To find the reason why the kingdom of God belongs to children in any subjective qualities of the children is surely to misunderstand; the reason is rather to be found in their objective humbleness: the fact that they are weak and helpless and unimportant, and in the fact that God has chosen "the weak things of the world" (1 Cor 1:26ff.; cf. Matt 9:25f.=Luke 10:21).[11]

I find it also striking how often children surface in the Gospels. One remarkable detail is that in all the Synoptic Gospels (Matt 17:14; Mark 9:14; Luke 9:37) the Transfiguration is immediately followed by the healing of a *boy* with an evil spirit. It is a climactic moment with Moses and Elijah, about the coming suffering, and the "restoration of all things." The restoration begins, it seems, with the healing of a little one!

And shortly thereafter, in Matthew and Mark, we hear how strongly our Lord feels about this point concerning the children when he speaks about those who cause "little ones who believe in [him] to sin." He says: "*If anyone [does that]. . . , it would be better for him to be thrown into the sea with a large millstone tied around his neck*" (Mark 9:42; Matt 18:6; cf. Luke 17:2). Obviously, it means: cursed are those who abuse children and lead them astray. It means: the church should not be the last but the first to see that this is horrendous stuff. The Lord of the church will not tolerate this. But it is no less of a stern voice when it comes to the matter of excluding children whom the Head of the Church means to include. Today's discussion needs to be considered also in the light of these words.

People sometimes accuse Canadian Reformed folk of teaching a version of presumptive regeneration. We presume our children are regenerate, they say. While we may not baptize them on the basis of presumptive regeneration, we do presume regeneration thereafter. Presume they are converted? Really? It's rather ironic, given our history. The truth is: it is wrong to presume that your children are all right just because they are born to you as a believing parent. But it is equally wrong to presume they are unbelievers, is it not? You don't talk to them the way you talk to your unbelieving neighbours, do you? They understand you.

---

11. Cranfield, *The Gospel According to Mark*, 324. Cf. Gundry, "Children in the Gospel of Mark," 150–54: "Why does the kingdom of God belong to little children? Apparently just because they need it. Need is the reason for Jesus' welcoming at his table tax collectors and sinners. It is those who recognize their need by coming to Jesus who benefit from his ministry, as also implied in his healing and exorcizing evil spirits for those who seek him out."

If you have taught them properly, then already at a young age they know who Jesus is. They know what he is all about. But as you address them, you presume neither absolute faith nor unbelief, but you address them as *covenant children*. Because they belong. They are people like you—they believe, but they have to continue to be called to faith!

In a wonderful article Robert S. Rayburn, a PCA pastor, argues that "grace runs in the line of generations." He provides all the biblical and historical support to be able to say, "I do not hesitate to claim that far and away the largest part of the Christian church at any time or place . . . are those who were born and raised in Christian families." The only exception to this is "that historical moment when the gospel first reaches a place and a people."[12] The Lord Jesus, to be sure, is in one line with the Old Testament and the later apostolic positions on children.

As James V. Brownson points out, "The New Covenant is not a *substitute* for a failed Old Covenant . . . but rather its extension and completion. . . . What was most central to the Old Covenant is deepened and expanded in the New."[13] Faith, allegiance, the work of the Spirit, family blessings are deepened and more central in the New.

The Kingdom Belongs to the Childlike

That leads us to a second point and conclusion here.

Our Lord is not only making it clear here that children are included. He is also making it clear here that *no one else will be included unless they are—in many respects—like these children.* For notice what else our Lord says. Mark 10:15: "*Whoever does not receive the kingdom of God like a child shall not enter it.*"

What is the point? This: if you read the Gospel of Mark by itself as one continuous book (as you really ought to do with each Gospel), you would see that for Mark this is the foremost question: does anyone know who Jesus is? Very strikingly, at the very beginning of the book, Mark makes it clear that the demons do. That is why Jesus shuts them up after the first chapter or two, and they don't speak again about the subject. But the great question of the book is: *does anyone else know what the demons*

---

12. Rayburn, "The Presbyterian Doctrines of Covenant Children, Covenant Nurture, and Covenant Succession," 96.

13. Brownson, *The Promise of Baptism*, 117.

know? And the point here is: *if anyone is going to get the answer right, they are going to have to have the attitude of a child.* They must have the faith of a child.

Already here, we are being told: access to the kingdom comes not by works, but by faith, of grace. The simplicity of a childlike faith is elevated. It's still true today. Children, properly instructed, will believe. In the process of growing up, they might waver and be tossed to and fro, but they will believe. Have you ever known a child who just heard about Adam and Eve, or about Noah and the ark, or about Jonah and the fish—have you ever known a child to stand up and say to mom or dad: now, I just can't believe that; it can't be true. No, the approach of a child is: this is my mom or my dad who tells me this; this is the Bible, God's book, this story in it—of course, it's true.

And that is what the Lord is talking about. It is in this respect that we have to become childlike. In our faith.

If we really take all the words of our Lord Jesus at face value, then we have to say that the great question of the Gospels is not whether children belong in the kingdom. But the greater question seems to be: *are there any adults here?* It is striking that in the Gospels there is not one time that our Lord puts children down. Instead, he is always lifting them up.

Throughout the Gospels the message of this passage is being reaffirmed: to such, *to persons like this,* belongs the kingdom of heaven. I think of Matthew 11, where he speaks to adults and tells them a hard truth—hard for proud adults—*that the things of God are hidden from the wise and learned . . . but they are revealed to little children* (11:25)! And how often don't we hear of him taking a *child*, putting that child in the midst of them and saying: See this? This is your model. *Unless you turn and become like this child, you will never enter the kingdom of heaven.*

So, too, later—even in his final days, when our Lord comes into Jerusalem riding on a donkey (Matthew 21) and the children are crying out, "Hosanna to the Son of David!" and the chief priests and the scribes are indignant, Jesus says it is music to his ears. He refers them to Psalm 8, to the fulfilment of prophecy, and says: "*Have you never read, 'From the lips of children and infants you have ordained praise'?*" It means: even the praise of children is a blessed thing to our Lord.

The strange truth of the gospel—hard for us adults—is: here it is not children who are to model themselves after adults, but *it is the adults who are to model themselves after children.* Covenant children are the ones who teach us faith, trust, and humility. But the adults? Covenant adults are the ones who reject him, remember? The adults were the ones who opposed him their whole life long and caused him so much grief. They were the ones who nailed him to the cross. Why, when you take a look at it all, you might very well be inclined to ask at times whether any *adults* were admitted to the circle of those who believe in him.[14]

The great problem of the Gospels is not *childhood*. The problem is *adulthood*. The problem is not that children cannot be adults. The problem is that *adults have difficulty staying like children in terms of faith, trust, and humility*. The challenge is for children and adults to keep believing with childlike simplicity and faith.

There is a wonderful paragraph in Cranfield's commentary on Mark again:

> The reference in ὡς παιδίον again is not to the receptiveness of humility or imaginativeness or trustfulness or unselfconsciousness of children, but to their objective littleness and helplessness. To receive the kingdom as a little child is to allow oneself to be given it, because one knows one cannot claim it as one's right or attempt to earn it. (To think of any subjective qualities of children here is to turn faith into a work.) Jn iii.3, 5 seem to be the Johannine version of this saying and provide an illuminating comment upon it. Nicodemus has to learn that he cannot enter the kingdom of God as a learned theologian and highly respected religious leader; if he is to enter it at all, it must be as one who is helpless and small, without claim or merit.[15]

You see, the great challenge of growing up in the church is not just: will the kids believe? But it is: will the adults *and* the kids believe? Will *everyone* embrace the promises of God, and be content to receive them—of grace, through faith, not because of merit, not because they are so good but just because of the perfect work of Christ? We see it repeatedly, don't we? It's a challenge to just remain at the simplicity of

---

14. A similar approach is taken by Bavinck, *Reformed Dogmatics*, 4:528: "Like John, Jesus appears on the scene with the message: 'Repent and believe the gospel!' He takes over John's baptism, thereby proclaiming that, despite their being circumcised, the Jews need repentance and forgiveness. The contrast gradually becomes so sharp that Jesus no longer expects anything from his people and they in turn reject him and hang him on a cross. Still, despite all this, he continues to regard their children as children of the covenant (Matt. 18:2ff.; 19:13ff.; 21:15–16.; Mark 10:13ff.; Luke 9:48; 18:15ff.). He calls them to himself, embraces them, lays hands on them, blesses them, tells them that theirs is the kingdom of heaven, marks them as an example to adults, warns the latter not to offend them, says that their angels watch over them, and reads their hosannas as a fulfillment of the prophecy that God has made the speech of children a power by which those who hate him are silenced, and he has ordained praise (αἰνον, ainon; LXX) from their lips."

15. Cranfield, 324.

childhood. Too often it is adolescence, teenage years, and adulthood that mess us up. Oh, to receive it like a child!

In many respects, then, children are not unlike the adults. They belong to God. They have the promises of God. But to all there is the call to continued faith and repentance. For all, the promises of God are received of grace, through faith. The faith of a child, even if you're an adult.

Conclusions

Let's draw some conclusions. Can one prove infant baptism from the Gospels? Clearly not. That would be saying too much. But one can draw some foundational conclusions that support that direction.

1. *The Lord Jesus maintains the Old Testament conviction that covenant children do belong to the community of God's people. Any other position fails to fully recognize both the words and the example of our Lord Jesus.*
2. *If it is true that the New Testament is silent about the baptism of children, the approach of the Gospels, like that of the Old Testament, continues to support the high probability and expectation that children are included in the circle of those baptized in the New Testament era.*
3. *The church must function as a body which does everything necessary to be a place where children are safe, and must continue to be called to humility, faith, and repentance.*
4. *All adults, called to live by grace, are called likewise to the same humility, faith, and repentance.*

Bibliography

Bauer, Walter, Frederick W. Danker, W. F. Arndt, and F. W. Gingrich. A *Greek-English Lexicon of the New Testament and Other Early Christian Literature*. 3rd ed. (BDAG). Chicago: University of Chicago Press, 2000.

Bavinck, Herman. *Reformed Dogmatics*. Edited by John Bolt. Translated by John Vriend. Vol. 4. Grand Rapids: Baker Academic, 2008.

Brownson, James V. *The Promise of Baptism: An Introduction to Baptism in Scripture and the Reformed Tradition*. Grand Rapids: Eerdmans, 2007.

Calvin, John. *Commentary on a Harmony of the Evangelists, Matthew, Mark, and Luke*. Calvin's Commentaries. Vol. 16. Translated by William Pringle. Grand Rapids: Baker, 1979.

Cranfield, C. E. B. *The Gospel According to Mark*. The Cambridge Greek Testament Commentary. Cambridge: Cambridge University Press, 1977.

Davies, W. D., and Dale C. Allison. *A Critical and Exegetical Commentary on the Gospel According to Saint Matthew*. The International Critical Commentary. Vol. 3. Edinburgh: T&T Clark, 1997.

Derrett, J. Duncan. "Why Jesus Blessed the Children (Mk 10:13-16 par.)." *Novum Testamentum* 25, no. 1 (1983): 1-18.

Encyclopedia Judaica. Jerusalem: Keter Publishing House, 1978.

France, R. T. *The Gospel According to Mark*. New International Greek Testament Commentary. Grand Rapids: Eerdmans, 2002.

Gieschen, Charles A. "The Value of Children According to the Gospels." *Concordia Theological Quarterly* 77 (2013): 195-211.

Gundry, Judith M. "Children in the Gospel of Mark, with Special Attention to Jesus' Blessing of the Children (Mark 10:13-16) and the Purpose of Mark." In *The Child in the Bible*, edited by Marcia J. Bunge, 143-78. Grand Rapids: Eerdmans, 2008.

MacDonald, Margaret Y. *The Power of Children: The Construction of Christian Families in the Greco-Roman World*. Waco, TX: Baylor University Press, 2014.

Postman, Neil. *The Disappearance of Childhood*. New York: Vintage Books, 1984.

Rayburn, Robert S. "The Presbyterian Doctrines of Covenant Children, Covenant Nurture, and Covenant Succession." *Presbyterion* 22, no. 2 (1996): 76-112.

Reading with Ancient Eyes: Children, Households, and Baptism in the First-Century World

William den Hollander

While reading Scripture may appear to be a straightforward matter to the average person in the pew, the reality is that any interpretation faces two inseparable challenges. The first is a matter of language; because we are not native speakers of biblical Hebrew or Koine Greek, we need to translate Scripture into our own language(s), which can never render the original perfectly. The second is a question of culture; because we do not inhabit the world of the author, we cannot bring the necessary cultural artifacts to bear on the text, upon which the author relies (subconsciously) to communicate meaning.

Despite these challenges, however, we need not despair of recovering the intended meaning of these important texts. The fundamental reason for this is that the Holy Spirit, who inspired the authors of the text, also illuminates the believing reader, "[so] that we might understand the things freely given us by God" (1 Cor 2:12). This profound and mysterious reality cannot be forgotten. But that is not the only answer to this challenge. Until more recent efforts to dislodge meaning from the text and relocate it in the reader, it was understood that the better we understand the ancient language and the better we understand the ancient culture, the better we will perceive the intended meaning of the text. The answer to the challenge was (and is), therefore, to situate the text as thoroughly as possible within its ancient environment. Of course, it needs to be acknowledged that the Spirit cannot be and is not absent in this process either.

This paper takes such an approach to the question of the composition of the households (οἶκοι) that Acts records as being baptized.[1] More specifically, my aim is to consider the antecedent likelihood that infants,

---

1. Acts 16:15, 31–34; see also Acts 2:38–39; 10:2; 11:14; 18:8; John 4:53; 1 Cor 1:16; see Jeremias, *The Origins of Infant Baptism*, 25.

or at least small children, were present among those who were baptized, by presenting a picture of the Graeco-Roman household that would have informed the way readers understood such passages.[2] I will note from the outset that my primary aim is not to demonstrate that the passages themselves leave open the possibility that infants were included. In my view, the arguments of Jeremias some time ago and other scholars since have adequately demonstrated that infants cannot be excluded in these passages on exegetical grounds alone.[3] What I am investigating is the question whether first-century readers of these household passages would, on the basis of their prior understanding (i.e., presupposition) of how households in their world worked, have (subconsciously) included or excluded infants when reading of these household baptisms.[4] That is, I will bring to bear on these passages our (admittedly limited) knowledge of ancient households in an attempt to read these passages with first-century eyes.

I will focus in particular on three areas: the Roman householder's *patria potestas* (i.e., his power as head of the household); the child's official initiation into the household; and the involvement of children in the ritual life of the household. Against this backdrop I will argue that the nature of children's involvement in the Graeco-Roman household suggests that the first-century reader would have assumed the presence of children among those baptized or, at the very least, could not have assumed their absence. Furthermore, if infants were not in fact included in these household baptisms, it would have been necessary for the author to signal as much to communicate effectively with his audience.

---

2. My paper rests on the common historical understanding that the audience of Luke-Acts, of whom we know only "most excellent Theophilus (κράτιστε Θεόφιλε)" (Luke 1:3; Acts 1:1) by name, was comprised of literate Greeks and Romans, among whom some were of elite status, perhaps even from the city of Rome itself. The honorific given to Theophilus demonstrates his high status (cf. Acts 23:26; 24:3; 26:25) and suggests the possibility that he himself was of Roman equestrian status. For an extensive analysis of the audience of Luke-Acts, see Keener, *Acts*, 423–34.

3. Jeremias, *Infant Baptism in the First Four Centuries*, esp. 19–23; Jeremias, *The Origins of Infant Baptism*, 12–16; contra Aland, *Did the Early Church Baptize Infants?* 87–94.

4. For a similar investigation, see the excellent article of Nicoletti, "Infant Baptism in the First-Century Presupposition Pool," 271–92, who uses the social-scientific concept of "presupposition pools" to make much the same point I will be making in this paper. See also Watt, "The Oikos Formula," 70–84, for similar conclusions from a different angle.

Household Baptism in the New Testament

Before I begin this investigation, however, it will be good to consider briefly the evidence for the baptism of entire households that appears in the New Testament. A quick survey reveals just how important these household baptisms were to the early Christian church and, consequently, how important they ought to be for us as we craft our understanding of baptism in our present church context.

The first instance of baptism in the New Testament is found in Acts 2:41, where we are told: "Those who received [Peter's] word were baptized, and there were added that day about three thousand souls."[5] The second instance occurs when the gospel has reached Samaria: "When they believed Philip as he preached good news about the kingdom of God and the name of Jesus Christ, they were baptized, both men and women. Even Simon [the magician] himself believed, and after being baptized he continued with Philip" (Acts 8:13). Later in the same chapter Philip encounters the Ethiopian eunuch whom he also baptizes (8:38). Then there is the account of the apostle Paul's baptism (9:18). It is after this that we read about the baptism of Cornelius' household (10:48; 11:14), of Lydia's household (16:15), and of the Philippian jailer's household (16:33). Later yet, we are told that the ruler of the synagogue in Corinth, Crispus, believed "with his whole household" (18:8), and that subsequently many Corinthians were baptized (including, presumably, the household of Crispus). From Paul's first letter to the Corinthians we learn that Crispus was certainly among these, and also on this occasion or a later one the household of Stephanas (1 Cor 1:16). Finally, we learn from Acts again that the adult male disciples of John were also baptized after Paul instructed them regarding the coming of the Holy Spirit (19:5).

This quick summary of actual baptisms recorded in the New Testament reveals a startling detail, that of the nine people or groups of people singled out as having been baptized, five had their households baptized as well.[6] This becomes even more significant when we consider that neither the Ethiopian eunuch nor the apostle Paul had households themselves, which brings the ratio to five household baptisms out of seven possible instances, the two exceptions being Simon Magus and the

---

5. Unless otherwise noted, all translations are from the English Standard Version.
6. See Strawbridge, *Infant Baptism: Does the Bible Teach It?* 20–21.

disciples of John the Baptist. Household baptism was therefore certainly not an isolated or marginal occurrence.

As significant as the apparent pervasiveness of the practice is, even more important to consider for our purposes is the careful way in which these baptisms are described in the narrative. For this it is important to turn to the Greek text itself, rather than translations, since the NIV obscures the precision of the original.[7] The first place to stop is the baptism of Lydia's household. There we read that when Lydia heard the apostle Paul speaking, "the Lord opened her heart" (16:14; ὁ κύριος διήνοιξεν τὴν καρδίαν). What follows is that she is baptized (singular verb), together with her household (16:15; ἐβαπτίσθη καὶ ὁ οἶκος αὐτῆς).[8] It is important to note that it is only *her* faith that is noted explicitly, and that the baptism of the household is associated with *her* baptism. That is, the baptisms of these members of the household were dependent on her profession of faith and baptism. They were baptized by virtue of their membership in the household. We are not told anything about their own faith.

The significance of this careful use of language is even clearer when we turn to the account of the Philippian jailer. First of all, the promise of salvation comes to the jailer himself but is extended *through him* to the entire household. The language is again precise: "Believe [singular verb] in the Lord Jesus, and you will be saved [singular verb], you and your household" (16:31; Πίστευσον ἐπὶ τὸν κύριον Ἰησοῦν, καὶ σωθήσῃ σὺ καὶ ὁ οἶκός σου). The focus is on the jailer himself, with the command and the promise given in the singular, while the household is associated with him in the promise. The same goes for the account of the household baptism: "And he was baptized [singular verb] at once, he and all his [household]" (16:33; καὶ ἐβαπτίσθη αὐτὸς καὶ οἱ αὐτοῦ πάντες παραχρῆμα). Most importantly, however, when it comes to the profession of faith, the only explicit testimony is what we read regarding the jailer: "And he rejoiced with his whole household that *he had believed* [singular verb] in God" (16:34; καὶ

---

7. I rely here on the excellent work of Scott, "Dynamic Equivalence and Some Theological Problems in the NIV," 351–61, who has demonstrated that the NIV translation misleadingly renders the Greek of certain passages in such a way as to suggest that all those who were baptized believed in response to the presentation of the gospel, which would omit infants from consideration within the household. The Greek itself, however, does not give these grounds for their exclusion, as Scott convincingly shows.

8. Cf. Acts 16:15 (NIV): "she and the members of her household were baptized"; this changes the singular verb into a plural.

ἠγαλλιάσατο πανοικεὶ πεπιστευκὼς τῷ θεῷ).[9] Again, it is the faith of the jailer that receives the attention, while the household is associated with his faith in their rejoicing. To say anything of the faith of the members of the household is an inference that needs to be substantiated. In both instances, then, we see the baptism of an entire household, but we encounter only one testimony of faith, that of the householder.

This same pattern, without reference to baptism, occurs in the account of the conversion of Crispus, the synagogue ruler in Corinth. There we are told that "Crispus, the ruler of the synagogue, believed [singular verb] in the Lord, together with his entire household" (18:8; Κρίσπος δὲ ὁ ἀρχισυνάγωγος ἐπίστευσεν τῷ κυρίῳ σὺν ὅλῳ τῷ οἴκῳ αὐτοῦ).[10] While the vocabulary varies in each of these instances, the grammatical construction remains the same.[11] Here, too, there is precision in the way faith is attributed only to Crispus, while his household is incorporated indistinctly in his individual testimony. This consistent pattern suggests that while a personal profession of faith was the *sine qua non* for the baptism of the head of the household, when it came to the members of the household it was the mere fact of their membership in the household that entitled them to receive the same sign along with the attending promises. As Scott states cogently, "Since households were baptized as such, anyone who could belong to a household could also be baptized. Since household baptism was evidently a fairly common apostolic practice, numerous infants must have been baptized."[12]

---

9. Cf. Acts 16:34 (NIV): "he was filled with joy because he had come to believe in God—he and his whole family." Here the crucial word πανοικεὶ is misleadingly applied to the faith of the jailer rather than to his joy.

10. Cf. Acts 18:8 (NIV): "Crispus, the synagogue ruler, and his entire household believed [plural verb] in the Lord."

11. See Scott, "Dynamic Equivalence and Some Theological Problems in the NIV," 352: "The Greek expressions translated 'with his whole household' are different, and a third is used at 16:32, but they are virtually identical in meaning."

12. Scott, 354.

Children in the Graeco-Roman Household

The Patria Potestas *of the Householder*

The next part of my paper is devoted to addressing the question whether or not ancient observers and ancient readers of these texts made the same inferences, based on their experience with and knowledge of households in their Graeco-Roman world. That is, was it conceivable to them that children should be baptized on the basis of the testimony of faith of the head of the household? Or, even more strongly, would they actually have expected this?

My investigation begins with considering the significance of *patria potestas*, the power of the ancient head of the household, the *paterfamilias*. His *potestas* officially constituted the household, since the *familia*, at least officially, consisted of all those who were under his legal authority.[13] Thus included were his wife, the daughters still under his power, and all agnatic descendants natural or adopted, while his *dominica potestas* extended over any slaves under his control, along with their own dependents, including children.[14] Complicating the situation even more were the freedmen and freedwomen still tied to wealthy households by moral, social, and economic ties rather than legal ones.[15] So, while it is difficult also in our day to speak of what constitutes a typical family or household, the inclusion of slaves and freedmen and women made the Roman situation particularly complex.[16] Usually the context would determine more precisely who were meant to be included. In fact, the jurist Ulpian specifically defined *familia* with six different categories in order to create clarity for the law.[17]

---

13. Gaius, *Inst.* 1.52, 55.

14. See especially Saller, *Patriarchy, Property, and Death in the Roman Family*, 102–32; Rawson, "The Roman Family," 1–57. It should be noted that only those wives that passed to the husband's *manus* in marriage were under his *potestas*. This was more common in the early Republic, but by the first century BC, most women remained under the *potestas* of their father; for these developments, see Gardner, *Women in Roman Law and Society*, 67–68.

15. See Mouritsen, *The Freedman in the Roman World*, 36–65.

16. Regarding the complications even in English of speaking about "family," see Bradley, *Discovering the Roman Family*, 3–4. Peskowitz, "'Family/ies' in Antiquity: Evidence from Tannaitic Literature," 12–18, discusses helpfully the importance of acknowledging the fluidity in the terms that are used and the difficulty in pinning down definitions.

17. *Dig.* 50.16.195.1–5; cf. 21.1.25.2; Bradley, *Discovering the Roman Family*, 11, n. 3.

Nevertheless, it would be a mistake to deny the significance of the single-stem family within the context of the household and, on that basis, to argue that when we read of households in the ancient texts we ought not to assume the presence of children. When Cicero outlines the founding blocks of society, he writes,

> For since the reproductive instinct is by Nature's gift the common possession of all living creatures, the first bond of union is that between husband and wife; the next, that between parents and children; then we find one home, with everything in common. And this is the foundation of civil government, the nursery, as it were, of the state. (*Off.* 1.54 [Miller, LCL])

What Cicero's words suggest, given the prominence he accords children within the household, is that if the author of Acts wished to exclude from the "household" any category of household members, he would have specified as much, all the more so if it was that of the children.

It is relevant to ask whether or not the *potestas* of the *paterfamilias* would have extended so far as to allow him to have his children baptized. The question is not a difficult one to answer. In our context—where the equal rights of children (apart from the unborn) are increasingly being championed, to the extent that very young children are expected to choose their own gender identity and parents are expected to respect their choice—it is difficult to imagine the extent of the Roman householder's control over those who belonged to his *familia*.[18] The near absolute character of his authority is most clear in the popular attribution to him of the right over the life and death of his children.[19] Roman legend rooted this *ius vitae necisque* ("right of life and death") in the very beginnings of Roman society. According to the Augustan Greek historian Dionysius of Halicarnassus, "[Romulus] the lawgiver of the Romans gave virtually full power (ἅπασαν ἐξουσίαν) to the father over his son, even during his whole life, whether he thought proper to imprison him, to scourge him, to put him in chains and keep him at work in the fields, or to put him to death" (*Ant. rom.* 2.26.4 [Cary, LCL]).

---

18. Rawson, "The Roman Family," 16–17, shares the telling story of the emperor Tiberius, who was adopted by Augustus while he was in his mid-40s and already the father of an adult son. When he became a member of Augustus' family, he not only changed his name from the Claudian to the Julian family name, but he also formally and officially passed into his adoptive father's *patria potestas*.

19. Here I am addressing matters other than the common and deplorable ancient practice of infanticide and the exposure of unwanted infants, regarding which see further below.

During the reign of Tiberius, the Latin historian Valerius Maximus confirmed the existence of this right and corroborated it with legendary examples (*Mir. dict.* 5.8). While these instances were viewed by ancient observers as peculiar and extreme,[20] and laws were passed that specifically curtailed this right,[21] so that we cannot find any formal, legal basis for this *ius*,[22] the fact remains that it occupied a place in the popular imagination and contributed to the ideology of the *patria potestas* of the *paterfamilias*. That is, while it is true, as Saller writes, that "there is no reason to believe that Roman children lived their daily lives conscious of this terrible paternal power,"[23] this hypothetical right is illustrative of the prevailing ideology. The jurist Gaius gives us the appropriate conclusion: "There are hardly any other men who have over their children a power such as we have" (*Inst.* 1.55).

While outside observers may have questioned the conversion of someone like the Philippian jailer to Christianity and his subsequent baptism because of their distaste for this "most mischievous superstition" (Tacitus, *Ann.* 15.44), no one would have found it unusual or objectionable on principle for him to include his children in the baptism of the household. In fact, given the nature and extent of his *patria potestas*, I would suggest that from an outside perspective it was to be expected.[24]

Religious Life in the Household

From this rather broad discussion of the rights of the father over his children, we can move easily into a narrower investigation of how the religious life of the household played into this reality. For our purposes, the most important place to begin is early on in the life of the Roman child with the ceremonies of the *dies lustricus* ("day of purification").[25]

---

20. See, e.g., Seneca, *De clem.* 1.15; cf. re this power over slaves, Cassius Dio 54.23.1ff.; Seneca, *De ira* 3, 40.2.

21. *Digest* 48.8.2; cf. 48.9.5.

22. See Shaw, "Raising and Killing Children," 31–77.

23. Saller, *Patriarchy, Property, and Death in the Roman Family*, 117.

24. Thus Betsworth, *Children in Early Christian Narratives*, 29, writes, "If a father converted to Christianity, it is reasonable to assume that his entire household did as well, since the father had the authority to choose the religion of his household. It is likely that children were baptized along with their parents in such cases."

25. It is unclear whether or not slave children would have undergone a formal *lustratio*.

This took place on the ninth day after birth for boys and the eighth day for girls and signified the formal initiation of the infants into the family by naming them, ritually purifying them, and so formally admitting and welcoming them into the family (see, e.g., Suetonius, *Nero* 6; Macrobius, *Sat.* 1.16.36; Festus, s.v. "*Lustrici*"; cf. Tertullian, *Idol.* 16).[26] While it is difficult to reconstruct what happened on these occasions, given the piecemeal nature of the evidence, what is clear is that it formed a regular part of the rhythm of Roman family life and served as an infant's "social birth."[27] Plutarch even goes so far as to state that prior to the *dies lustricus*, the infant was considered to be "more like a plant than an animal" (*Quaest. rom.* 288), because the umbilical cord had often not yet fallen off. More important for our purposes, however, is the fact that "social birth" included entrance into the cultic life of the family and the state—not surprisingly, given the embedded nature of religious ritual in the social lives of the ancient Romans.[28] This was marked clearly by the ceremonial proceedings of that day, which included offerings to various gods judged to be significant for the health and well-being of the child and the family.[29]

In such a context, then, the baptism of Christian infants shortly after birth would not have been unusual. Indeed, outside observers may well have understood it or made sense of it within the framework of their own pagan practices.[30] In that regard it is interesting to note what McWilliam writes of the ongoing importance of the ritual: "It is likely that memory

---

Presumably this would have depended on the approval of the master. See McWilliam, "Socialization of Roman Children," 268.

26. For more detailed discussion of the sources for this event, see Rawson, "Adult-Child Relationships in Roman Society," 7-30; Garnsey, "Child Rearing in Ancient Italy," 48-65; Laes, *Children in the Roman Empire*, 65-66.

27. See Corbier, "Child Exposure and Abandonment," 58-60; Laes, *Children in the Roman Empire*, 66; Nicoletti, "Infant Baptism in the First-Century Presupposition Pool," 285.

28. Nicoletti, "Infant Baptism," 286, makes this important point, "What is important for us to note is that since both the state and the family were cultic and religious in nature, the *dies lustricus* cannot be thought of as *merely* a secular-social initiation, but must be considered a religious initiation as well. Even if the emphasis on the ritual was often on its social aspects, the *dies lustricus* still accomplished the function of initiating infants into the religious and cultic life of the state and family."

29. See, e.g., Laes, *Children in the Roman Empire*, 66-67, for a description of the proceedings.

30. An intriguing thought occurs in response to the following statement of Laes, *Children in the Roman Empire*, 67: "This initiation and purification ritual provides yet another indication of how concerned the Romans were with protecting infants during the most vulnerable stage of their lives." How much more precious was the baptism of infants in a culture where infants were so vulnerable and parents needed assurance?

of the *dies lustricus* was preserved by adults and older child attendees, who may have reminded younger family members of their *dies lustricus* at other gatherings such as birthdays, coming of age ceremonies, betrothals, and weddings."[31] This is just the sort of preservation of social memory I have experienced and encouraged regarding baptism within the Reformed Christian circles in which I was born, raised, and continue to serve.

The fact that children were thenceforth seen to belong formally and functionally to the household and to the state—not to put too fine a point on the distinction between the two—can be recognized also in their subsequent involvement in religious ritual.[32] The first thing to be noted is that children were expected to follow the manner of life of their parents (in particular their father, who had them under his *potestas*), including the family's specific religious rituals.[33] It was a question of *pietas*—loyalty and respect towards the gods, the state, and the family—one of the highest Roman virtues.[34] These rituals were tied directly and uniquely to the individual family, since each household recognized and honoured its own divine powers, including the *Genius* of the master, the *Juno* of his wife, and then also the household *penates* (gods of the storeroom), *Vesta* (goddess of the hearth), and *lares* (guardian deities).[35] Alongside these common household deities, each household would ensure its health and safety by honouring any number of other spirits (*numina*) by established family rituals.

When a child was formally initiated into the family, therefore, he was by extension welcomed into a complex family religious life that was already established by the *paterfamilias* (and, before him, his ancestors)

---

31. McWilliam, "Socialization of Roman Children," 268.

32. The question of exactly how integrated children were in the household is a significant one. Wiedemann, *Adults and Children in the Roman Empire*, has famously argued for their marginal nature, but Laes, *Children in the Roman Empire*, has more recently and helpfully demonstrated that while there is some evidence to suggest that, they ought better to be seen as "outsiders within." See also the response of Golden, "Chasing Change in Roman Childhood," 92, to Wiedemann.

33. See Horns and Martens, *Let the Little Children Come to Me*, 33; Wiedemann, *Adults and Children in the Roman Empire*, 181; Green, "'She and Her Household Were Baptized,'" 75; Betsworth, *Children in the Early Christian Narratives*, 21–29.

34. McWilliam, "Socialization of Roman Children," 269–70.

35. Inscriptions: ILS 3025=CIL III.6456 (Genius); ILS 3644=CIL VIII.3695 (Genius, Juno); ILS 3598=CIL VII.237 (Penates); ILS 3643=CIL VI.259 (Genius); ILS 3604=CIL II.1980 (Lares, Genius); ILS 3608=CIL IX.723 (Lares).

and that was, as Beard, North, and Price put it, "destined to be passed on to his descendants (the *sacra familiae*)."[36] It is in this vein that Plutarch advises prospective brides:

> A woman ought not to make friends of her own, but to enjoy her husband's friends in common with him. The gods are the first and most important friends. Hence, it is becoming for a wife to worship and to know only the gods that her husband believes in, and to shut the door tight upon all strange rituals and outlandish superstitions. For with no god do stealthy and secret rites performed by a woman find any favour. ("Advice to Bride and Groom" 19, *Moralia* 140D [Babbitt, LCL])

Even clearer for our purposes is Cicero's description of the ideal state: "Let no one have gods of their own, neither new ones nor from abroad, unless introduced to Rome publicly; let their private worship be for those gods whose worship they have duly received from their fathers. . . . Let them preserve the rituals of their families and of their fathers" (*Leg.* 2.19 [Keyes, LCL]). Thus, the cardinal virtue of *pietas* towards one's ancestors, which included honouring their traditions and following the *paterfamilias* in everything, reinforced the unity of the household in domestic rituals and beliefs.[37]

There was great danger, therefore, in anything that would damage the cohesion in the religious life of a household. That was the threat posed by the spread of the Bacchic cult in 186 BC, which caused significant upheaval in Roman society and may have set a precedent for dealing with later religious disturbances.[38] As Beard, North, and Price observe, "It would have been disturbing and quite unacceptable that a man, or still worse a woman or child, of this community should take action that transferred their obedience to new and unauthorized groups, such as Bacchists."[39] The possibility that such changes in allegiances could cause tension in the household is evident also in the early Christian writings, in particular where advice is offered to women who have converted to Christianity apart from their husbands.[40] The fact that these situations

---

36. Beard, North, and Price, *Religions of Rome*, 1.49.

37. See Osiek, "The Family in Early Christianity," 15; Barclay, "The Family as the Bearer of Religion," 68.

38. E.g., the expulsions from the city of Rome of groups like the Jews, the astrologers, magicians, or worshippers of Isis; see Beard, North, and Price, *Religions of Rome*, 1.228–44; Gruen, *Diaspora*, 29–41, 52–3; Den Hollander, *Josephus, the Emperors, and the City of Rome*, 242.

39. Beard, North, and Price, *Religions of Rome*, 1.96.

40. See, e.g., 1 Cor 7:12–16; 1 Pet 3:1–2.

are addressed underscores the reality that the most common situation—and the safest situation, from the standpoint of Roman moralists—was that the entire household should be bound together in their domestic religious rituals. That was the expected way.

In the context of this paper, it also important to stress that children were not simple observers in all of this. On the contrary, there were specific roles for children, although it is difficult to tell in any given instance precisely how old the children were.[41] In his poem on the festivals and sacred rites of the Roman calendar, Ovid imagines a common household scene:

> An altar is built. Hither the husbandman's rustic wife brings with her own hands on a potsherd the fire which she has taken from the warm hearth. The old man chops wood, and deftly piles up the billets, and strives to fix the branches in the solid earth: then he nurses the kindling flames with dry bark, the boy stands by and holds the broad basket in his hands. When from the basket he had thrice thrown corn into the midst of the fire, the little daughter presents the cut honeycombs. Others hold vessels of wine. A portion of each is cast into the flames. The company dressed in white look on and hold their peace.[42] (*Fasti* 2.645-65 [Frazer, LCL])

While in Ovid's account the children are merely involved in the ceremonial presentation of offerings, for perhaps no specific reason, Columella suggests that children by their very nature were well suited to act as intermediaries between the adult members of the household and the *penates* (household gods), since they were still sexually pure. They should, therefore, be the only ones handling the food stock of the household (*penora*) (*Rust.* 12.4.3). Not only were they well suited to interact with the *penates*, but also the *lares*. In his *Satyricon* Petronius offers up a parody of a regular mealtime ritual at the infamous dinner of Trimalchio. He writes, "While all this was going on, three boys in brief white tunics came in. Two of them set down on the table the household deities (*lares*), which had amulets around their necks; the other, carrying a bowl of wine, kept shouting, 'God save all here!'" (60 [Sullivan]). As in Petronius' imaginary scene, it was the children of the household who would announce that the household gods were propitious when the

---

41. Regarding the various stages of life of children, see Laes and Strubbe, *Youth in the Roman Empire*, 23-30.

42. For similar scenes, see Horace, *Ep.* 2.1.139-44; Virgil, *Aen.* 7.71-2; Tibullus 1.10.23-4, 2.1.59-60; Ovid, *Trist.* 5.5.11-12; Mantle, "The Role of Children in Roman Religion," 100-102.

paterfamilias offered sacrifices during the meal (see Servius *ad Aen.* 1.730).[43]

Given their involvement at the household level, it is no surprise to find them involved in more public rituals and ceremonies as well.[44] Children's choirs frequently played a role in religious festivals, such as those associated with the Secular Games of 17 BC (Augustus) and AD 88 (Domitian), or at the dedication of a temple or a shrine. Certain children could serve as acolytes (*camilli*, *camillae*) for public sacrifices, just as they did in the household setting, provided they were under 12 years old, were of upper-class stock, and had both parents still living.[45] But perhaps the most evocative image of the child's participation in the religious life of the household comes from the fourth-century Christian observer Prudentius, who writes that the reason for the persistence of what he calls *superstitio* (i.e., non-Christian religious practices) was that pagan infants drank in their parents' errors with their mother's milk (*puerorum infantia primo errorem cum lacte bibit. Symm.* 1.201–2). To his mind at least, children from their infancy were fully immersed in the religious life of the household.

The Graeco-Roman View of the Jewish Household

I have been attempting to create a mental backdrop for the audience members of Luke-Acts to help us understand what they heard or read when presented with household baptisms. There is one final piece I want to add and that is the Graeco-Roman perception of the Jewish household. While Christianity was of course new on the scene for the audience members of Luke-Acts, they were acquainted already with Jewish households, perhaps even as God-fearers.[46] Now, in general terms, Cohen is probably right when he observes, "The Jewish family in antiquity seems not to have been distinctive by the power of its Jewishness; rather, its structure, ideals, and dynamics seem to have been

---

43. See Wiedemann, *Adults and Children in the Roman Empire*, 181.

44. See especially Mantle, "The Role of Children in Roman Religion," 85–106; Mantle, "Addendum: The Religious Roles of Children in the Provinces," 117–21; Betsworth, *Children in the Early Christian Narratives*, 24–25.

45. See Plutarch, *Numa* 7.5; Macrobius 3.8.6–7; Servius, *ad Aen.* 11.543, 558; see Wiedemann, *Adults and Children in the Roman Empire*, 184; Mantle, "The Role of Children in Roman Religion," 91.

46. See, e.g., Bock, *Luke*, 14–15; Keener, *Acts*, 427.

virtually identical with those of its ambient culture(s)"; and later on, "The Jewish values and expectations governing parent-child relationships were entirely consonant with, and almost indistinguishable from, those of Graeco-Roman society."[47] But he glosses over one particular feature of Jewish family life that was noted specifically by at least two outside observers. The Jews distinguished themselves from their contemporaries by refusing to abandon or dispose of unwanted children by exposing them or practising abortion and infanticide,[48] which was an otherwise pervasive practice in the ancient world.[49] Tacitus regarded as noteworthy the fact that they did not do so and attributed the size of the Jewish population to this principle (*Hist.* 5.5.3), while Hecataeus of Abdera made much the same observation (*apud* Diodorus 40.3.8). While Tacitus reserves judgment here of the Jews' refusal to practise infanticide, elsewhere he commends the German tribes for nurturing their offspring well, writing, "To limit the number of their children or to destroy any of their subsequent offspring is accounted infamous" (*Germ.* 19). So, it would seem that Tacitus' observation regarding the Jews was also a positive one. Other ancient writers downplayed the extent of infant exposure,[50] which suggests that this was a sensitive moral issue for at least some and that the Jewish avoidance of the practice would have reflected positively on them in the eyes of these contemporaries.

It is not surprising, then, that the Jewish historian Josephus highlighted just this detail when he undertook to defend Jewish customs and practices against the slanderous accusations of individuals like Apion.[51] He writes, "Above all we take pride in raising children (παιδοτροφία)" (*Ag. Ap.* 1.60 [Barclay]), and later on states more explicitly, "[The law] gave orders to nurture all children, and prohibited women from causing the seed to miscarry and from destroying it. But if it

---

47. Cohen, "Introduction," 2, 3.

48. Schwartz, "Did the Jews Practice Infant Exposure and Infanticide in Antiquity?" 61–95, notes that while there would no doubt have been Jews who joined their contemporaries in this practice, these were exceptions; cf. Horn and Martens, "*Let the Little Children Come to Me*," 214–17; Reinhartz and Shier, "Josephus on Children and Childhood," 370–71.

49. Musonius Rufus, frag. 15; Didache 2.2; Tertullian, *Apol.* 9.8; Minucius Felix, *Oct.* 30.2; Origin, *Cels.* 8.55; see Boswell, "Expositio and Oblatio," 10–33; Wiedemann, *Adults and Children in the Roman Empire*, 36–37; Barclay, *Against Apion*, n. 288 at Josephus *Ap.* 2.202.

50. Polybius 36.17.5–12; Dionysius of Halicarnassus, *Ant. rom.* 2.15.2.

51. See also Ps.-Phocylides 185; *Sibylline Oracles* 3.765–66; Philo, *Virt.* 131–32; Philo, *Spec.* 3.110–19 (re Exod 21:22).

were to become evident, she would be an infanticide, obliterating a soul and diminishing the [human] race" (Ag. Ap. 2.202). He also extolled their desire to educate their children from birth: "Indeed, not even on the occasion of the birth of children did [the law] permit laying on feasts and making pretexts for drunkenness, but it ordered that from the very beginning their upbringing should be in sober moderation" (Ag. Ap. 2.204). In this treatise then, in which Josephus sought not only to defend the reputation of his fellow Jews but also to win the sympathy and perhaps even devotion of his non-Jewish audience,[52] he bolstered the perception that the Jews were even more concerned about their children than their Gentile counterparts. When it came to household activities, therefore, it is reasonable to argue that outsiders would have assumed more extensive involvement of the children in the life of the Jewish household than in the Graeco-Roman household—certainly not less. That is to say, when the audience of Luke-Acts heard or read of households being baptized, knowing what they did of Jewish households, they would have had no reason to imagine that the children would be excluded. After all, at this point the ways had not yet parted, and the early Christians were still intimately tied to the Jewish communities from which they first came.

Concluding Thoughts

What went through the minds of the first audience members when they read of the baptism of Lydia and her household, or the Philippian jailer and all his household? What mental picture of the life of the first century household did they bring to the text that informed the way they received Luke's message? The evidence presented above suggests, at the very least, that there was no reason for these ancient readers to assume the complete absence of children. I would argue, in fact, that it suggests more, namely that the reader would have presumed not only the presence of children in these households, but also their participation in the baptisms of the whole household.

---

52. Regarding the aim and audience of Josephus' *Against Apion*, see Mason, "The *Contra Apionem* in Social and Literary Context," 187–228; Barclay, *Against Apion*, lii–liii; Den Hollander, *Josephus, the Emperors, and the City of Rome*, 248–49, 279–93.

Moreover, the initiation of infants into the ritual life of the first-century household, and their active participation early on, make the silence of our earliest Christian texts on the issue of infant baptism even more acute. Surely, in this ancient context and in the wake of the old covenant practice of circumcision on the eighth day, the denial of baptism to the children of believing parents would have warranted a defence or at least a clarifying note. Instead, we have only indicators that they still belonged fully in the covenant community, from Peter's speech in Acts—"the promise is for you and for your children" (Acts 2:34)—to Paul's letter to the *saints* (τοῖς ἁγίοις) in Ephesus—"children, obey your parents in the Lord" (Eph 6:1).[53] And so, the burden of proof ought to lie on the shoulders of those who would argue a break not only from the old covenant tradition but also from contemporary expectations that children did indeed belong fully in the religious life of the household.

---

53. Regarding the significance of these passages, see further in this volume, Visscher, "Peter, Paul, and the Promises of God to the Children of Believers," and Van Vliet, "Let the Children Receive the Sign of the Covenant."

Bibliography

Aland, Kurt. *Did the Early Church Baptize Infants?* 1961. Translated by G. R. Beasley-Murray. Eugene, OR: Wipf & Stock, 2004.

Babbitt, F. C. *Plutarch: Moralia*. Loeb Classical Library 222. Cambridge, MA: Harvard University Press, 1928.

Barclay, John M. G. "The Family as Bearer of Religion in Judaism and Early Christianity." In *Constructing Early Christian Families: Family as Social Reality and Metaphor*, edited by Halvor Moxnes, 66–80. London: Routledge, 1997.

———. *Against Apion. Flavius Josephus: Translation and Commentary*. Vol. 10. Leiden: Brill, 2007.

Beard, Mary, John North, and Simon Price. *Religions of Rome*. Vol. 1, *A History*. Cambridge: Cambridge University Press, 1998.

Betsworth, Sharon. *Children in Early Christian Narratives*. Library of New Testament Studies 521. New York: Bloomsbury T&T Clark, 2015.

Bock, Darrell. L. *Luke*. 2 vols. Baker Exegetical Commentary on the New Testament. Grand Rapids: Baker Academic, 1994.

Boswell, John Eastburn. "*Expositio* and *Oblatio*: The Abandonment of Children and the Ancient and Medieval Family." *The American Historical Review* 89, no. 1 (1984): 10–33.

Bradley, Keith R. *Discovering the Roman Family: Studies in Roman Social History*. Oxford: Oxford University Press, 1991.

Cary, Earnest. *Dionysius of Halicarnassus: Roman Antiquities Books 1–2*. Loeb Classical Library 319. Cambridge, MA: Harvard University Press, 1937.

Cohen, Shaye J. D., ed., *The Jewish Family in Antiquity*. Atlanta, GA: Scholars Press, 1993.

Corbier, Mireille. "Child Exposure and Abandonment." In *Childhood, Class and Kin in the Roman World*, edited by Suzanne Dixon, 52–73. London: Routledge, 2005.

Den Hollander, William. *Josephus, the Emperors, and the City of Rome. From Hostage to Historian*. Ancient Judaism and Early Christianity 86. Leiden: Brill, 2014.

Frazer, James G. *Ovid: Fasti*. Loeb Classical Library 253. Cambridge, MA: Harvard University Press, 1931.

Gardner, Jane F. *Women in Roman Law and Society*. London: Croom Helm, 1986.

Garnsey, Peter. "Child Rearing in Ancient Italy." In *The Family in Italy from Antiquity to the Present*, edited by David I. Kertzer and Richard P. Saller, 48–65. New Haven, CT: Yale University Press, 1991.

Golden, Mark. "Chasing Change in Roman Childhood." *The Ancient History Bulletin* 4, no. 4 (1990): 90–94.

Green, Joel B. "'She and Her Household Were Baptized' (Acts 16:15): Household Baptism in the Acts of the Apostles." In *Dimensions of Baptism: Biblical and Theological Studies*, edited by Stanley E. Porter and Anthony R. Cross, 72–90. London: Sheffield Academic, 2002.

Gruen, Erich. *Diaspora: Jews Amidst Greeks and Romans*. Cambridge, MA: Harvard University Press, 2002.

Horn, Cornelia B., and John W. Martens. *"Let the Children Come to Me": Children and Childhood in Early Christianity*. Washington, DC: Catholic University of America Press, 2009.

Jeremias, Joachim. *Infant Baptism in the First Four Centuries*. 1958. Translated by David Cairns. Eugene, OR: Wipf & Stock, 2004.

———. *The Origins of Infant Baptism. A Further Study in Reply to Kurt Aland*. Translated by Dorothea M. Barton. 1962. Eugene, OR: Wipf & Stock, 2004.

Keener, Craig S. *Acts: An Exegetical Commentary*. Vol, 1, *Introduction and 1:1–2:47*. Grand Rapids: Baker Academic, 2012.

Keyes, Clinton W. *Cicero: On the Republic; On the Laws*. Loeb Classical Library 213. Cambridge, MA: Harvard University Press, 1928.

Laes, Christian. *Children in the Roman Empire: Outsiders Within*. Cambridge: Cambridge University Press, 2011.

Laes, Christian, and Johan Strubbe. *Youth in the Roman Empire: The Young and the Restless Years?* Cambridge: Cambridge University Press, 2014.

Mantle, I. C. "The Roles of Children in Roman Religion." *Greece & Rome* 49, no. 1 (2002): 85–106.

———. "Addendum: The Religious Roles of Children in the Provinces." *Greece & Rome* 57, no. 1 (2010): 117–21.

Mason, Steve. "The *Contra Apionem* in Social and Literary Context: An Invitation to Judean Philosophy." In *Josephus' Contra Apionem: Studies in Its Character and Context with a Latin Concordance to the Portion Missing in Greek*, edited by Louis H. Feldman and John R. Levison, 198–228. Leiden: Brill, 1996.

Miller, Walter. *Cicero: On Duties*. Loeb Classical Library 30. Cambridge, MA: Harvard University Press, 1913.

McWilliam, Janette. "The Socialization of Roman Children." In *The Oxford Handbook of Childhood and Education in the Classical World*, edited by Judith Evans Grubbs and Tim Parkin, 262–85. Oxford: Oxford University Press, 1991.

Mouritsen, Henrik. *The Freedman in the Roman World*. Cambridge: Cambridge University Press, 2011.

Nicoletti, Steven A. "Infant Baptism in the First-Century Presupposition Pool." *Tyndale Bulletin* 66, no. 2 (2015): 271–92.

Osiek, Carolyn. "The Family in Early Christianity: 'Family Values' Revisited." *The Catholic Biblical Quarterly* 58, no. 1 (1996): 1–24.

Peskowitz, Miriam. "'Family/ies' in Antiquity: Evidence from the Tannaitic Literature and Roman Galilean Architecture." In *The Jewish Family in Antiquity*, edited by Shaye J. D. Cohen, 9–38. Atlanta, GA: Scholars Press, 1993.

Rawson, Beryl. "The Roman Family." In *The Family in Ancient Rome: New Perspectives*, edited by Beryl Rawson, 1–57. Ithaca, NY: Cornell University Press, 1986.

———. "Adult-Child Relationships in Roman Society." In *Marriage, Divorce, and Children in Ancient Rome*, edited by Beryl Rawson, 7–30. Oxford: Clarendon Press, 1991.

Reinhartz, Adele, and Kim Shier. "Josephus on Children and Childhood." *Studies in Religion/Sciences Religieuses* 41, no. 3 (2012): 364–75.

Saller, Richard P. *Patriarchy, Property and Death in the Roman Family*. Cambridge: Cambridge University Press, 1996.

Schwartz, Daniel. "Did the Jews Practice Infant Exposure and Infanticide in Antiquity?" *The Studia Philonica Annual* 16 (2004): 61–95.

Scott, J. W. "Dynamic Equivalence and Some Theological Problems in the NIV." *Westminster Theological Journal* 48, no. 2 (1986): 351–61.

Shaw, Brent D. "Raising and Killing Children: Two Roman Myths." *Mnemosyne* 54, no. 1 (2001): 31–77.

Strawbridge, Gregg. *Infant Baptism: Does the Bible Teach It?* Brownstown, PA: WordMp3.com, 1999.

Sullivan, J. P. *Petronius: The Satyricon; Seneca: The Apocolocyntosis.* London: Penguin, 1986.

Watt, Jonathan M. "The *Oikos* Formula." In *The Case for Covenantal Infant Baptism*, edited by Gregg Strawbridge, 70–84. Phillipsburg, NJ: P&R, 2003.

Wiedemann, Thomas. *Adults and Children in the Roman Empire.* New Haven, CT: Yale University Press, 1989.

Peter, Paul, and the Promises of God to the Children of Believers

Gerhard H. Visscher

Beyond a doubt, the concept of "promise" captures the whole of Scripture. God made promises to Adam, to Abraham, and subsequent generations. The fulfilment of all these promises comes in Christ and all his work. Walter C. Kaiser, for example, says that "there is only one single promise that, according to NT writers, has been unfolding as the plan of God since it was first announced in the OT." He points out that forty times, when the New Testament wants to summarize the Old Testament message, it just uses the word "promise." He says that this was the promise to Abraham, fulfilled in Christ, and "it is that same promise in which we Christians share as 'heirs together with Israel' (Eph. 3:6)."[1] Similarly, Thomas McComiskey argues for the unity of the promise in all Scripture and writes: "The promise-oath continues unchanged in essence throughout the history of redemption. It is thus the vehicle that expresses the unity of the divine redemptive purpose."[2]

Now I have no doubt that these scholars are correct. Paul before Agrippa, for example, rests his whole defence on this promise: "*It is because of my hope in what God has promised our fathers that I am on trial today*" (Acts 26:6, 7). And he says to the Galatians, "*If you belong to Christ, then you are Abraham's seed, and heirs according to the promise*" (3:29).

While we agree with all of this, the interesting, and perhaps alarming, thing is that these scholars have Baptist roots and affiliations and say nothing about the relation between this promise and *children*. What about the children and that promise, we wonder?

---

1. Kaiser, *Toward Rediscovering the Old Testament*, 88–89.
2. McComiskey, *The Covenants of Promise*, 188.

Acts 2:39

There seems to be a bit of a pattern in this regard. Consider the well-respected F. F. Bruce, who has similar roots;[3] he gives only a passing comment on the verse, saying, "The promise of the 'covenant of grace' is not only to the present generation but also to those yet to come . . . ."[4] Consider Craig S. Keener, an associate pastor at an African-American Baptist church in Philadelphia who holds a teaching position at Asbury Seminary.[5] He wrote the most massive commentary ever written on the Book of Acts, if not on any book of the Bible: four big volumes, a total of no less than 4,459 pages. But when it comes to "the children" in Acts 2:39, he spends all of two sentences, in which he simply notes: "'Your children' may develop 'your sons and daughters' in 2:17 (cf. Luke 13:34)."[6] To be fair to Keener, he sees the "promise" here as hooked in with 1:4–5, 8 and the promise of "baptism with the Holy Spirit" and therefore he will understand it in a Pentecostal fashion as an additional gift given to some believers. Now I agree that "the promise" makes immediate reference to "the baptism with the Spirit,"[7] but I would argue that "the baptism of the Holy Spirit" is a reference to all believers who are incorporated into the church rather than the select few.[8]

Two further points: First, it makes no sense to understand "children" here in some general kind of way without regard to the children of those who were right there on the day of Pentecost. For, as everyone seems to agree, this text is hooked in with the earlier passage from Joel 2 (Joel 2:28–31) as the phrase "for all whom the Lord our God will call" comes from Joel 2 as well (Joel 2:32 [LXX Joel 3:5]). Further, Joel's very point is that it will be the children of Israel who will prophesy (your "sons" and "daughters"). So how can it be that the children of those who believed right then and there are not in view as well? How is it going to involve future generations, as Bruce suggests, if it does not also

---

3. Open Brethren, holding to believer's baptism.

4. Bruce, *The Acts of the Apostles*, 98.

5. An interdenominational seminary in the Wesleyan-Arminian tradition.

6. Keener, *Acts: An Exegetical Commentary*, 1:987, quoted in full as follows: "Initially, the promise is to all Israel ('your children'), as in the Scriptures (cf. also Acts 3:20, 25–26). 'Your children' may develop 'your sons and daughters' in 2:17 (cf. Luke 13:34)."

7. Cf. Marshall, *Commentary on the New Testament Use of the Old Testament*, 543.

8. Gaffin, *Perspectives on Pentecost*. See, e.g., 29–32.

impact the children of present generations? Peter's very point is that the promises of God were for those who believed that day, *and their children*, and all whom God would call in future generations and other places. The word *teknon* that is used in Act 2:39 does not designate the age of the child; it simply refers to the offspring of parents, their posterity, whatever their age. It is saying: the God who is going to reach out worldwide is also reaching in to the families and the communities he has already embraced. The crucifixion has changed neither the nature of the promises nor the expected recipients of the promises.

And secondly, as C. K. A. Barrett puts it:

> The promise here is in the first instance the promise of the Holy Spirit (v. 33 as well as v. 38). It would probably however be mistaken to confine it to this sense . . . . It covers the covenant into which God entered with his people, to which he continues to be faithful . . . . Notwithstanding the crucifixion of Jesus, God has not cast off his people (cf. Rom. 11.1, 2); the promise remains open—for those represented by the crowd surrounding Peter (cf. Rom. 11:28f.) and for their children, and for those far off. The scope of the promise is thus extended in time and space.[9]

More popularly, Gregg Strawbridge expresses it this way:

> Let us read our New Testaments with an understanding of the original audience. If we stand in the sandals of the First Century Jewish (and proselyte) followers of Jesus, how would they have reacted to the Baptist claim that believers' little children are excluded from the people of God? Imagine the shock of Crispus, the synagogue leader (Acts 18:8), who believes on Friday, let's say, his children are in covenant with God and fully part of the people of God. Then after Paul preaches, he finds out that—in the fulfillment of all the promises, in the fullness of time, in the Messianic kingdom and glory of Israel . . . now his little children have no part in the people of God!
>
> Or, imagine the new proselyte family who has recently undergone the painful passage to covenant membership (circumcision), only to discover now their children have less of a place than in the shadows of Judaism! This view of the new covenant would be more than disappointing to the original audience: it would be biblically inconceivable. The clearly stated objections of the Judaizers (e.g., circumcision is required as a covenant sign) are plain (Acts 15:1). If the Apostles actually had taught that the infant children of Jews (and Gentiles) are now excluded, this would have been an outrage. It is very remarkable that no hint of this discussion arises in the pages of the New Testament. But the reason this is not in the New Testament is best

---

9. Barrett, *Acts*, 155. Cf. McDowell, *Christian Baptism*, 90.

explained by the view that the Baptist practice and belief was not the Apostles' teaching.[10]

In his booklet *You and Your Household*, Gregg Strawbridge quotes fourteen Old Testament texts that reference children as having a part in the great future God has in store for his people. Many of these are from the passages of Jeremiah very central in the promises of the New Covenant.[11] Also note Isaiah 59:20 and 21:

> "The Redeemer will come to Zion...."
> "As for me, this is my covenant with them," says the LORD. "My Spirit... and my words... will not depart from your mouth, or from the mouths of your children, or from the mouths of their descendants from this time on and forever," says the LORD.

Is it not clear, then, that we have to see also Acts 2:39 as fulfilment of these prophecies? The covenantal ways set out with Abraham find their extension into the new covenant with Acts 2:39. In the words of Romans 4:16–17, "the promise comes by faith, so that it may be by grace and may be guaranteed to all Abraham's offspring—not only to those who are of the law but also to those who are of the faith of Abraham. He is the father of us all."

Ephesians 6:1–4

How about Paul? Turn with me, then, first to Ephesians 6:1-4. I have argued elsewhere that Paul, in his letter writing, takes a corporate approach that is not unlike the Old Testament approach to the people of Israel. Just as the Old Testament prophets spoke to the nation of Israel collectively, without suggesting that all in Israel were purely regenerate in Israel, so Paul does in his letters.[12] We see that clearly in Ephesians. He is writing to a church, or to a group of churches.[13] Chapter 1:1: "To the saints in Ephesus, the faithful in Christ Jesus," and then in chapter

---

10. Strawbridge, *You and Your Household*, loc. 414–26.

11. He cites Jer 31:1, 17, 36, 33-37, 37-40; 33:22-26 as allusions to Deut 30:6. And then also Ezek 37:24-26; Zech 10:6-9;Joel 2:1-29; Isa 44:3, 54:10-13, 59:20-21; Mal 4:5-6.

12. Visscher, "How Should the Pulpit Address the Pew?" 557–61.

13. These letters were generally circular in nature (cf. Col. 4:16); this factor may explain the disputed reference "in Ephesus"in Eph 1:1. Comfort, *New Testament Text and Translation Commentary*, 578, posits that something must complete the *tois ousin* and that the best explanation may be that each church would supply the name of its own city.

6, he speaks to some of those saints in particular: "*Children, obey your parents in the Lord, for this is right.*" In actuality, the whole matter of the position of children in the New Covenant community is stated in the frequent reference here to the parent-child relationship as one that is "in the Lord." Children are to obey their parents "in the Lord" (6:1), and fathers are to raise them in "the discipline and instruction of the Lord" (6:4). Strikingly, both Bauer[14] and Silva[15] take these as references to "the Lord Jesus Christ." S. M. Baugh says: "That Christ is the referent of *kurios* ('Lord') here is clear from the fact that 6:1–4 is following up from the general notion of submission in 5:21 'in the fear of Christ.'"[16] This does not necessarily suggest that these children are all sufficiently age and repentant to be identified as believers. Rather, it is based upon what the dogmaticians call *positional sanctification*, or *definitive sanctification* (Murray), or *passive regeneration* (Bavinck). We'll come back to this, but it's a reference to the fact that *as a body* parents and their children, along with the congregation, have been set apart, dedicated to God. It's not a suggestion that each of those children has already been justified and sanctified; collectively, they have been set apart. Parents and children are urged to a higher standard of mutual co-operation in the family because they share this relationship in Christ. Children are called to acknowledge the Christocentric basis of their obedience, and parents see the Christocentric nature of their instruction. It is not personal preferences that shape a Christian family; it must be the promises and commands of the Lord Jesus Christ. Just as the old covenant people had children who were rebellious but still belonged to God's people, so the

---

14. BDAG suggests that most of the New Testament references are to the Lord Jesus and notes, s.v. "κύριος": "δ. In some places it is not clear whether God or Christ is meant, cp. Ac 9:31; 1 Cor 4:19; 7:17; 2 Cor 8:21; Col 3:22b; 1 Th 4:6; 2 Th 3:16 al."

15. Silva, s.v. "*kurios*," *New International Dictionary of New Testament Theology and Exegesis*, 2:777: "The phrase 'in the Lord' is freq. in Paul and means the same as 'in Jesus Christ.' It is used in a wide variety of contexts: a door was opened for mission (2 Cor 2:12); Paul is convinced, affirms, exhorts (Rom 14:14; Eph 4:17; 1 Thess 4:1); believers are told to receive others (Rom 16:2; Phil 2:29), to rejoice (3:1), to stand firm (4:1), to work (Rom 16:21), to greet one another (Rom 16:22; 1 Cor 16:19), to be strong (Eph 6:10), to walk (Col 2:6), to undertake service (Col 4:17). Christians who marry should do so 'in the Lord,' i.e., they are to enter marriage as a Christian act, presumably by marrying a believer (1 Cor 7:39); Paul was a prisoner 'in the Lord' (Eph 4:1); people are chosen (Rom 16:13) and beloved (16:8; 1 Cor 4:17); their work is not in vain (1 Cor 15:58); the Christian has eternal life (Rom 6:23); the church is a light (Eph 5:8). The whole of life, both in the present and the future, is determined by the fact expressed by the formula 'in the Lord': Paul and his churches stand in the presence and under the power of the κύριος." Cf. Fitzmyer, s.v. "*kurios*," *Exegetical Dictionary of the New Testament*, 2:328–31.

16. Baugh, *Ephesians*, 505. Cf. Hoehner, *Ephesians*, 786.

children of believers in the new covenant belong and must, along with the adults, regularly be called to faith and repentance—also in the home. Fathers and mothers can address their children in the Lord long before they have professed their faith, because in a significant sense they are "in the Lord." Christian parents don't speak to their children as they might speak to unbelieving neighbours. They speak to them as people who belong in that privileged circle of believers.

Murray references this text and says:

> We are ... compelled to take account of the fact that the language of sanctification is used with reference to some decisive action that occurs at the inception of the Christian life, and one that characterizes the people of God in their identity as called effectually by God's grace. It would be, therefore, a deflection from biblical patterns of language and conception to think of sanctification exclusively in terms of a progressive work.[17]

The second factor corroborating all of this is the reference to "promise" in 6:2. What often fails to receive our full attention is the way in which the promise of the fifth commandment is applied here. Douglas Wilson rightly posits that we should not imagine that the promises of God to children hit a brick wall at the coming of Christ. He references Mary, the mother of our Lord, who quotes from Psalm 103: "*From now on all generations will call me blessed .... His mercy extends to those who fear him, from generation to generation*" (Luke 1:48, 50). Did this suddenly change at Pentecost? Certainly not. In Ephesians 6:2 and 3 new covenant children are urged to honour their parents precisely because the "first commandment with a promise" applies to them. A promise which had been applied first to the children of the old covenant in the promised land, and which Jewish people continue to count on as valid, is now also applied to the children of Gentile families living in Asia Minor under the new covenant. "We have flesh-and-blood Jewish children in Deuteronomy and flesh-and-blood Gentile children in Ephesus. And the promise covers both groups *in this life*."[18] In truth, a position which denies that children are included today is really quite contrary to the clear teaching of Scripture.

---

17. Murray, "Definitive Sanctification," 278. Cf. Bavinck, *Reformed Dogmatics*, 4:252–56; Hoekema, *Saved by Grace*, 202–06.

18. Wilson, "Baptism and Children: Their Place in the Old and New Testaments," 295.

1 Corinthians 7:14

When we now turn to the famous text of 1 Corinthians 7:14 ("*Otherwise your children would be unclean, but as it is, they are holy*"), we see more of the same. It's noteworthy, by the way, that in all three texts (Acts 2:39; Eph 6:1; 1 Cor 7:14) Paul uses the same word "*tekna*" ("offspring"). But what is the single possible basis for Paul's view that children of believers are holy? It obviously cannot be that all the offspring of believers are known to be regenerate and therefore justified and sanctified. It must be the very same reason as in Ephesians. Closer scrutiny does indeed show such to be the case. 1 Corinthians is written "To the church of God in Corinth, *to those sanctified in Christ Jesus and called to be holy*" (1:2).

In a very significant study on the subject of sanctification and holiness, David Peterson has argued, especially out of Corinthians, that in the New Testament, sanctification should not first of all be understood as the corollary and consequence of justification, but again, that it should primarily be viewed in this *positional sense*—as an act of God whereby he sets aside his people in Christ in a manner very much like the way he sets aside Israel in the Old Covenant. Says Peterson:

> Just as Israel was made holy by God's saving activity in the time of Moses, and again in the restoration after the Babylonian Exile, so sanctification in the New Testament is an integral part of the redemptive work of Jesus Christ. It is regularly portrayed as a once-for-all, definitive act and primarily has to do with the holy status or position of those who are 'in Christ.'[19]

For example, when Paul writes in 1 Corinthians 1:30 about our Lord Jesus, who became for us "*wisdom from God, and righteousness, and sanctification*," he is not speaking about three attributes that we bring about through our experience and will power, but he is speaking about the fact that all three of these and more exist in our lives only because we receive them "in Christ":

> The sanctification in view here is not a process of moral change. The context is about belonging to God and being given a holy status. The focus is on God's saving activity, not on our response."[20]

---

19. Peterson, *Possessed by God*, 24.

20. Ibid., 43. Cf. also "you were sanctified" (1 Cor 6:11), of which Peterson writes: "This verb does not refer to a process of ethical development but highlights the fact that God claimed them as his own and made them members of his holy people. He turned them around and brought them to himself in faith and love. In ethical terms, however, such a separation from previous

So too, then, when Paul writes in 1 Corinthians 1:2 "*to those sanctified in Christ Jesus and called to be holy*," he is not speaking about a body of people who have grown in righteousness and holiness to the extent that now they can be regarded as saints, but he is addressing those in Corinth who have been set aside by God in Christ as his possession—people who are now also called to be holy in a progressive sense according to the new status that they have received in Christ in that positional sense of the word. Everything is rooted in God's action. Paul is apostle because he has been called to be an apostle (1:1); they are people of God only because they have been called by God to be such.[21] The new Israel is not unlike the old in this regard.

Time and again, there have been those who maintain that the New Testament community is a "pure" community, consisting only of those who are converted. Stephen J. Wellum, for instance, states:

> Baptist theology ... argues that the NT church, by definition, is constituted by a regenerate community, so that under the new covenant the locus of the covenant community and the elect are the same.[22]

That is very doubtful. These criteria actually exclude any church that the apostle Paul is gathering. In an important work Wayne A. Meeks has shown us that the household was the "basic cell" of the church, as reflected in the Pauline phrase "the church that meets in their house" (1 Cor 16:19; cf. Rom 16:5; Phlm 2; Col 4:15). He points out that the household included "slaves, freedmen, hired workers, and sometimes tenants and partners in trade or craft,"[23] and suggests that "if the existing household was the basic cell of the mission, then it follows that motivational bases for becoming part of the *ekklesia* would likely vary from one member to another."[24] But the point is: it is this community of people whom Paul addresses as "saints" and "holy ones," and it is with reference to this kind of motley group that he uses words like "elect," "called," "loved," and

---

attachments and values has profound implications." This becomes, then, argues Peterson, the basis for Paul's call to holy living. See ibid., 46.

21. Ibid., 40–41.

22. Wellum, "Baptism and the Relationship Between the Covenants," 98, n. 3. Comments to this effect are also scattered throughout the book.

23. Meeks, *The First Urban Christians: The Social World of the Apostle Paul*, 76.

24. Ibid., 77.

"known by God."[25] To suggest that the early Christian church consists only of the converted is in contradiction with the facts.[26] Paul addresses his congregations in a manner similar to the way in which the Old Testament addressed Israel; all members of the community are urged to repent and believe in response to the preaching of the Word and through the work of the Holy Spirit. Over time, of course, this motley group of people would be called to decide whether they and their children were part of the believing community. Somehow, those lines of division would need to be drawn; Scot McKnight suggests that it was probably exactly the rite of baptism that was used for this purpose.[27]

So too, then, in 1 Corinthians 7:14 we are informed that also in cases where sanctified believers are married to those who do not believe, the unbelieving partner is still "sanctified" through the believing partner. "The unbelieving partner is brought into a relationship of special privilege and opportunity with respect to God but is not yet converted."[28]

If we take this one step further, the same obviously applies to the children.[29] They, too, belong to those who are set apart in Corinth, even though they may not yet be converted. They, too, are "*sanctified in Christ*

---

25. Ibid., 85.

26. Cf. Silva, s.v. "*ekklesia*," New International Dictionary of New Testament Theology and Exegesis, vol. 2, 139: "Paul's teaching is consistent with the recognition that both hypocrisy and self-deceit may exist in the church. Therefore, the church that is visible to human beings does not correspond exactly to the group that constitutes those who truly belong to God. The latter are clearly visible to God alone: 'The Lord knows those who are his' (2 Tim 2:19). This truth extends to the church what Paul says of Israel: 'For not all who are descended from Israel are Israel' (Rom 9:6); the true Israel consists rather of those who are 'the children of the promise' (9:8). Thus the apostle recognizes the existence of false believers within Christian congregations (2 Cor 11:26; Gal 2:4), and when writing to the Corinthian church he can cite the command given to the Israelite community: 'Expel the wicked person from among you' (1 Cor 5:13, quoting Deut 17:7 et al.)."

27. McKnight, *It Takes a Church to Baptize: What the Bible Says About Infant Baptism*, 82–83.

28. Peterson, 87.

29. In his later work, however, Peterson state that he believes the baptism of the children of believing parents to be consistent with his theology, "especially having regard for the covenantal implications of baptism." *Encountering God Together: Leading Worship Services that Honor God, Minister to His People and Build His Church*, 155. Ciampa and Rosner, *The First Letter to the Corinthians*, 301–2, do work this out with respect to the children. They comment: "In calling these children 'holy' Paul does not mean that they are automatically saved (any more than the unbelieving spouses), but that rather than being held at arm's length by members of the church they are to be fully embraced in exactly the same way as children born into families where both parents are believers. As a result of this, those children 'will be marked by an element of shaping and "difference" from a wholly pagan environment.' This result should bring great blessings that would otherwise be lost to the children of such families, but they are not what make them 'holy' rather than 'unclean.' It is the Lord's sanctioning of their parents' marriage which accomplishes that and allows them to experience the blessing of living within a community inhabited by the Spirit of God. Both parts of v. 14 serve to support Paul's injunction to believers in mixed marriages not to divorce their partners (vv. 12b and 13b)."

... and called to be holy." Gordon Fee also defends the view that, in keeping with the Jewish tradition, proselyte children were members of Israel in full standing,[30] and that Paul views such children as included in the church community.[31] This, by the way, must be the origin of the expression in question in the classic Reformed Form for Baptism, "Do you confess that our children ... are sanctified in Christ and thus as members of his church ought to be baptized?"[32] The parents are not being called upon to attest to the idea that these newborn children are already justified and sanctified, but that they are "set apart in Christ" together with the rest of the congregation.

Other Indications

There are also other epistolary indications of childhood inclusion in the community and the expectation of Christian behaviour among them.

Children are never regarded as being exempt from Christian behaviour until their later conversion. It is the children of the *ungodly* who are regarded as being "disobedient to parents" (Rom 1:30; 1 Tim 5:4; 2 Tim 3:2), while better things are expected of the children of the Christian communities (Eph 6:1-4; Col. 3:20; 1 Tim 5:4, 10-14; 1 John 2:12-14).

In a wonderful classic article, in reference to Titus 1:6, which expects of elders that "their children are believers," Robert S. Rayburn says:

> There is the very important evidence of Titus 1:6 where Paul lays down the requirement that to qualify for consideration for the eldership a man must have believing children. Upon this rock must finally shatter every attempt to argue that parents are not directly accountable for the spiritual issue of their children's lives. A man with unbelieving children is a man with a defect which disqualifies him from the leadership of the church.[33]

---

30. m. Ketub.4.3; m. Yeb.11.2.

31. Says Fee, *The Epistle to the Corinthians*, 301-2: "If you are correct, he [Paul] argues, then your children lie outside the covenant; but as it is, through their relationship with the children, they too can be understood to be 'holy' in the same way as the unbelieving spouse. Thus in both cases Paul is setting forth a high view of the grace of God at work through the believer toward members of his/her own household (cf. 1 Pet. 3:1)." Fee also references Romans 11:16, where Israel is regarded as holy despite the unbelief of some. See Peterson, 161, n. 37.

32. *Book of Praise*, 598.

33. Rayburn, "The Presbyterian Doctrines of Covenant Children, Covenant Nurture, and Covenant Succession," 105.

While Rayburn is not unsympathetic to the challenges of unbelief in the children of believers, in another section he writes:

> It is emphatically clear from Deuteronomy to Proverbs to Ephesians that nurture, not evangelism, is the paradigm of child-rearing in the covenant home, a nurture which presupposes a heart, however young, set free, or soon to be set free, from the native blindness and opposition to the truth into which the fall has cast all mankind from conception (Ps 51:5). It can only be thought remarkable that the contrary paradigm—adolescent unbelief overcome in an experience of new birth—now so securely fixed in the evangelical mind, never once appears in Scripture in an exemplary role and almost never appears at all. Instead, there is everywhere the assumption that the covenanted grace will overtake covenant children at the headwaters of life so that, in response to a faithful parental and ecclesiastical nurture, they will both claim the promises made to them and respond to the summons issued to them in a way appropriate to each stage of life according to the measure of faith.[34]

Conclusion

The words of Dr. Rayburn are a worthy conclusion to this essay. There remains only this thought of which the study of this subject has convinced me. And that is that when everything is added up in the Gospels and the letters, the challenge to children in the Christian community is not very different from the challenge to the adults. Contrary to such brothers as Stephen J. Wellum, the children are inside the community where all are regularly called to faith and repentance. Baptism, you see, is not a prophecy, or a prediction, or a guarantee. It is the sign of a promise. And that which is promised becomes a reality through faith alone. Neither Jesus, nor Paul, nor Peter know of a community made only of believers. Actually, I wonder how that even works out in a Baptist church. Do the adults never doubt there? Do they never stray from the faith? Don't the adults, too, have to live by hope in the promise of God? Do they not need to be called all the days of their life to faith and repentance?

At the same time, Wellum is clearly motivated by the fear that infant baptism "may even lead, if we are not careful, to a downplaying of the need to call our children to repentance and faith."[35] That is a valid concern, and I do really wonder in that regard whether in our midst that

---

34. Ibid., 99.
35. Wellum, 144.

call to faith and repentance is heard clearly enough by all our children and adults. The truth is that unless this call is heard clearly and with authority, the youth of our churches only really hear a question which is saying: Are you content to continue in this community in which you have lived now for some years, with all its social and religious expectations, for the rest of your life? What they need to hear is: Do you know what it means to be "in Christ" and to devote the rest of your lives to Jesus Christ, in a spirit of love, faith, repentance, and humility under his dominion? Collectively, the people of God are so blessed in Christ. But collectively and individually, we need to do everything possible to cultivate faith and repentance. *Positional* sanctification—being sanctified in Christ—should never decrease the urgency of the call to repentance and *progressive* sanctification—being what we are, growing in holiness and dedication to our glorious and gracious God. The call to faith and repentance continues to beckon throughout our lifetime, repeatedly and always. There is not a fallen human being in the universe who will receive all the benefits of Christ without rebirth and regeneration. But the blessing of being born to Christian parents is that children are placed at a young age into a context in which they hear the gospel from trusted and loving sources who are similarly called to display the gospel in an exemplary way with every manner of integrity.

Bibliography

Balz, H., and G. M. Schneider. *Exegetical Dictionary of the New Testament*. Grand Rapids: Eerdmans, 1981.

Barrett, C. K. A. *Critical and Exegetical Commentary on the Acts of the Apostles*. Edinburgh: T&T Clark, 1994.

Bauer, Walter, Frederick W. Danker, W. F. Arndt, and F. W. Gingrich. *A Greek-English Lexicon of the New Testament and Other Early Christian Literature*. 3rd ed. (BDAG). Chicago: University of Chicago Press, 2000.

Baugh, S. M. *Ephesians: Evangelical Exegetical Commentary*. Edited by H. Wayne House. Bellingham, WA: Lexham Press, 2016.

Bavinck, Herman. *Reformed Dogmatics*. Vol. 4. Grand Rapids: Baker Academic, 2008.

Book of Praise: Anglo-Genevan Psalter. Winnipeg: Premier, 2014.

Booth, Robert R. *Children of the Promise: The Biblical Case for Infant Baptism*. Phillipsburg, NJ: P&R, 1995.

Bruce, F. F. *The Acts of the Apostles: The Greek Text with Introduction and Commentary*. Grand Rapids: Eerdmans, 1975.

Ciampa, Roy E., and Brian S. Rosner. *The First Letter to the Corinthians*. The Pillar New Testament Commentary. Grand Rapids: Eerdmans, 2010.

Comfort, Philip W. *New Testament Text and Translation Commentary*. Carol Stream, IL: Tyndale, 2007.

Fee, Gordon. *The Epistle to the Corinthians*. Grand Rapids: Eerdmans, 1987.

Fitzmyer, J. A. "κύριος, ου, ὁ." In *Exegetical Dictionary of the New Testament*, edited by H. Balz and G. Schneider, vol. 2, 328–31. Grand Rapids: Eerdmans, 1991.

Gaffin, Richard B. *Perspectives on Pentecost: New Testament Teaching on the Gifts of the Holy Spirit*. Phillipsburg, NJ: P&R, 1979.

Green, Michael. *Baptism: Its Purpose, Practice, and Power*. Downers Grove, IL: IVP, 1987.

Gross, Edward N. *Will My Children Go to Heaven? Hope and Help for Believing Parents*. Phillipsburg, NJ: P&R, 1995.

Hoehner, Harold. *Ephesians: An Exegetical Commentary*. Grand Rapids: Baker Academic, 2002.

Hoekema, Anthony A. *Saved by Grace*. Grand Rapids: Eerdmans, 1989.

Kaiser, Walter C., Jr. *Toward Rediscovering the Old Testament*. Grand Rapids: Zondervan, 1987.

Keener, Craig S. *Acts: An Exegetical Commentary*. Vol. 1. Grand Rapids: Baker Academic, 2012.

Marshall, I. Howard. "Acts." In *Commentary on the New Testament Use of the Old Testament*, edited by G. K. Beale and D. A. Carson, 513–606. Grand Rapids: Baker Academic, 2007.

McComiskey, Thomas E. *The Covenants of Promise: A Theology of the Old Testament Covenants*. Grand Rapids: Baker, 1985.

McDowell, Bruce A. *Christian Baptism: The Sign and Seal of God's Covenant*. Indianapolis, IN: Dog Ear Publishing, 2017.

McKnight, Scot. *It Takes a Church to Baptize: What the Bible Says About Infant Baptism*. Grand Rapids: Brazos, 2018.

Murray, John. "Definitive Sanctification." In *Collected Writings of John Murray*, vol. 2, 557–61. Carlisle, PA: Banner of Truth, 1983.

Meeks, Wayne. *The First Urban Christians: The Social World of the Apostle Paul*. New Haven, CT: Yale University Press, 1983.

Peterson, David. *Possessed by God: A New Testament Theology of Sanctification and Holiness*. Grand Rapids: Eerdmans, 1996.

———. *Encountering God Together: Leading Worship Services that Honor God, Minister to His People and Build His Church*. Phillipsburg, NJ: P&R, 2014.

Rayburn, Robert S. "The Presbyterian Doctrines of Covenant Children, Covenant Nurture, and Covenant Succession." *Presbyterion* 22, no. 2 (1996): 76–112.

Silva, Moisés, ed. *New International Dictionary of New Testament Theology and Exegesis*. Vol. 2. Grand Rapids: Zondervan, 2014.

Strawbridge, Gregg. *You and Your Household: The Biblical Case for Infant Baptism*. Kuyperian Press, 2015. Kindle edition.

Visscher, Gerhard H. "How Should the Pulpit Address the Pew? Some Lessons from Paul." *Clarion* 55, no. 23 (2006): 557–61.

Wellum, Stephen J. "Baptism and the Relationship Between the Covenants." In *Believer's Baptism: Sign of the New Covenant in Christ*, edited by Thomas R. Schreiner and Shawn D. Wright, 97–161. Nashville, TN: B&H Publishing, 2007.

Wilson, Douglas. "Baptism and Children: Their Place in the Old and New Testaments." In *The Case for Covenantal Infant Baptism*, edited by Gregg Strawbridge, 286–302. Phillipsburg, NJ: P&R, 2003.

Growing Up into Christ: Renewing the Pathway to Maturity in the Church

Bill DeJong

Though there is much about today's adolescents to admire in terms of their energy, creativity, and technological prowess, there is also much to warrant concern. One needs to think only of the soaring rates of teen anxiety and depression, confusion about gender identity and sexual orientation, widespread exposure to porn, frequent instances of callous bullying, and, worst of all, the irremediable tragedy of suicide.[1]

How are Christian adolescents faring? What can the church do to build trust and demonstrate support? How can adolescents be shepherded along the pathway to maturity so as to equip them for a lifetime of fidelity? Are the current practices of Reformed churches vis-à-vis adolescents helpful or harmful? What are the implications of the widespread exclusion of adolescents within continental Reformed churches from the Lord's table? Should the typical age (i.e., 17 to 19) at which one professes his or her faith in such churches be reassessed? Most importantly, what insight does Scripture provide regarding the process of maturation?

In what follows I will survey some prominent psychological and sociological perspectives on adolescence before offering a biblical perspective and then concluding with some recommendations for renewing ministry to adolescents today. Throughout this paper I will argue for the importance not simply of imparting doctrine but of unveiling the gospel of Christ so that youth, seeing and embracing that gospel, might experience the transformative work of the Spirit through whom a new self can emerge with which youth can live "authentic" lives.

---

1. The American Psychological Association's "Stress in America" survey (2014) reported that 30 percent of teenagers acknowledged feelings of sadness or depression.

Age of Adolescence

It is commonly, though incorrectly, alleged that prior to industrialization the world knew only two stages in life development—namely, childhood and adulthood. Ancient Rome, for example, distinguished three stages of youth—namely, childhood (*infantia*), pre-puberty (*impuberes*, sometimes called *pueritia*), and post-puberty (*pubertas*, sometimes called *adolescentia*).[2] It is the case, however, that the transition from childhood to adulthood is celebrated in many cultures through a particular rite of passage (e.g., the Jewish bar and bat mitzvah). In agrarian societies this transition was often tied to variables that transcended age. If a boy was big enough to do a man's work, he was regarded as a man, and if a girl was biologically ready for motherhood, she was regarded as a woman.[3] The industrialization movement precipitated the rise of factories and mass migration to cities and, in their wake, the destiny of youth began to change. Child-labour laws prohibiting children from working were enacted, education for children between the ages of 6 and 18 became compulsory, and separate legal measures were introduced to address juvenile delinquency with corrective rather than punitive means.[4] In the second half of the twentieth century the automobile became common, suburbia was born, and teenagers became far more mobile, affluent, and consumeristic. Though the term "adolescence"—derived from the Latin verb *adolescere*, "to grow up, to come into maturity"—existed for centuries prior, the concept of an age of adolescence was first popularized in 1904 by G. Stanley Hall, who linked its onset with biological maturation.[5] Even today it is aptly and often said that adolescence "begins in biology and ends in culture."[6]

Age of Identity Formation

How should adolescence be conceived from a developmental perspective? James W. Fowler (1940–2015), who reflected on faith

---

2. See, for example, Laes, *Children in the Roman Empire*, 92–95.
3. Hine, *The Rise and Fall of the American Teenager*, 11.
4. Berard, Penner, and Bartlett, *Consuming Youth*, 23–25.
5. See Hall, *Adolescence*.
6. See Clark, "The Changing Face of Adolescence," 45–47.

development in particular, argued that toddlers operate with what he termed a Mythic-Literal Faith, with which they interpret reality naively, read literature literally, and are inclined to stories, make-belief, and fantasy.[7] The ethical world young children inhabit is black and white and strictly regulated by commands. This phase corresponds, in Lawrence Kohlberg's theory of human ethical development, to the punishment-obedience phase, where the morality of children is activated by the promise of reward or the threat of punishment.[8]

Young children then move in Fowler's conception to the next stage, which he dubbed Synthetic-Conventional Faith—a stage that persists into the early teens. By going to school, meeting people beyond their family, and learning from teachers, such youth become aware of the opinions and viewpoints of others. Often meaningful friendships are forged in which for the first time they experience a relationship of trust with a non-family member.[9] Here they begin to "construct an image of the self one sees others seeing."[10] The ethical world in this stage becomes more complex as individuals are introduced to moral dilemmas, ethical scenarios neither black nor white. This corresponds to Kohlberg's Mutual Interpersonal Relations phase, where one's morality transcends mere obedience to commands and envisions what a good person would do. This stage ends with disappointment with traditional authorities. Exhibiting flaws, making mistakes, and being unable at times to provide satisfactory answers, parents and teachers are no longer idealized.

In the Individuative-Reflective Faith stage which follows, often apparent in later adolescence and early adulthood, one discards the naive literalism and legalism of the past and becomes increasingly confident of one's critical reasoning and arguments. Faith commitments

---

7. Fowler, *Stages of Faith*. See also Fowler, *Faith Development and Pastoral Care*. Influenced by Paul Tillich and Richard Niebuhr, Fowler defined faith as "the human quest for relation to transcendence" and "an orientation of the total person, giving purpose and goal to one's hopes and strivings, thoughts and actions," involving "commitment to centers of value and power." See Fowler, *Stages of Faith*, 14, 18. Fowler's theory has been criticized for, among other things, accenting cognitive dimensions of faith to the neglect of affective and relational dimensions and for presenting as stages of faith what may in fact simply be styles of faith.

8. Kohlberg famously devised a model for understanding especially ethical development. See Kohlberg, "The Development of Children's Orientations Toward a Moral Order," 11–33. See also Kohlberg, *Essays on Moral Development*.

9. Selfhood is "acutely attuned to the realm of the interpersonal." Fowler, *Faith Development and Pastoral Care*, 66.

10. Ibid., 64.

are scrutinized, and authorities are challenged in a quest to distil the truth from its cultural husk. Though this phase is marked by scepticism and cynicism, youth find themselves over time yearning for the very things they once naively embraced and relishing the world of their childhood for its simplicity, order, fantasy, and mystery.[11] Attempts are made to understand self apart from relationships with others. A third-person perspective is sought from which to assess the evaluations of others (i.e., who are we when not defined by our profession or our relationships or friendships?).[12] Congruence is sought between one's identity, affiliations, and beliefs in what might be termed "authenticity."[13]

Prior to Fowler, the brilliant psychiatrist Erik Erikson engaged in considerable reflection on the subject of adolescence. In his life-cycle theory of eight stages, adolescence (the fifth stage) was characterized by a striving for identity. Erikson coined the term "identity-crisis" to denote the experience adolescents have of trying, in the midst of radical changes, to reconcile who they are (identity, the image they have of themselves) with whom society expects them to be or become (role, the image society mirrors back).[14] One begins in adolescence a process that is completed in adulthood of differentiating oneself from one's parents and family of origin in terms of residence, career, family (e.g., as boyfriend or girlfriend, or in marriage), and relationships (e.g., as being a father, not just a son). The period of adolescence concludes when the conflict between identity and role is resolved by the acquisition of the virtue of fidelity, by which Erikson means a psychosocial capacity to make adult commitments and the strength to be true to oneself. Erikson called fidelity the "vital strength which [a person] needs to have an opportunity to develop, to employ, to evoke—and to die for."[15]

---

11. Faith in the fifth stage, Conjunctive Faith, typically not apparent until mid-life, features a new appreciation for tradition, stories, and mystery, entering what Paul Ricoeur called "the second naïveté." The notion that faith transcends rational and logical categories to include other ways of knowing is embraced. The final stage, Universalizing Faith, apparent in few, is observable in the transformers of culture (e.g., Ghandi, Martin Luther King Jr., and Mother Teresa) and features consciousness and appropriation of universal values such as justice and peace.

12. Fowler, *Faith Development and Pastoral Care*, 69.

13. Ibid., 70.

14. By identity, Erikson has in mind "the capacity of ego to sustain sameness and continuity in the face of changing fate . . . maintaining essential patterns in the processes of change. Erikson, *Insight and Responsibility*, 96.

15. Fidelity, for Erikson, is the centre of youth's "most passionate and most erratic" striving. Erikson, *Identity, Youth, and Crisis*, 233.

Adolescents, in other words, are searching for a cause worthy of suffering and worthy of a lifetime.[16] They "do not want to suffer," Kenda Creasy Dean avers, "but they do desperately want to love something worthy of suffering, and to be so loved."[17]

For Erik Erikson adolescence is a society-sanctioned "moratorium" on adulthood, a reprieve for youth from adult roles and responsibilities, to enable youth to form an identity. Whereas the fifth stage typically caps at age 20, Erikson argued that in technological and industrial societies identity formation can persist much longer because of the time it takes to acquire the requisite skills for one's career.[18] This is precisely the phenomenon we are witnessing today: delays in all the major markers of entering adulthood—namely, leaving home, finishing school, becoming financially independent, getting married, and having children.[19]

- In 1960 more than two-thirds of young adults had attained all five of these markers by the age of 30; in 2000 this was true of less than half of females and less than a third of males (US Data).[20] In 1960, 70 percent of 25-year-old women had attained all these markers; in 2000 only 25 percent had (US Data).[21]
- In 1960 the average age of first marriages was 20 for women and 22 for men; in 2010 it was 26 for women and 28 for men (US Data).[22] In 1974 the average age of first marriages was 22.5 for women and 24.8 for men; in 2008 it was 29.6 and 31, respectively (Canadian Data).[23]

---

16. This phenomenon accounts for the popularity of the jihadist groups not simply among those raised in Muslim cultures in the Middle East but also among some in North America. Raised in American suburbia, John Walker Lindh, for example, converted to Islam at age 16, travelled to Yemen to study the Qur'an, and eventually joined an al-Qaeda training camp in Afghanistan.

17. Dean, *Practicing Passion*, 2. Of John Walker Lindh, Dean writes, "His parents allowed him to choose his own ideological boundaries—and he did, with a vengeance. . . . John Walker Lindh discovered what every teenager is hard-wired to seek: an object he deemed worthy of passion. And he invested his all in it." See *Practicing Passion*, 5.

18. "Erikson does note that the time of identity crisis for persons of genius is frequently prolonged. He further notes that in our industrial society, identity formation tends to be long, because it takes us so long to gain the skills needed for adulthood's tasks in our technological world. So . . . we do not have an exact time span in which to find ourselves. It doesn't happen automatically at eighteen or at twenty-one. A *very* approximate rule of thumb for our society would put the end somewhere in one's twenties." Gross, *Introducing Erik Erikson*, 47.

19. Clark, "Delayed Transitions of Young Adults," 13.

20. Setran and Kiesling, *Spiritual Formation in Emerging Adulthood*, 2.

21. Ibid.

22. Ibid.

23. Hiemstra, Dueck, and Blackaby, *Renegotiating Faith*, 27.

- In the mid 1960s the average age of a Canadian woman giving birth for the first time was 23.5; in 2011 it was 28.5.[24]
- In 1986 only 15 percent of those 25 to 35 had a university degree; in 2016, 35 percent did.[25]
- In 1981, 50 percent of men and 42 percent of women aged 15 to 24 were employed full time; in 2008, 32 percent of men and 25 percent of women.[26]
- In 1981, 42 percent of those 20 to 24 lived at home and 11 percent of those 25 to 29; in 2018, 63 percent of those 20 to 24 lived at home and 29 percent of those 25 to 29.[27]

To capture this growing chasm between adolescence and the attainment of traditional adult milestones, psychologist Jeffrey Arnett posited in 2000 a new life stage he called "emerging adulthood."[28] Emerging adults are characterized by five interrelated markers.

1. They pursue identity formation and consider meaning in love, work, and worldview.
2. They live with instability in terms of residence, work, and life plans.
3. They tend to be self-focused and free from parental oversight and responsibility toward others.
4. They feel they're in a liminal phase between adolescence and adulthood.
5. They see it as a time of possibility and want to keep all the doors open.[29]

Postmodern youth are accustomed to the fluctuating self. "Adolescence itself," Dean writes, "has become a life*style* as well as a life*stage*, an equally viable choice for fourteen- and forty-year olds."[30]

---

24. Ibid., 29.
25. Ibid., 21.
26. Ibid., 25.
27. Ibid., 23.
28. Arnett, "Emerging Adulthood," 469–80.
29. These markers are identified by Arnett, "Emerging Adulthood," 7–9. Cf. Setran and Kiesling, *Spiritual Formation*, 2.
30. Dean, *Practicing Passion*, 61.

Age of Authenticity

The identity-crisis phase of adolescence involves the pursuit of authenticity (Fowler) or fidelity (Erikson). This particular quest can take shape in two different ways. Many adolescents, and especially emerging adults, are unnerved by hypocrisy and yearn for congruence between profession and practice, creed and conduct. They are sensitive to, and offended by, the insincerity of claims to be Christian that are not backed by a complementary lifestyle. The congruence sought here is between what one *professes* and how one lives. This is what might be termed positive authenticity.[31]

The quest for authenticity, however, can also imply something negative (i.e., harmful)—namely, congruence between what one *desires* and how one lives. According to Charles Taylor, ours is "a culture of authenticity," which he defines as "the understanding of life which emerges with the Romantic expressivism of the late-eighteenth century, that each one of us has his/her own way of realizing our humanity, and that it is important to find and live out one's own, as against surrendering to conformity with a model imposed on us from the outside, by society, or the previous generation, or religious or political authority."[32]

Morality in an age of (negative) authenticity is internal and intuitive, no longer external and revealed. It is alleged that there is a voice deep within us which is the voice of nature, and therefore the voice of morality. It is this voice, which can be heard through a connection with one's deeper and inner self, that provides the moral compass to be followed. To deny this voice and follow another—the voice of parents, teachers, pastors—is immoral. The slogans of the age of authenticity are: find yourself, realize yourself, release your true self, follow your heart, be true to yourself, follow your heart, believe in yourself, live out your desires![33] It is often alleged in this connection that anything

---

31. The terms "negative authenticity" and "positive authenticity" are invoked in a slightly different way in Penner et al., *Hemorrhaging Faith*, 58.

32. Taylor, *A Secular Age*, 475, where he goes on to say, "But it is only in the era after the Second World War, that this ethic of authenticity begins to shape the outlook of society in general. Expressions like 'do your own thing' become current; a beer commercial of the early 70s enjoined us to 'be yourselves in the world of today'.... Therapies multiply which promise to help you find yourself, realize yourself, release your true self, and so on." This is true of ethical systems that associate authentic morality with freedom and autonomy—namely, existentialism and situationalism, and what Alasdair MacIntyre and others have called "emotivism."

33. "It cannot be emphasized enough that for many young adults the measure of authenticity is

is permissible that does not infringe on the freedom of others, as if goodness were the sum of individual desires and choices.

The leading American sociologist in this area, Christian Smith, alleges that corollaries of this quest are a determination to be happy and to see people get along. Smith contends that many American teenagers are gripped by a common religious perspective quite distinct from that of their parents—what he denominates Moral Therapeutic Deism (MTD), the five components of which are:

1. A God exists who created and ordered the world and watches over human life on earth.
2. God wants people to be good, nice, and fair to each other, as taught in the Bible and by most world religions.
3. The central goal of life is to be happy and to feel good about oneself.
4. God does not need to be particularly involved in one's life except when God is needed to resolve a problem.
5. Good people go to heaven when they die.[34]

Smith alleges that MTD is a new religion—found among Christian, Jewish, and Muslim youth—and one that youth feel is close enough to the religion of their parents that their parents need not be alarmed by their embrace of it. Smith's claim is corroborated in my own experience as a pastor in an evangelical Reformed church. Youth interviewed for profession of faith (and thereby communicant membership) speak freely about God and how helpful he is and hesitantly about Christ and how he is Lord of their lives.

Canadian researchers have recently made a slightly different discovery, though it is difficult to determine whether the difference is attributable to the gap in time between the two research projects (2006 and 2018) or to the difference in locale (the United States and Canada). In a research publication titled *Renegotiating Faith*, Canadian researchers argued that Moral Therapeutic Deism is giving way to what they term a Universal Gnostic Religious Ethic (or UGRE).[35] In UGRE there is the

---

the degree to which one is *true to oneself*." Penner et al., *Hemorrhaging Faith*, 91. Films produced by Disney and Pixar, for example, are full of these slogans.

34. Smith and Denton, *Soul Searching*, 162. This perspective, interestingly, was held by American teenagers almost irrespective of religious affiliation.

35. "We counterpose the UGRE against the concept of moralistic therapeutic deism." See Hiemstra, Dueck, and Blackaby, *Renegotiating Faith*, 107.

notion that behind all religions there is a reality, a core philosophy, a universal set of standards or ethic regarding what it means to be a good person, that previous generations allegedly could not perceive (thus Gnostic, i.e., "secret," knowledge that emerges in moments of enlightenment). All religions, from this perspective, try to promote this "reality," albeit imperfectly, and the extent to which conduct is recommended beyond this "reality" is considered "extreme." The value of religions in UGRE is functional, rendering the peculiar teachings of religion unimportant and culturally relative (i.e., matters of cultural preference). Unlike MTD, which still clings to a notion of God, UGRE regards God (or a higher power, and religion in general) as unessential for a moral outlook. Those expressions of religion that correspond to the physical world (thus Manichean duality) and link religion to space and time, are unwelcome—e.g., religious pomp and circumstance.[36]

A Biblical Perspective on Adolescence

Having probed psychological and sociological accounts of adolescence in terms of human development and societal changes, we will now consider the interesting perspective that Scripture provides. From one vantage point there are in Scripture only two stages: childhood and adulthood (or maturity). This child/adult paradigm is invoked in Scripture to account for personal spiritual growth: though there are aspects to childhood celebrated as ideal for believers (see, e.g., Mark 10; 1 Pet 2:2), there is also the clear sense that one must mature beyond childhood (see, e.g., Heb 5:13–14; cf. 1 Cor 3:2). This paradigm, however, is also assumed in Galatians 3:23–4:11, where Paul explains that the law was a pedagogue or tutor to lead Israel to Christ.[37] The implication here is that the law is uniquely suited for children who have not yet entered into maturity (cf. Isa 28:9–10). Maturity, for God's people, is attainable through Christ, the new man. While Israel was in her minority she was guided and guarded by the law; now that Christ has come, she has come

---

36. Ibid., 107–09.

37. This verse is frequently and mistakenly cited by Reformed theologians to provide biblical support for the law's function to convict us of sin and drive us to Christ for forgiveness. It is an instance of "right doctrine, wrong text." See, for example, Berkhof, *Systematic Theology*, 612–15, and Spykman, *Reformational Theology*, 342–44.

of age (thus entering maturity) and no longer needs the oversight of guardians (Gal 4:1–2). For the Galatian Christians to revert back to the law's restrictions on foods and festivals was, therefore, to revert back to childhood.

If one were to extrapolate from this redemptive-historical development, one could also envision Adam and Eve at the outset of human history as infants or toddlers. This perspective comports well with their prelapsarian state of nakedness. Like newborns, Adam and Eve first appeared naked, and like toddlers they were unabashed about being naked (Gen 2:25). The notion that Adam and Eve would have remained naked apart from sin or that the redeemed will inhabit the new creation in a naked state finds little support in Scripture. Clothing is often associated in Scripture with beauty and glory, so much so that God himself is robed with glory. Sin sometimes requires individuals to grow up fast, and Adam and Eve's transgression introduced them to clothing quickly (although their early coverings were an attempt to recover lost glory).

It is clear from Scripture, therefore, that human development from childhood to adulthood is a metaphor for redemptive-historical development. There is, however, another paradigm for understanding development in both a redemptive-historical sense and in a personal sense—namely, a development from childhood to adolescence to adulthood corresponding to the three offices of priest, king, and prophet.[38] The *munus triplex* can be utilized to understand three progressive stages in redemptive-history in the Old Testament as well as three stages in spiritual growth.[39]

---

38. It was one of the remarkable contributions of the reformer John Calvin to present Christ's work in terms of the *munus triplex*. This particular model for understanding the ministry of Christ was also valued as a way to understand the calling of all Christians. The Heidelberg Catechism, for example, explains how those "in Christ" are similarly called to be prophets, priests, and kings (LD 12, Q&A 32). Much of what follows derives from the creative and fruitful insights of James B. Jordan, though distilled in places by Peter J. Leithart and Alistair Roberts. See Jordan, "Biblical Theology Basics #5." See also Jordan, *From Bread to Wine: Toward a More Biblical Liturgical Theology*. It should be noted that Jordan sees the three phases as childhood, adulthood, and eldership.

39. These three stages are cumulative, often overlapping, and increasingly glorious. Attempts to press these stages into tidy boxes all fail. Though the prophetic phase is Israel's final phase prior to Christ, both Abraham (e.g., Gen 20:7) and Moses (e.g., Deut 34:10), for example, are called prophets.

The first stage of Old Testament history was *priestly*. Priests were household servants who represented Yahweh in serving his bride.[40] They ministered within his temple-palace, the central sanctuary (first tabernacle and then temple) located at the heart of Israelite society, and there they welcomed guests and assisted in the offering of sacrifices. Much like Adam in the Garden of Eden, the proto-sanctuary, priests were called to guard the sanctuary from unlawful intrusion and to serve. Their job was relatively simple: inspecting animals brought for sacrifice, for instance, or inspecting leprosy, or fulfilling carefully prescribed rituals. The priest had to judge between right and wrong, clean and unclean, holy and common. In this connection, they taught the people the law, which, much like the commands Adam received in the garden, was clear, black and white. The priests had to say to Israel: don't do this and don't do that; you either obey, for which blessings are promised, or you do not, for which curses are threatened. This phase in Israel's history ran from Moses to Saul and was associated with the Pentateuch, in which both the priests and law feature prominently.

The second stage of Old Testament history was *kingly*. Just as there were prototypical priests who offered sacrifices before the priesthood was officially formed, so there were prototypical kings—namely, warrior-judges like Gideon. If the priest was a household servant, the king was a vicegerent who ruled under and for Yahweh. The palace was situated within the larger complex associated with the temple. If the priest's work involved guarding the central sanctuary, the king's calling involved guarding the entire land of Israel. If the priest was tasked with guarding the faithfulness of the bride, the king represented the whole nation as chief worshipper (e.g., Solomon in 1 Kings 8).

What was key to faithful kingship was *wisdom* and not simply *law*. When Solomon prepared to rule, he asked for wisdom and received knowledge of good and evil. The king was more mature than the priest, and he applied the law in new and challenging ways through wisdom. He was expected to make judgments in scenarios not specifically addressed by the law (e.g., 1 Kings 3), sometimes to make life and death decisions, and to know the times in order to determine what was necessary when (e.g., Eccl 3). Society under the kings could no longer be regulated simply

---

40. The Hebrew word for priest, *kohen*, can also be translated as "servant" (*Targum* to Jer 48:7). The Mosaic priesthood, in Heb 3:1–5, is associated with being a servant of God's palace.

by the "do this" and "don't do that" commands of the priestly stage. If the priestly stage was characterized by faithful reception of the law, the kingly phase was characterized by *wise perception*. Kings had to write out a copy of the law for themselves, and good kings were so familiar with the law that they internalized its principles. Not surprisingly, the kingly phase of Israel's history, which ran from Saul to the end of the kingdom, was associated with wisdom literature (e.g., Psalms, Proverbs, Ecclesiastes, and Song of Solomon).

The third stage of Israel's history was *prophetic*. If the kingly office was anticipated by the judge, the prophetic office was anticipated by the seer who knew the will of God and communicated it to the people. If the priest was a household servant in the temple and the king a vicegerent, a ruler under God, the prophet was a member of the divine council, one who represented the people and consulted with God, thereby transcending the vocation of the seer (Amos 3:7; 7:1-6; cf. Gen 20:7; 18:16-33). Whereas *judgment* was passed by the priest according to the law and by the king according to wisdom, it was especially the prophet's domain, applied sometimes to entire nations. If the priest issued commands ("do this" and "don't do that") and the king provided wisdom ("time for this" or "time for that"), the prophet's word was *powerful*: destructive and constructive (he could tear down and build up; e.g., Jer 1:10). More so than the king, the prophet internalized the Word of God by consuming it (e.g., Ezek 3:3) so that it burned within him. Prophets did not merely repeat what had been said (as, e.g., priests) or apply existing principles in new ways (as, e.g., kings) but cast a vision for something better. The power of the prophetic word, to root up kingdoms and tear them down, exceeded the power both of the law and of wisdom.

The realm that preoccupied the prophet exceeded the realms of the priest (sanctuary within Israel) and the king (land of Israel) to include the wider world. Jonah was sent to Nineveh, Daniel laboured in Babylon, and several prophets delivered judgments on foreign nations. The prophet was often itinerant, moving as the Spirit did, and was hard to pin down. The prophetic phase of Israel's history ran from Elijah to Jesus and was associated with the prophetic books of the Bible. In Israel's maturation process, therefore, there was a widening of geographical concern from sanctuary to land to world as there was a deepening of literary power, from law to wisdom to judgment/mission. Full maturity is of course enjoyed in Christ (Col 2:9–10). Jesus himself grew into adulthood and now is fully mature in heaven, where he is pictured with white hair (Rev 1:14).

The progression from priest to king to prophet approximates some of the phases in developmental psychology. The priestly phase, in which obedience to law invites blessing and disobedience curses, corresponds well to Kohlberg's Punishment-Obedience level, where the morality of children is activated by the promise of reward or the threat of punishment, and Fowler's Mythic-Literal Faith, with which children inhabit a black and white ethical world regulated by commands. The kingly phase, in which law is internalized in wisdom, approximates Kohlberg's Mutual Interpersonal Relations level, where one's morality transcends mere obedience to commands and envisions what a good person would do, and Fowler's Individuative-Reflective Faith, where one, inhabiting an ethical world no longer black and white, seeks truth for oneself and a convergence within oneself that gives the sense of authenticity. The prophetic phase, in which transcendent judgments are issued beyond those of law and wisdom, approximates Kohlberg's final stage, the stage of Universal-Ethical Principles, during which one operates in terms of universal moral principles, and especially Fowler's final stage, Universalizing Faith, which features consciousness and appropriation of universal values such as justice and peace and is observable in those who transform culture.

The progression here is a parallel with the sequence of educational stages embraced by the classical education tradition in terms of the trivium. Corresponding to priestly law, grammar involves learning the basic "parts" of a subject. Corresponding to kingly wisdom, logic or dialectic involves discerning relationships and patterns between the "parts." Corresponding to prophetic vision, rhetoric involves communicating and applying those "parts" creatively and beautifully. Analogously, the piano student moves from learning the basic scales ("law") to improvising ("wisdom") to composing ("mission").

The Ministry to Adolescents Today

In this final section I will unpack the implications of the data above in terms of recommendations for ministry to adolescents today and conclude with a specific proposal regarding the ecclesiastical practice within continental Reformed churches of youth publicly professing their faith and being admitted to the Lord's table.

Six Recommendations for Adolescent Ministry

Given what we know about human development generally and North American adolescents in particular, ministry to adolescents today will be enhanced, I believe, by embracing the following five injunctions.

First, *present the person, ministry, and claims of Christ so that adolescents know who Jesus is (person) and ultimately trust in his work (ministry) and surrender to his Lordship (claims)*. To challenge the impulse to moral therapeutic deism or, worse, a universal gnostic religious ethic, the person, work, and claims of Jesus Christ must be central in all catechesis. The identity of Christ as loving and eternal Son of God who became human and gave his life to pay for human sin, defeat the power of evil, renew humanity, and ultimately renovate the cosmos must be unveiled in clarity.

Second, *forge meaningful relationships with adolescents*. Adolescents should be respected, identified by name, mentored, and engaged in terms of their desires, dreams, and ambitions in order to help them distinguish good from bad. One must probe into their answers, dig deeply, and not easily be satisfied. Moreover, the gospel message should be conveyed by those with whom adolescents have or can have meaningful relationships—namely, sound and relational mentors. Youth think a lot about their desires, dreams, and ambitions, and our society encourages them to accept, follow, and pursue them without critique. In many cases youth are unable to offer critique, and therefore their mentors must help them discern.

Third, *expose the myths of negative authenticity and personal autonomy*. Adolescents need to hear that the cultural ideal of authenticity (i.e., being true to yourself) is in fact a myth. In moments of honesty, people recognize that they should not be absolutely true to themselves because of the detestable things they see in themselves, not least desires to slander, lie, betray, envy, etc. One's authentic self might in fact be quite evil and quite enslaving. Dreams of behaviours that are self-destructive or harmful should not be pursued. The only ones to believe their own propaganda about their innate moral greatness are narcissists.[41] Analogously, the penchant for autonomy and freedom must also be deconstructed.[42] Goodness is not the sum of individual desires and choices. Such a position leads to self-deception, because it is impossible for anyone to live in a way that does not impinge on the liberty of others. This self-deception in turn generates manipulation as we attempt to locate "moral" ways to satisfy self-interest. The family bond between parents and children, for instance, is not conducive (perhaps "opposed") to self-interest and generates resentment and bargaining.[43]

Fourth, *emphasize not simply moral conformity but character transformation*. The happy life is not the fulfilment of human desire, nor is it merely the development of desire, as Aristotle posited. Corrupted by sin, our thoughts, desires, and attitudes must be thoroughly reshaped and reformed into the form of Christ. To become a believer, biblically speaking, is not to add religion to one's identity but to become a thoroughly new person ("new creation," 2 Cor 5:17).[44]

One should recommend to adolescents in this connection the practice of virtue (good and better) in addition to the observance of law (right and wrong). What should be accented in terms of the Christian life is not simply commandments (the priestly phase), but virtue or wisdom, the internalizing of the law (the kingly phase). Rules must be kept, not simply as an imposition from the outside, but through a Spirit-transformed character inside (Gal 5:16–26; Eph 5:18).[45] Jesus recommends transformation as a kind of via media between external and internal ethical models because it generates a lifestyle that both transcends mere alignment with rules and conforms to oneself, though this self is a new and redeemed self. This accent is apparent, for N. T. Wright, in the story in the Gospels of the rich young ruler (Matt 19:16–30; Mark 10:17–22;

---

41. Some of my thinking on this has been generated by insights from Kyle Hackmann, pastor of Christ Church in Toronto.

42. Some of what follows reproduces or reworks material from my *Eucharistic Reciprocity: A Practical Theological Inquiry into the Virtue of Gratitude*.

43. Hauerwas, *Peaceable Kingdom*, 10.

44. Believing the gospel message, therefore, must be transformative. "If no one was transformed," Peter Leithart writes, "then the message that announced the transformation could not possibly be true." *Against Christianity*, 99. The language of "accepting Jesus into your heart" is also problematic in this regard because it implies that Jesus is simply something you add to your existing life. (I am indebted to Sinclair Ferguson for this insight.)

45. "An account of the virtues," Jonathan Wilson argues, "is a description of how Christ is being formed in us by the Holy Spirit." *Gospel Virtues*, 45.

Luke 18:18–30) who poses the question: what must I do to inherit eternal life? For a Jew, Wright explains, this is analogous to asking: what kind of person must I be to enjoy the age to come? This in turn is not so different from the question: how do I experience fulfilment, meaning, and happiness in life? The young man viewed his life as one of compliance with the Ten Commandments but feels incomplete. Jesus' answer—namely, sell your possessions, give proceeds to the poor, and follow me—does not set the moral bar higher by adding commandments, but summons a character transformation. Throughout his entire ministry, Jesus resocializes human habits, desires, and affections to be godly.[46]

In order to help translate "head knowledge" into "heart knowledge," youth should be encouraged in the practice of virtue. Whereas Aristotle's virtues make a person a hero, a moral giant who should be applauded, the virtues prized by Christ are just the opposite. Consideration should be given in catechesis, therefore, to practising the virtues Jesus recommends in the Sermon on the Mount (e.g., meekness and poverty in spirit) and, as in the Catholic Catechism, to exhibiting the fruit of the Spirit—love, joy, peace, forbearance, kindness, goodness, faithfulness, gentleness, and self-control (Gal 5:22–23). By habituating strengths of character, extraordinary challenges are simplified, and the virtuous life becomes nearly inescapable.[47]

One is helped tremendously, in terms of teaching the Heidelberg Catechism, by Zacharias Ursinus's commentary, which, after each exposition of a commandment, identifies associated virtues and vices. An even better resource is the wisdom literature in Scripture. If the above thesis about human development occurring along the lines of priest-king-prophet is valid and if adolescence corresponds to the kingship phase, then adolescents should be encouraged to read especially Psalms, Proverbs, and Ecclesiastes. Here we find not simply law, but wisdom (law internalized). Wisdom recognizes the patterns embedded in the world as God's created order in terms of cause and effect, root and fruit, etc.

---

46. I really like the term "resocialization," which is used by Leithart, *Against Christianity*, 16, and by Jonathan Pennington. The latter defines it as "an intentional re-forming of our habits, desires, affections (a proper ordering of loves), a re-making of disciples to be like their Father God ('to be holy as I am holy'), to be god-like/godly." Pennington, "The Sermon on the Mount and the Kingdom of God, 3.

47. In the ancient world, virtues spoke to your identity, whether as a free man or a courageous woman or a merciful person. See Vos, "Christelijke deugden in de gemeente," 27.

Lastly, *underscore the radical summons of Jesus to "die for" him*. At the heart of Jesus' ministry is his summons to deny oneself, take up one's cross, and follow him. The cross-bearing demand of discipleship should not be softened or diminished but presented for what it is. "With nothing left 'to die for' in Christian teaching," Kenda Creasy Dean writes, "it became increasingly unclear whether or not Christianity offered something worth *living for.*"[48]

A Modest Proposal Regarding Profession of Faith

In addition to these five recommendations, I conclude by proposing a change in ecclesiastical practice—namely, that baptized youth who have grown up in the church should be admitted to the Lord's table in Reformed churches at a much younger age than they presently are (i.e., age 17 to 19) without simultaneously being assigned all the responsibilities of church membership. Before making that proposal, however, I will rehearse the origin and meaning of the profession of faith ceremony.

History, Meaning, and Biblical Basis

The Reformed ecclesiastical practice of having youth publicly profess their faith was first introduced to replace the Roman Catholic sacrament of confirmation.[49] According to Roman Catholic sacramentology, through confirmation one receives the gift of the Holy Spirit more abundantly than at baptism and one's bond with the church is rendered "more perfect."[50] In order to become a candidate for communion in the

---

48. Dean, *Practicing Passion*, 9.

49. Anglicans retain the language of confirmation but deny its categorization as a sacrament. Evangelical Anglicans also dispute the role confirmation plays in conferring the Holy Spirit. See Cornwall, "The Rite of Confirmation in Anglican Thought," 365. Both Anglicans and Catholics understand confirmation to involve the affirmation (or ratification or renewal) of vows made on one's behalf by sponsors or godparents at one's infant baptism. John Stott points out that confirmation has a double meaning. The candidate "confirms" commitment to Christ, and God "confirms" the candidate. *Your Confirmation*, 10–11.

50. Van Slyke, "Confirmation: A Sacrament in Search of a Theology," 533, 527. One also receives the seven gifts of the Spirit—namely, wisdom, understanding, counsel, knowledge, fortitude, piety, and fear of the Lord (534). The medieval theologian Thomas Aquinas compared the sequence of baptism, confirmation, and the Eucharist to birth, growth, and nourishment. See *Summa Contra Gentiles* 4.58.

Roman Catholic Church and not have the promised blessings forfeited, one must be confirmed.

The alleged biblical basis for such confirmation is Acts 8:14–17, where Peter and John, as Christ's apostles, confer the Holy Spirit on those already baptized (see also Heb 6:2). The Catholic Catechism stresses that individuals are best confirmed by the bishop as successor of the apostles, "mindful that the celebration of Confirmation has been temporally separated from Baptism for this reason."[51] The magisterium, Van Slyke avers, "has consistently encouraged the faithful to be strengthened by confirmation near the age of discretion or reason, that is, around the age of seven."[52]

The Strasbourg reformer Martin Bucer criticized the Catholic sacrament of confirmation for adding to the ceremony of the laying on of hands the anointing of oil, which Bucer judged to be superstitious.[53] In 1531, therefore, he introduced the practice of an evangelical confirmation, Burnett argues, to correspond to Roman Catholic confirmation and as "a means of countering the Anabaptists' insistence on a public profession of faith."[54] Those who have been "given" to Christ in baptism, he argued, should subsequently "give" themselves publicly to Christ and his church.[55] Children should not be denied baptism because they could not make a profession of faith (contra the Anabaptists), Bucer argued, but once they had mastered their catechism, they should make their own profession and be confirmed through the laying on of hands.[56] For Bucer this profession was "a personal affirmation of the covenantal

---

51. *Catechism of the Catholic Church*, 1313.

52. Van Slyke, "Confirmation," 545. The Fourth Lateran Council had mandated all Christians beyond "the age of reason" to receive communion every Easter. See Burnett, "The Social History of Communion," 82.

53. Burnett, "Church Discipline and Moral Reformation," 445. The Second Helvetic Confession (19:3) regards "extreme unction and confirmation" as "mere devices of men, which the Church may very well spare, without any damage or inconvenience at all; and, therefore, we have them not in our churches, because there are certain things in them which we can by no means allow." Calvin writes, "How will they assure us that their chrism is a vessel of the Holy Spirit? We see the oil—the gross and greasy liquid—nothing else." *Institutes* 4.19.5.

54. Burnett, "Church Discipline and Moral Reformation," 445. Scholars surmise that Bucer may have embraced Erasmus's suggestion in his *Paraphrase of Matthew* that children be instructed in the fundamentals of the faith and only then confirmed. See Burnett, "Church Discipline and Moral Reformation," 445.

55. Burnett, "Confirmation and Christian Fellowship," 207.

56. Ibid. The core of the ceremony, for Bucer, was the profession of faith and not the laying on of hands, and he defend this public profession biblically with appeals to profession of faith references in the Psalms. See Burnett, "Church Discipline and Moral Reformation," 446.

bond established at baptism" analogous to the Israelites' renewing their covenant with Yahweh.[57]

Like Bucer, John Calvin also rejected Roman Catholic confirmation in favour of a testimony on the part of the covenant child—namely, the "testimony of a good conscience" mentioned in 1 Peter 3:21. For adults, Calvin argued, this testimony precedes baptism, but for children it follows, and thus children are enjoined "to confirm and ratify the covenant made with them by the Lord."[58] To make this testimony, youth must first be catechized, and having given the testimony, they ought to be admitted to the Lord's table.[59] Like the Passover, which admitted only "those old enough to be able to inquire into its meaning [Exod 12:26]," the Lord's Supper, Calvin argued, is only for those "capable of discerning the body and blood of the Lord, of examining their own conscience, of proclaiming the Lord's death, and of considering its power."[60] This point is echoed by the Westminster Larger Catechism (Q 177), which distinguishes the Lord's Supper from baptism in part by designating the former as fitting "only to such as are of years and ability to examine themselves."[61] In fact, this catechism, which recommends denying the

---

57. Burnett, "Confirmation and Christian Fellowship," 215.

58. Calvin, Institutes 4.16.21. Not insignificantly, Calvin misquotes the apostle Paul in speaking of discerning "the body and blood of the Lord" where Paul speaks only of discerning "the body of the Lord," i.e., the congregation. (For an alternate view of this passage, see the chapter by Cornelis Van Dam in this volume, "Children, Passover, and Lord's Supper.") In a position similar to Calvin's, Karel Deddens refers to profession as "delayed" from the moment of baptism. Deddens, Response to Your Baptism, 8.

59. "But the best method of catechizing would be to have a manual drafted for this exercise, containing and summarizing in simple manner most of the articles of our religion, on which the whole believers' church ought to agree without controversy." Calvin, Institutes 4.19.13. The Genevan church order stipulated that each Sunday at 12 noon the children be catechized in the three town churches: St. Pierre, Madeleine, and St. Gervais. Four times a year on the Sunday before the Lord's Supper children would be questioned in public and were expected to answer or cite a summary of the catechism. The catechism was divided (from the printing of 1548) into 55 sections so that the content could be covered in the course of a year. See Calvin: Theological Treatises: LCC XXII, 84–87. This practice was later followed by the Palatinate church order for the Heidelberg Catechism. The summary Calvin may have used is published in Johannis Calvini Opera Selecta II, 152–57 (much shorter than his catechism), possibly derived from summaries drafted by Martin Bucer in 1537. See Saxer, "Der Genfer Katechismus von 1545," 6. The standard for requisite knowledge for participation in the Lord's Supper became, in the Reformation tradition, familiarity with the contents of a catechism. Note in this regard the stated purpose of, for example, the Heidelberg Catechism. See Verboom, "The Heidelberg Catechism: A Catechetical Tool," 232.

60. Calvin, Institutes 4.16.30.

61. The Westminster Shorter Catechism (Q 97) teaches that worthy participation in the Lord's Supper requires those who commune to "examine themselves of their knowledge, to discern the Lord's body, of their faith to feed upon Him, of their repentance, love, and new obedience; lest, coming unworthily, they eat and drink judgment to themselves." Cf. Westminster Larger Catechism 170.

Lord's Supper to the "ignorant or scandalous, notwithstanding their profession of faith" (Q 173), is the only Reformed confession to mention profession of faith explicitly.[62]

The precise meaning of profession of faith varies considerably in the continental Reformed tradition. For Abraham Kuyper it was the ceremony that denoted the attainment of "moral responsibility."[63] For Idzerd Van Dellen and Martin Monsma it was for those of "years of understanding" who have given evidence that their faith is not simply potential, but actual, who are truly regenerate and demonstrate the fruits of that regeneration in a godly walk.[64] Furthermore, the one professing his faith must "declare that he believes the Reformed interpretation to be correct, Biblical."[65] For William W. J. VanOene, a person professing his or her faith acknowledges that he or she believes the Word of God because it is the truth and not simply because one's parents or the church said it is.[66]

In the history of public profession of faith in the Reformed tradition, therefore, there have been two accents that are not mutually exclusive. The first is to see profession of faith as the testimony of one's personal commitment to Christ which typically precedes adult baptism but in the event of infant baptism is delayed until one has sufficient knowledge to make this testimony credibly. The second is to see profession of faith as the testimony to mark one's acquisition of the requisite knowledge and maturity to partake meaningfully in the Lord's Supper and to commit to

---

62. The Belgic Confession indicates that at the Lord's Supper we, among other things, "make confession of our faith" (Art. 35).

63. "A child is morally too irresponsible to appropriate the blessings of his baptism to himself by a public confession. . . . [S]ome years must elapse between [baptism and Lord's Supper] in the life of every individual; as many years, in fact, as are required to make his confession and his approach to the Lord's table a morally responsible action." Kuyper, *The Implications of Public Confession*, 16.

64. Van Dellen and Monsma, *The Church Order Commentary*, 251–52. The Lord's Supper, they also argued, "should be given only to those concerning whom we have reasons to believe that they are true believers" and the elders have the duty to "only admit those whom they believe to be worthy" (250). The Belgic Confession indicates that the Lord's Supper is instituted "to nourish and sustain those whom he has already regenerated and incorporated into his family, which is his church" (Art. 35).

65. Van Dellen and Monsma, *Church Order Commentary*, 251. They further comment: "We do not desire to separate ourselves from the general Christian Church, although we take a decided stand when testing those who ask to be admitted to the Lord's Supper" (252). "The consistories must have a good reason to believe that applicants are children of God, and that they have such a measure of knowledge and understanding of biblical doctrine as may reasonably be expected" (252–53).

66. VanOene, "The Way You Came," 18. Cf. Deddens, who regarded profession as a response to God's election. See *Response to Your Baptism*, 6.

the church and assume all responsibilities of membership. In the former perspective, profession of faith corresponds to infant baptism; in the latter, it qualifies one for the Lord's Supper.

Age of Accountability

At what age is one sufficiently mature to profess faith publicly and so be admitted to the Lord's table? One of the remarkable episodes in the earthly ministry of Jesus is his healing of a man blind from birth. The Pharisees were troubled not so much by the healing as they were by the healer. In their minds Jesus' apparent violation of the Sabbath called into question his credentials as one divinely empowered and commissioned. Unhappy with the healed man's testimony about Jesus, the Pharisees turned to his parents, who in turn redirected the Pharisees back to their son: "Ask him. He is of age; he will speak for himself" (John 9:21 [NIV]). What does it mean to be "of age"? Biblical scholars will argue this meant he was at least 13 years old, the legal voting age for first-century Palestinian Jews.

The phrase "of age" surfaces in the Scots Confession (1560) as a category for those children too old for infant baptism (i.e., baptism without profession) and old enough for credobaptism (i.e., baptism upon profession).[67] Precisely how old a child should be before baptism without profession is no longer appropriate is addressed by the Dutch church historian and polity expert F. L. Rutgers (1836–1917), who indicates that typically in the "southern countries" children between the ages of 10 and 12 were admitted to the Lord's table and in the "northern countries" children at the age of 14.[68] Rutgers indicates that in his day it was rare for

---

67. The Scots Confession (1560) says, "We hold that baptism applies as much to the children of the faithful as to those who are *of age and discretion*, and so we condemn the error of the Anabaptists, who deny that children should be baptised before they have faith and understanding" (Art. 23).

68. Rutgers, *Kerkelijke Adviezen* II, 68–69. Burnett, "Confirmation and Christian Fellowship," 212: "Bucer suggested that children should make a public profession of faith between the ages of 10 and 12." See also Burnett, *The Yoke of Christ*, 102–94. The early teens marked, for Bucer, the onset of "the age of reason." See Burnett, "Confirmation and Christian Fellowship," 208. It is thought that in the Palatinate children typically professed their faith when they were fourteen. See Verboom, "The Heidelberg Catechism," 232, n. 12). "A child of ten," Calvin wrote, "would present himself to the church to declare his confession of faith, would be examined in each article, and answer to each." *Institutes* 4.19.13. According to Cornelis Venema, "Only those children of believers who had professed their faith (at the age of ten to twelve) were to be received at the Table." "Paedocommunion in History (2)," 26. Cornelis Van Dam alleges on the grounds that mastering the content of early Reformation catechisms would have been too demanding for young teenagers that professions of faiths were made, in Calvin's time at least, by mid-teenagers

a child of 15 to be admitted to the Lord's table and that it was increasingly common to wait until the age of 18 or 20. He refers to a rule with which the church has operated, that an unbaptized person who is 14 and older would not be baptized without simultaneously being admitted to the Lord's Supper upon a profession of faith.[69]

Reformed pastor Johannes Jansen, whose commentary on the church order has become a standard text, argues that the development of a child occurs in three stages. Between the ages of 1 and 7, an individual is clearly a child and from 15 and beyond one clearly is not. Whether an unbaptized child between the ages of 8 and 14 should be baptized as infant or an adult (upon a profession of faith) is complex, especially if the child is between 12 and 14. The consensus in the Reformation, according to Jansen, was that a child of 15 should make profession of faith and so be baptized as an adult.[70] "Some are qualified for public confession at sixteen," Abraham Kuyper argues, "others at twenty-three years of age, but all reach a morally responsible age sometime during this interval of seven years. Hence it is the duty of each to respect these boundaries."[71]

It is noteworthy that, within continental Reformed churches at least, the age at which one professes faith has increased from 10–12 at the time of the early Reformation to 17–19 today. Implicit in this trajectory is the assumption that one does not attain maturity today at the rate at which one did in previous centuries.

A Proposed Distinction

I am of the conviction that the question how old one must be to commit to the church and assume all the responsibilities of church membership is quite distinct from the question how old one must be to be admitted to the Lord's table. If profession of faith is designed to mark the maturity with which one can be admitted to the Lord's table, such profession can and should be done at a young age (and need not be done before the

---

(e.g., at the age of 15). See Van Dam, "Children, Passover, and Lord's Supper," elsewhere in this volume. There is, however, little historical evidence for such a conjecture.

69. Rutgers, *Kerkelijke Adviezen*, 2:69. Because "knowledge of the essentials" of the Christian faith is necessary, K. de Gier argues in line with the tradition of his day that the most appropriate time for making public profession of one's faith is between 17 and 21. See his commentary on Article 61 of the Dordt Church Order in *De Dordtse kerkorde: Een praktische verklaring*.

70. Jansen, *Handleiding Gereformeerd Kerkrecht*, 60–61.

71. Kuyper, *The Implications of Public Confession*, 17.

congregation).[72] If profession of faith is designed to mark the maturity with which one can commit to the church, know its teachings, and assume all membership responsibilities, it should be later (and before the congregation).

In critiquing paedocommunion, John Murray argued that the elements of the Lord's Supper themselves suggest that some maturity is required for participation.[73] Unlike water, which is baby friendly, and bread, which is young child friendly, wine is typically an adult beverage. Furthermore, it is noteworthy, given the priest-king-prophet progression mentioned above, that priests (representing children) had to abstain from wine while serving in the temple. There was no restriction, however, on kings (representing adolescents) enjoying wine (cf. Prov 31:4). When is it reasonable for a young person to have a sip of wine? The age of 10 does not seem too young.

Reformed churches, therefore, should consider the advantages of admitting early adolescents to the Lord's table (perhaps as young as age 10, as in the early Reformation). In the volatility of life when their very identities are being forged through crisis it would be faith-confirming for such adolescents to enjoy communion and so have the constancy of Christ's love communicated through Word and sacrament. So far as I can tell, there is no biblical warrant for depriving adolescents of this life-shaping, identity-forming ritual Christ himself instituted to convey his love and grace. Moreover, inviting young adolescents to the Lord's table reinforces the notion that access to the Lord's table is provided, in God's gracious economy, not on the basis of theological, developmental, or cerebral proficiency, but simply on the basis of faith. To deny young adolescents access to the Lord's table on the grounds that their faith is inadequate or superficial is to convey a message as demoralizing as it is unbiblical. Lastly, parents could appeal in the discipline and instruction of their children not only to their baptism but to their participation in the Lord's Supper.

This having been said, it is also true that a 10-year-old child, for example, is unprepared to commit to the local church, to understand with sufficient maturity its doctrines and practices, and to assume the

---

72. For this proposal to be accepted in the Canadian Reformed churches (where I serve), Article 61 of the Church Order would need to be amended.

73. Murray, *Christian Baptism*, 77. Similarly, Calvin: "The Supper is given to older persons who, having passed tender infancy, can now take solid food." *Institutes* 4.16.30.

responsibilities of church membership (e.g., voting for office-bearers). For this reason, membership vows should not be affirmed until the age of 18, at which point an individual can finally assume all the responsibilities of church membership.[74]

In conclusion, adolescents are situated in a critical time period in life for which special pastoral ministry is required. Attention must be given to the prevailing culture in which such adolescents find themselves immersed, and godly, biblical direction must be provided from mentors they trust. One way for continental Reformed churches to assist adolescents on the pathway to maturity in Christ is to admit them to the Lord's table at a younger age, not simply to dignify their young faith but to provide them the means for spiritual enrichment from Christ.

---

74. Only after I worked out this proposal did I discover that this is precisely the approach some in the Presbyterian Church in America have adopted (private correspondence with Paul VandenBrink, pastor of Grace Valley Church in Dundas, Ontario).

Bibliography

Arnett, Jeffrey. "Emerging Adulthood: A Theory of Development from the Late Teens Through the Twenties," *American Psychologist* 55, no. 3 (2000): 469–80.

Berard, John, James Penner, and Rick Bartlett. *Consuming Youth: Leading Teens Through Consumer Culture*. Grand Rapids: Zondervan, 2010.

Berkhof, Louis. *Systematic Theology*. Grand Rapids: Eerdmans, 1941.

Burnett, Amy Nelson. "Church Discipline and Moral Reformation in the Thought of Martin Bucer." *Sixteenth Century Journal* 21, no. 3 (1991): 438–56.

———. "Confirmation and Christian Fellowship: Martin Bucer on Commitment to the Church." *Church History* 64, no. 2 (1995): 202–17.

———. "The Social History of Communion and the Reformation of the Eucharist." *Past & Present* 211, no. 1 (2011): 77–119.

———. *The Yoke of Christ: Martin Bucer and Christian Discipline*. Sixteenth Century Essays & Studies 26. Kirksville, MO: Northeast Missouri State University Press, 1994.

Calvin, John. *Calvin: Theological Treatises: LCC XXII*. Edited by J. K. S. Reid. London: Westminster, 1954.

———. *Institutes of the Christian Religion*. Edited by John T. McNeill. Translated by Ford Lewis Battles. Library of Christian Classics. Philadelphia: Westminster, 1960.

———. *Johannis Calvini Opera Selecta*. Vol. 2. Edited by Petrus Barth and Dora Scheuner. Munich: Christian Kaiser, 1952.

Catechism of the Catholic Church. 2nd ed. Washington, DC: United States Catholic Conference, 2000.

Clark, Chap. "The Changing Face of Adolescence: A Theological View of Human Development." In *Starting Right: Thinking Theologically about Youth Ministry*, edited by Kenda Creasy Dean, Chap Clark, and Dave Rahn, 41–61. Grand Rapids: Zondervan, 2001.

Clark, Warren. "Delayed Transitions of Young Adults." *Canadian Social Trends* 84 (2007): 14–22.

Cornwall, Robert. "The Rite of Confirmation in Anglican Thought During the Eighteenth Century." *Church History* 68, no. 2 (1999): 359–72.

Dean, Kenda Creasy. *Practicing Passion: Youth and the Quest for a Passionate Church*. Grand Rapids: Eerdmans, 2004.

Deddens, Karel. *Response to Your Baptism*. London, ON: Inter-League Publication Board, 1986.

De Gier, K. *De Dordtse kerkorde: Een praktische verklaring*. Houten: Den Hertog, 1989.

DeJong, A. William. *Eucharistic Reciprocity: A Practical Theological Inquiry into the Virtue of Gratitude*. Eugene, OR: Pickwick, 2019.

Erikson, Erik. *Identity, Youth, and Crisis*. New York: Norton, 1968.

Fowler, James W. *Faith Development and Pastoral Care*. Philadelphia: Fortress, 1987.

———. *Stages of Faith: The Psychology of Human Development and the Quest for Meaning*. New York: HarperCollins, 1981.

Gross, Francis L. *Introducing Erik Erikson: An Invitation to His Thinking*. Lanham, MD: University Press of America, 1987.

Hall, G. Stanley, *Adolescence: Its Psychology and Its Relations to Physiology, Anthropology, Sociology, Sex, Crime, Religion and Education*. New York: Appleton, 1904.
Hauerwas, Stanley. *Peaceable Kingdom: A Primer in Christian Ethics*. Notre Dame, IN: University of Notre Dame Press, 1993.
Hiemstra, Rick, Lorianne Dueck, and Matthew Blackaby. *Renegotiating Faith: The Delay in Young Adult Formation and What It Means for the Church in Canada*. Toronto: Faith Today Publications, 2018.
Hine, Thomas. *The Rise and Fall of the American Teenager: A New History of the American Adolescent Experience*. New York: Harper Perennial, 1999.
Jansen, Joh. *Handleiding Gereformeerd Kerkrecht*. Kampen: Kok, 1947.
Jordan, James B. "Biblical Theology Basics #5" (September 3, 2011). https://biblicalhorizons.wordpress.com. Accessed September 3, 2018.
———. *From Bread to Wine: Toward a More Biblical Liturgical Theology*. Niceville, FL: Biblical Horizons, 2001
Kohlberg, Lawrence. "The Development of Children's Orientations Toward a Moral Order: I. Sequence in the Development of Moral Thought." *Vita Humana* 6, no. 1–2 (1983): 11–33.
———. *Essays on Moral Development*. Vol. 1: *The Philosophy of Moral Development*. San Francisco: Harper & Row, 1981.
Kuyper, Abraham. *The Implications of Public Confession*. Translated by Henry Zylstra. Grand Rapids: Zondervan, 1934.
Laes, Christian. *Children in the Roman Empire: Outsiders Within*. Cambridge: Cambridge University Press, 2011.
Leithart, Peter J. *Against Christianity*. Moscow, ID: Canon, 2003.
Murray, John. *Christian Baptism*. Phillipsburg, NJ: P&R, 1962.
Penner, James, Rachael Harder, Erika Anderson, Bruno Desorcy, and Rick Hiemstra. *Hemorrhaging Faith: Why and When Canadian Adults Are Leaving, Staying and Returning to Church*. Toronto: EFC Youth and Young Adult Ministry Roundtable, 2012.
Pennington, Jonathan. "The Sermon on the Mount and the Kingdom of God." Paper presented at IBR-SBL Annual Meeting, San Antonio, TX, November 19, 2016.
Rutgers, F. L. *Kerkelijke Adviezen*. Vol. 2. Kampen: Kok, 1922.
Saxer, E. "Der Genfer Katechismus von 1545." In *Calvin-Studienausgabe*. Band 2: *Gestalt und Ordnung der Kirche*, edited by E. Busch, A. Heron, C. Link, P. Opitz, and E. Saxer, 1–135. Neukirchen-Vluyn: Neukirchener, 1997.
Setran, David P., and Chris A. Kiesling. *Spiritual Formation in Emerging Adulthood*. Grand Rapids: Baker, 2013.
Smith, Christian, and Melinda Lindquist Denton. *Soul Searching: The Religious and Spiritual Lives of American Teenagers*. New York: Oxford University Press, 2005.
Spykman, Gordon J. *Reformational Theology: A New Paradigm for Doing Dogmatics*. Grand Rapids: Eerdmans, 1992.
Stott, John. *Your Confirmation*. London: Hodder & Stoughton, 1991.
Taylor, Charles. *A Secular Age*. Cambridge, MA: Belknap, 2007.
Van Dellen, Idzerd, and Martin Monsma. *The Church Order Commentary*. Grand Rapids: Zondervan, 1961.
VanOene, William W. J. "The Way You Came." In J. Geertsema et al., *Before Many Witnesses*, 14–18. Winnipeg: Premier, 1974.

Van Slyke, Daniel G. "Confirmation: A Sacrament in Search of a Theology." *New Blackfriars* 92, no. 1041 (2011): 521–51.

Venema, Cornelis. "Paedocommunion in History (2)." *The Outlook* 55, no. 11 (2005): 26–30.

Verboom, W. "The Heidelberg Catechism: A Catechetical Tool." In *A Faith Worth Teaching*, edited by J. D. Payne and S. Heck, 230–36. Grand Rapids: Reformation Heritage, 2013.

Vos, Pieter. "Christelijke deugden in de gemeente." In *Oefenen in discipelschap: de gemeente als groeiplaats van het goede leven*, edited by James Kennedy and Pieter Vos, 27–29. Zoetermeer: Boekencentrum, 2015.

Wilson, Jonathan. *Gospel Virtues: Practicing Faith, Love, and Hope*. Eugene, OR: Wipf & Stock, 1998.

Children, Passover, and Lord's Supper

Cornelis Van Dam

When the Old Testament is brought into the discussion of children and the church, then very quickly the question can come up whether children should not participate in the Lord's Supper celebration since they did apparently take part in the celebration of the Passover. This reasoning was also on display during the conference whose papers this book is publishing.[1] Typically in such reasoning a direct line is drawn from the Passover feast described in Exodus 12, which was celebrated within Israelite households, to the institution of the Lord's Supper during Christ's last Passover with his disciples. It has even been said that we are Reformed in accepting infant baptism but Baptist when denying paedocommunion, the practice of allowing children at the Lord's table.[2] Is this true?

An examination of the issues involved shows that the above is a rather superficial way of reasoning which does not do justice to the biblical evidence. Within the space allowances available, this chapter will consider the Passover as instituted in Egypt and as celebrated in the Promised Land and in New Testament times with a view to the participation of children. The significance of Christ's instituting the Lord's Supper on the occasion of a Passover celebration and the relationship of the one meal with the other will be considered. The last major sections will deal with the issue of who qualifies for participation in the Lord's Supper. Some concluding remarks will round off this chapter.

---

1. This chapter was written after the conference, which did not feature a speech on the Old Testament and children. There are many aspects to this topic that cannot be discussed in an adequate manner here. Some helpful fairly recent detailed studies which cover all the main arguments for and against paedocommunion and give further bibliography include Sinia, "From the Least to the Greatest"; Waters and Duncan, *Children and the Lord's Supper*: Venema, *Children at the Lord's Table?* Two important articles which raised the issue of paedocommunion in the Reformed-Presbyterian community and which helped spawn the current debate are Keidel, "Is the Lord's Supper for Children?" (in favour of paedocommunion) and Beckwith, "The Age of Admission to the Lord's Supper," a response to Keidel.

2. E.g., Keidel, "Is the Lord's Supper for Children?" 305; Rayburn, "Defense of Paedocommunion," 15–156.

The Passover in Egypt

The LORD had commanded that on the final night that Israel was in Egyptian bondage each household was to slaughter, roast, and eat a lamb along with unleavened bread and bitter herbs. The blood of the lamb was to be spread on the door frames of the home, and everyone was to remain indoors until morning. The LORD would go through Egypt to kill all its first born, but he would pass over the homes with the blood on the door posts and save the first born of those families from death. This Passover was clearly a family event. The use of the term "household" (Exod 12:3–4)[3] and the mention of children who could ask about the significance of this meal (Exod 12:26) make this familial character of the meal clear. This does not, however, mean that every young infant or child necessarily partook. It is difficult to imagine infants typically weaned at age three and thus unaccustomed to solid food sharing in lamb and bitter herbs (2 Macc 7:27; cf. 1 Sam 1:24).

At the same time this celebration was more than a family event. In God's eyes, this meal was also a congregational happening. "The whole assembly of the congregation of Israel" or "all the congregation of Israel" (Exod 12:6, 47) was involved. This broad participation was nevertheless limited to those who truly belonged. Those not part of the covenant community first had to be circumcised before being allowed to share in this meal (Exod 12:48). This was therefore a covenant meal of the people of God, and children who were old enough to handle the food participated in this meal as members of the covenant by circumcision. Similar Passover feasts were held in the wilderness (Num 9:1–5) and on the plains of Jericho after Israel had crossed the Jordan (Josh 5:10–12).

We can assume that all these Passovers were held within the context of the home and family. With the settlement in the Promised Land some important changes took place.

The Passover at the Central Sanctuary

In preparation for the time that Israel would be in the land of Canaan, the LORD gave modified instructions for the celebration of the

---

3. Scripture quotations are from the English Standard Version.

Passover—instructions which deviated significantly from the first celebrations of the Passover according to the rules of Exodus 12. With Israel's settlement in the Promised Land the killing and consuming of the sacrificial lamb was no longer to take place in the homes of the Israelites, but at the central sanctuary. "You shall offer the Passover sacrifice to the LORD your God, from the flock or the herd, at the place that the LORD will choose, to make his name dwell there" (Deut 16:2). This injunction was repeated in both negative and positive forms. "You may not offer the Passover sacrifice within any of your towns that the LORD your God is giving you, but at the place that the LORD your God will choose, to make his name dwell in it, there you shall offer the Passover sacrifice" (Deut 16:5–6). With the Passover taken out of the homes, the blood could no longer be spread on the door frames of the houses. Instead, it was sprinkled on the side of the altar as was customary for the sin offerings (2 Chron 35:11; cf. 29:22).[4]

This change of venue for the Passover celebration from the home to the tabernacle or temple meant that the original family setting was pushed into the background. The new location for the feast had consequences for who would regularly attend such Passover sacrifices. God commanded that "three times a year all your males shall appear before the LORD your God at the place that he will choose: at the Feast of Unleavened Bread, at the Feast of Weeks, and at the Feast of Booths" (Deut 16:16; also Exod 23:17; 34:23). Although the Passover is not specifically mentioned, it was subsumed under the Feast of Unleavened Bread, which followed immediately after the Passover (Exod 12:14–15; Lev 23:5–6). Consequently, the two feasts are sometimes even identified with each other, as in the Gospel of Luke: "Now the Feast of Unleavened Bread drew near, which is called the Passover" (Luke 22:1).

With the centralization of worship, the Passover became a pilgrimage festival which only the males were required to attend. The word for "male" (*zəkûr*) that is used in the passages requiring them to come to the central sanctuary for the Passover festival (Exod 23:17; 34:23; Deut 16:16) suggests that the reference is to mature males. This meaning of the term is evident from the only other place where this term is used, namely in Deuteronomy 20. In this passage God commanded that all the men (*zəkûr*) in a town be killed, but the women and little ones be spared, if

---

4. Also see Keil, *Manual of Biblical Archaeology*, 2:21–22; Klein, *2 Chronicles*, 521.

that town rejected the terms of peace that were offered (Deut 20:13-14). So what would be considered a mature male in ancient Israel? The biblical record suggests the age of twenty.[5] One indicator out of many is that all those twenty and older who rebelled in the wilderness were held responsible for their actions and were excluded from entry into the Promised Land (Num 14:29-31).[6] The reason for holding them responsible was that they were expected to have the necessary discernment. Those below the age of twenty "have no knowledge of good and evil" (Deut 1:39). Other indications of twenty as the age of maturity include the fact that those twenty and older were included in the census of the people of Israel and had the obligation to "give the LORD's offering" (Exod 30:14). That was also the age for military service (Num 1:3).

Although only mature males were commanded to go and were thus expected, it is conceivable that women and even children would attend when possible. After all, the celebration of the Feast of Weeks and the Feast of Booths at the central sanctuary was expected to include sons and daughters, as well as others (Deut 16:9-15; cf. 12:7). Although we are not told of the occasion, we do read of "Elkanah and all his house" going up to the tabernacle at Shiloh to offer the yearly sacrifice and to pay his vow (1 Sam 1:21, also vv. 3-7). Once Samuel was weaned, probably about the age of three (2 Macc 7:27), his wife Hannah took their son and journeyed to Shiloh with him (1 Sam 1:24). It was not unprecedented for women and children to travel, so they may have attended the Passover festivities at the central place of worship as well.

With respect to this celebration, it is remarkable that after the text of Deuteronomy 16 mentions that the Passover lamb was to be eaten "at the place the LORD your God will choose," it goes on to say: "In the morning you shall turn and go to your tents" (Deut 16:7). This cannot refer to the Israelites going home but, rather, must relate to the temporary lodgings outside Jerusalem where they stayed for the duration of the feast of Passover-Unleavened Bread. In that case, if more members of the family came along for the Passover, they would have had their private home-

---

5. For a full discussion, see Fleishman, "The Age of Legal Maturity in Biblical Law,"and Avraham, "On the Question of Male Maturity in Israelite Society During Biblical Times."

6. It is noteworthy that the term for "male" (zəkûr) is used of these men in the ancient Damascus Document parts of which were found near Qumran, confirming again that mature males are referred to. CD 3.7 = 4Q269 2.7. See Garcia Martínez and Tigchelaar, *The Dead Sea Scrolls*, 164-65; Rabin, *The Zadokite Documents*, 10-11.

like lodgings at the central sanctuary for the duration of the feast. The fact that the people had to prepare themselves according to their fathers' houses (2 Chron 35:5-6) might also suggest that smaller family units were present in Jerusalem for the Passover.[7] However, when all has been said, the law clearly required as a minimum that only the mature males needed to come to the three festivals at the central sanctuary (Exod 23:17). The Passover was no longer legally characterized as a nuclear family event. The national dimensions of the feast were in the forefront.

After the conquest of Canaan, Scripture only specifically refers to four Passover feasts. Brief mention is made of Solomon's having the Passover celebrated (subsumed under the Feast of Unleavened Bread, 2 Chron 8:13). Considerable attention is paid to the great Passover feasts held in times of revival and a return to the true worship of the LORD during the reigns of King Hezekiah (2 Chron 30:1-27) and King Josiah (2 Kings 23:21-23; 2 Chron 35:1-19). Enormous multitudes came to celebrate. Considering the nature of the religious fervour with the desire to honour the LORD, those attending probably included at least some women and children besides the mature men. A similar composition of worshippers may have attended the Passover celebrated in the days of Ezra after the return from exile (Ezra 6:19-22; 1 Esd 7:10-15). Josephus at least comments on this celebration that "all the people streamed from their villages to the city and celebrated the festival [Passover] in a state of purity with their wives and children, according to the law of their fathers."[8]

The Passover in the Intertestamental and New Testament Times

There is considerable continuity with the Passover legislation found in Deuteronomy and the way the Passover was celebrated in intertestamental and New Testament times. The Book of Jubilees, written in about the mid-second century BC, notes that the Passover should be eaten at the sanctuary of the LORD: "And all the men who come

---

7. Craigie, *Deuteronomy*, 244; McConville, *Law and Theology in Deuteronomy*, 109-10; cf. McConville, *Deuteronomy*, 274.
8. Josephus, *Antiquities* 11.109; the quotation is from *Josephus: Jewish Antiquities, Books 9-11*, 367.

on its day will eat it [the Passover] in the sanctuary of your God before the LORD, whoever is twenty years or older, because it is written and decreed that they shall eat it in the sanctuary of the LORD" (Jub 49:17; also vv. 18–21). However, the Book of Jubilees does not restrict the celebration to those males twenty and over. They need to celebrate, but others are encouraged to do so as well. The requirement to celebrate the Passover is for "all the children of Israel" and for "all the people of congregation of Israel," that is, the nation as a whole (Jub 49:8, 14–16).[9]

As far as can be reconstructed on the basis of the available historical resources, the relevant details for our purpose about the Passover celebration in the intertestamental and New Testament times are as follows.[10] The paschal lamb was slaughtered in the inner court of the temple by worshippers who formed groups of at least ten men—Jesus and his disciples totalled thirteen participants (Matt 26:20). There were also groups that included women and slaves. A priest scattered the blood of the slaughtered lamb on the altar. The groups of worshippers ate the sacrificial lamb in different places in Jerusalem: in homes, or in a room reserved for the occasion (cf. Matt 26:17–19), or in a courtyard. The meal was shared by all in attendance, including an entire household, with children if present, according to the instructions of Exodus 12:43–48. A critical part of the Passover and an important element of instruction was the point when, in accordance with tradition, the youngest son asked the father: "Why is this night different from all the other nights?" His father helped him to ask this question if that was necessary.[11] Tradition, possibly from the time of Jesus, held that boys raced up the hill to Jerusalem for the right to bring the Passover to the temple.[12] In summary, although the law required males over twenty years of age to participate (Deut 16:16), there is no evidence that other Israelites could not attend. This conclusion is confirmed in the New Testament.

---

9. The quotation is from Wintermute, in Charlesworth, *The Old Testament Pseudepigrapha*, 141; on the date, see 43–44; VanderKam, "Jubilees, Book of," 434–35.

10. For the sources and what follows in this section, see the text and discussion of the rabbinic tradition in the Mishnah in Instone-Brewer, *Feasts and Sabbaths*, 115–200; also see Safrai, "The Temple," 891–93, and Wilson, "Passover," 677–78.

11. Perhaps this would explain the dissension among the disciples about who was the greatest and who the youngest (i.e., who would ask the question). Instone-Brewer, *Feasts and Sabbaths*, 183–84.

12. Instone-Brewer, *Feasts and Sabbaths*, 153–54, 200.

Luke informs us that the parents of Jesus "went up to Jerusalem every year at the Feast of the Passover. And when he [Jesus] was twelve years old, they went up according to custom" (Luke 2:41–42). Rather than honouring the minimum of the law with respect to the Passover, the entire family went up to Jerusalem from Nazareth. Such a journey was a considerable undertaking on foot. It would have taken three or four days to travel the approximately eighty miles or one hundred and twenty-eight kilometers involved. Much has been made of the age of Jesus being twelve as if it marked a beginning of adulthood and was somehow related to the age of accountability and the ceremony of Bar Mitzvah, which normally took place at age thirteen.[13] However, Jesus was twelve, not thirteen, and this ceremony was unknown in New Testament times. Jesus is described as a baby (Luke 2:16), a little child (Luke 2:40), and a child or boy (Luke 2:43), that is, one below the age of puberty.[14] He was not yet a man at this particular Passover. In view of the customs of the time as noted above, it is probably deducing too much from the text to assume that this was the first time that Jesus was at a Passover in Jerusalem because he was now nearing the age of taking responsibility before God for his behaviour. In any case, for our purposes it makes little difference whether this was his first trip or not. Jesus as a young boy partook of the Passover festivities.[15]

If this is the case, why can children today not attend the Lord's Supper? To answer that question, we need to see clearly how the Lord's Supper relates to the Passover.

Passover and Lord's Supper

There is both continuity and discontinuity between the Passover and the Lord's Supper. The continuity is evident in the fact that the Lord Jesus instituted the Lord's Supper during his last Passover meal (Mark 14:12–16; Luke 22:7–15).[16] Elsewhere Christ is called "our Passover lamb"

---

13. See, e.g., the summary in Bock, *Luke 1:1—9:50*, 264. Bock does recognize that the custom of Bar Mitzvah "began at a period after the time of Jesus."

14. BDAG, s.v. "παῖς."

15. See the discussion in Van Bruggen, *Lucas*, 99–100.

16. For a discussion of some of the issues dating this Passover meal, see Venema, *Children at the Lord's Table?* 85–86; Lane, *Mark*, 496–98; also see Instone-Brewer, *Feasts and Sabbaths*, 129–35.

(1 Cor 5:7). Central to both the Passover and the Lord's Supper is the command to remember the great acts of salvation that God has done for his people (Exod 12:14, 26–27; 1 Cor 11:24–26). However, in spite of the obvious elements of continuity, we also need to recognize major points of discontinuity.

The Lord's Supper Is Not a Christian Passover

The Lord's Supper is not a Christian Passover feast. It is, rather, a fulfilment of the Passover and cannot be equated with it.[17] The unleavened bread of the Passover was "the bread of affliction" because Israel "came out of the land of Egypt in haste" (Deut 16:3). Christ, however, gave this element of the Passover a new meaning. Instead of relating the bread to the afflictions of Egypt and the hasty departure of the Israelites to freedom, Christ broke the bread and said, "This is my body, which is given for you. Do this in remembrance of me" (Luke 22:19; 1 Cor 11:24). These words must have been startling to the disciples. Here was something completely new![18] The bread was now identified with Christ's body (cf. John 6:35–58), and taking and eating it was to make them remember Christ's sacrifice of himself. Him they had to think of when breaking the bread according to Christ's command and not the hasty flight from Egypt so many centuries ago.

Christ thus used the bread of the Passover in establishing one element of the Lord's Supper, but he also employed something that was not part of the original Passover. For that feast the LORD God had included and specified only three elements: the lamb, the unleavened bread, and the bitter herbs (Exod 12:8). For all these elements there was an explanation (cf. Exod 1:14; 12:13, 39). Eventually cups of wine became part of the official Passover ritual, but the LORD had never specifically asked for this.[19] But now Christ included this element of wine in the Lord's Supper. The apostle Paul in recounting the institution of the Lord's Supper speaks of "the cup of blessing" (1 Cor 10:16). This may have been the third

---

17. So, e.g., Versteeg, "Het avondmaal volgens het Nieuwe Testament," 34, and many others.
18. A point made in detail by Coppes, *Daddy, May I Take Communion?* 200–208.
19. It is interesting to note that the introduction of wine produced a problem for the participation of women and children. See the discussion in Beckwith, "The Age of Admission," 147–48.

cup in the Passover meal as it was celebrated in the time of Jesus.[20] The Lord Jesus also connected this element to himself. When he gave the cup to his disciples, he said: "Do this in remembrance of me!" (1 Cor 11:25). Christ said more, however, and so underlined the newness of what he was instituting. He also said of the wine: "This is my blood of the covenant, which is poured out for many" (Mark 14:24) and "Drink of it, all of you, for this is my blood of the covenant, which is poured out for many for the forgiveness of sins" (Matt 26:27–28). These words, too, must have been a shock to the disciples. If one thing was ingrained in the Israelite mind, it was that the drinking of blood was strictly forbidden (e.g., Lev 17:11). By introducing this meaning to the cup, the Lord Jesus divorced the Lord's Supper decisively from the Passover feast, in which no blood, not even symbolically, was shared with the guests at the table.

More needs to be mentioned, however, in considering the significance and background of Christ's establishing the Lord's Supper. With the cup the Saviour alluded to another Old Testament event and meal when he said of the wine, "This is my blood of the covenant" (Mark 14:24), and when he "took the cup, after supper, saying, 'This cup is the new covenant in my blood" (1 Cor 11:25). The expressions "my blood of the covenant" and "the new covenant in my blood" would have reminded the disciples of the confirmation of the covenant as recorded in Exodus 24. In that chapter we read that God invited Moses, Aaron, Nadab, Abihu, and seventy elders of Israel to come up Mount Sinai to the LORD. However, before that happened, sacrifices were made, and Moses read the Book of the Covenant to Israel. Then he took half the blood of the sacrifices "and threw it on the people and said, 'Behold the blood of the covenant that the LORD has made with you in accordance with all these words'" (Exod 24:8). After that, the select few men invited by God went up the mountain and had fellowship with God. "They saw the God of Israel" and "they beheld God and ate and drank" (Exod 24:10, 11). Thus, when Christ said at the institution of the Lord's Supper, "This is my blood of the covenant," he clearly had in mind that awesome event of the blood of animals being sprinkled on God's people as "the blood of the covenant" and the accompanying meal. But he himself was now the one providing this blood with his sacrifice on the cross and so initiating the

---

20. Instone-Brewer, *Feasts and Sabbaths*, 188; Garland, *1 Corinthians*, 476.

new covenant in his blood for the forgiveness of sins (Matt 26:28; 1 Cor 11:25; Heb 9:11–28).

This reality places Christ's sacrificial death in a far wider framework than only the paschal offering. It also refocuses the issue of children participating and makes the argument for their inclusion at the Lord's table on the basis of a Passover analogy far less persuasive. After all, the Passover is only part of the background of the Lord's Supper. There was also that unique meal at Mount Sinai. It was a foreshadowing of the celebration of the Lord's Supper. The significance of that meal before the face of God for the Lord's Supper must not be underestimated.[21]

Christ's death as remembered in the Lord's Supper is therefore not only the fulfilment of the Passover lamb, but also of the meal that took place on Mount Sinai. But one can go further. The Lord's Supper is in fact the fulfilment of the entire Old Testament sacrificial service which signified the forgiveness of sins that made life with God in the covenant possible. As Herman Ridderbos puts it in commenting on the institution of the Lord's Supper: "The great and central thought is that Jesus' death is the eminently propitiatory sacrifice, the fulfilment of everything that had been symbolized as such under the old covenant. And it is the fruit of this all-embracing, all-fulfilling propitiatory sacrifice which he gives to his disciples to eat and to drink as his body and blood."[22]

Since the words of the institution of the Lord's Supper refer more broadly to reconciliation and covenantal fellowship with the living God as also alluded to and seen in the sprinkling of blood and the meal with God at Mount Sinai, an element which the Lord's Supper brings to the fore much more forcefully than the Passover is the communion one has with the Lord and with each other (1 Cor 10:16–17). This emphasis on communion with the living God is not specifically associated with the Passover, nor reflected in the words spoken at that meal. But the notion of communion is certainly central in the Lord's Supper as a fulfilment, not just of the Passover, but also of the meal in Exodus 24 and, indeed, of the entire sacrificial service of the old dispensation. "The cup of blessing that we bless, is it not a participation in the blood of Christ? The bread

---

21. According to Venema, "the New Testament views the event recorded in Exodus 24 as one, if not *the most important*, of the Old Testament precedents for the Lord's Supper" (emphasis his). Venema, *Children at the Lord's Table?* 64.

22. Ridderbos, *The Coming of the Kingdom*, 426.

that we break, is it not a participation in the body of Christ?" (1 Cor 11:16–17).

In terms of the discontinuity between the Passover and the Lord's Supper, it is also noteworthy how the apostle John consciously placed a distance between the Passover meal and the Christian faith. In his Gospel he speaks of the Passover as "the feast of the Jews" (John 6:4; also 2:13, 11:55), suggesting that Christians no longer identify with this feast. It is for John's Christian readers a Jewish festival. Christians now have something quite different in the Lord's Supper.

The Place of Children

Considering all of the above, it is surely not only simplistic but also unwarranted to say that children should partake of the Lord's Supper simply because they partook of the Passover meal. The Lord's Supper is not a Christian Passover, as if the two can be equated in some way. The Lord's Supper is a new sacrament with new requirements, and what is true of the one is not necessarily true of the other.[23]

In this connection it is good to note that already in the Old Testament there were divinely directed changes in the celebration of the Passover which made the attendance of children optional and not a high priority. As we saw above, while the Passover was originally for the entire family, the LORD had removed it from its immediate family setting once Israel was in the land of Canaan and placed the celebration in the larger context of the family of Israel as a nation. The celebration now had to take place at the central place of worship. As a result, only mature males who had reached the age of discretion were obligated to attend. The new sacrament of the Lord's Supper is also not a family event but a congregational feast that takes place during a worship service. In view of the Old Testament Passover analogy, it should not be surprising if the LORD did not obligate or expect every single member of the covenant community to attend. Indeed, Scripture makes clear that a limitation has been put in place with regard to the Lord's Supper.

---

23. One can also in this connection think of how circumcision was replaced by baptism—two completely different sacraments, but both spoke of covenant promises to those who belonged to the covenant.

With the progression of the history of redemption and the fulfilment of the Passover in the Lord's Supper, the Lord restricted attendance to the table of the Lord. Whereas every single soul of Israel, young and old, had participated in the exodus out of Egyptian bondage and thus in the Passover celebration, not everyone in the congregation necessarily participates in the new exodus from the bondage of sin through the Passover lamb, Jesus Christ. Only those who "have participated in the new exodus, those who by faith in Christ can testify that they have passed from bondage to freedom, may participate in the Lord's Supper."[24] The Lord's Supper is a sacrament of the new covenant and it is for those in whose hearts the Lord has written his law (Jer 31:33). Participants of the Lord's Supper need to be actively involved by remembering and believing that Christ died as the atoning sacrifice for all their sins.[25] This reality sets the Lord's Supper apart from the sacrament of infant baptism. A child is passive in receiving baptism, but a participant in the Lord's Supper needs to be active and make a conscious choice to respond to God's saving grace in Christ by seeking admission to the table of the Lord. God's Word gives guidance for who can be admitted to this sacrament. Certain expectations must be fulfilled that in effect limit access to the Lord's Supper.

1 Corinthians 11

The classic passage that restricts access to the sacrament occurs in the context of the apostle Paul's admonishing the Corinthian believers for their reprehensible behaviour at the Lord's Supper.[26] After his rebuke, he rehearsed the institution of the Lord's Supper and then reminded them: "As often as you eat this bread and drink the cup, you proclaim the Lord's death until he comes" (1 Cor 11:26). These words are followed by this admonition and instruction:

---

24. John Stek's thoughts as articulated in Sinia, "From the Least to the Greatest," 470; see further Stek, "Children and the Lord's Supper," 4.

25. A point rightly emphasized by Venema, *Children at the Lord's Table?* 80–81, 83.

26. Discussions on 1 Cor 11:17–34 pertinent to our topic can be found in Sinia, "From the Least to the Greatest," 473–507; Knight III, "1 Corinthians 11:17–34," 75–95; Gentry, "Pauline Communion," 163–210; and Venema, *Children at the Lord's Table?* 101–25, where he interacts with Gallant, *Feed My Lambs*.

> Whoever, therefore, eats the bread or drinks the cup of the Lord in an unworthy manner will be guilty concerning the body and blood of the Lord. Let a person examine himself, then, and so eat of the bread and drink of the cup. For anyone who eats and drinks without discerning the body eats and drinks judgment on himself. That is why many of you are weak and ill, and some have died. But if we judged ourselves truly, we would not be judged. (1 Cor 11:28–31)

Notice how the apostolic instructions are not limited to only the Corinthian believers in their particular situation. He gives general guidelines that are applicable to all times and places wherever the Lord's Supper is administered, as indicated by his use of terms rightly translated as "whoever," "a person," and "anyone."[27]

For our purposes we will briefly consider two elements that are interrelated: the need to examine and judge oneself and the need to discern the body.

Examine and Judge

To avoid coming to the Lord's table in an unworthy, that is, disrespectful and sinful, way, one must examine oneself. "Let a person examine himself, then, and so eat of the bread and drink of the cup" (1 Cor 11:28). The reason for this self-examination is that "anyone who eats and drinks without discerning the body, eats and drinks judgment on himself" (1 Cor 11:29).

In the original Greek the word translated as "examine" (*dokimazō*) means "to critically examine something to determine its genuineness." In this case, those who contemplate going to the Lord's Supper need to do more than engage in a simple introspection. They need to examine themselves, as Anthony Thiselton puts it, "to confirm that their understanding, attitude, and conduct are genuine in sharing … in all that the body and blood of Christ proclaims, both in redemption and in social terms."[28] The apostle Paul sheds further light on the self-examination when he more or less equates it with judging oneself. After enjoining the Corinthians to examine themselves (1 Cor 11:28), he later elaborates by saying: "If we judged ourselves truly, we would not be

---

27. See further Knight III, "1 Corinthians 11:17–34," 84–86.
28. Thiselton, *First Corinthians*, 891.

judged" (1 Cor 11:31). Examining oneself is thus like judging oneself to make sure that one measures up to Christ's expectations. The Greek word for "judge" (*diakrinō*) used here (1 Cor 11:31) is the same as that translated as "discern" in the requirement to discern (*diakrinō*) the body (1 Cor 11:29). So the requirement to examine oneself and the requirement to judge and discern are closely related.

The verb translated as "discern" and "judge" (*diakrinō*) means "to differentiate by separating; to conclude that there is a difference; to judge; to render a legal decision; to pay careful attention."[29] The point that the apostle stresses in the immediate context is that if the Corinthians rightly examine and judge themselves, they will be able to break with the practices of disorderly conduct at the Lord's table which he had condemned (1 Cor 11:21). More generally such self-examination means that they must see their sins, ascertain whether the fruits of faith are evident in their life, and be committed to a life of holiness in the Lord. Such demands are more appropriate for adults than for children. There is no evidence of children participating in the Lord's Supper in Corinth[30] and the question can be fairly asked whether children have the necessary discernment to follow up on the apostolic exhortation.

Discerning the Body

Besides examining and judging oneself, another requirement for attending the Lord's Supper is to be able to discern the body, that is, the Lord's body. The point seems to be that participants must be able to distinguish the Lord's Supper clearly from other meals and treat it as holy. Discerning the body therefore includes being able to appreciate the reality of Christ's presence at this sacrament and to act accordingly. The weightiness of this responsibility is evident from the fact that "anyone who eats and drinks without discerning the body eats and drinks judgment on himself" (1 Cor 11:29).

---

29. BDAG, s.v. "διακρίνω."

30. The argument that, since the Lord's Supper exhibits the unity and fellowship of the congregation (1 Cor 10:16–17), children must have been included in the celebration draws much more from the text than is warranted. Gallant, *Feed My Lambs*, 31–34, 82–83, and the response by Venema, *Children at the Lord's Table?* 108–11; also see Gentry, "Pauline Communion," 173–79.

Such discerning has traditionally been understood to mean seriously considering the significance and implications of the Lord's Supper. This requirement demands a certain level of maturity, and so this passage has been a long-standing argument against paedocommunion. A more recent and increasingly popular interpretation of this passage, however, argues that "discerning the body" refers not to the sacrificial body of Christ but to the body of believers. Justification for this identification is sought in the fact that the previous chapter uses the word "body" in speaking of the congregation at Corinth: "we who are many are one body" (1 Cor 10:17). Since the apostle admonished this church about divisions in connection with the Lord's Supper, he now asks them to discern the body, that is, according to this interpretation, to recognize it and pay attention to each other's welfare. Furthermore, it is noted that the term "body" is the object of "discerning" (in 1 Cor 11:29)—not the full phrase found in a previous verse, namely, "the body and blood of the Lord" (1 Cor 11:27), which does clearly refer to the physical body of Christ. So, the use of the term "body" by itself (in v. 29) can refer to the congregation.[31] If "discerning the body" does indeed mean "recognizing and being mindful of one another," then a traditional reason for excluding children from the Lord's table is removed.

Although some are convinced by this reasoning, the vast majority of commentators remain with the traditional interpretation, which is, as noted above, that Paul is admonishing the Corinthians that they must distinguish the Lord's Supper from their everyday meals and recognize its holiness. There are at least two good reasons for staying with this interpretation. In the first place, a critical problem with the non-traditional interpretation is that in order to understand "the body" as referring to the congregation, the verb "to discern" must be understood as "to be mindful of each other" or, more expansively, "to perceive and give due weight to the church, assembled at the Supper as the body of Christ."[32] But as C. K. Barrett notes, this "strains the meaning of the verb" (*diakrinō*).[33] The verb in question, as noted earlier, means "to differentiate by separating; to conclude that there is a difference; to

---

31. These arguments are summarized in Weima, "Children at the Lord's Supper," 8; for a fuller treatment, see Fee, *1 Corinthians*, 622–24; for a survey of the interpretation of 1 Cor 11 in the Dutch Reformed tradition, Sinia, "From the Least to the Greatest," 496–504.

32. Barrett, *The First Epistle to the Corinthians*, 274.

33. Ibid.

judge; to render a legal decision; to pay careful attention." No standard Greek lexicon gives a meaning that would make obvious and facilitate the notion that the body referred to is the congregation or church.[34] Not surprisingly, the various arguments for "discerning the body" as referring to the body of the congregation fail to convince scholars like Anthony Thiselton on lexical and other grounds.[35]

The second major problem with identifying the body in 1 Corinthians 11:29 with the congregation is the immediate context. The reference to the body (in "discerning the body") is too far removed from the reference to the body of believers in the preceding chapter (1 Cor 10:16–17). With an entire discussion of women's head coverings intervening, it is expecting too much for the reader to readily connect the "body" in chapter 11 with that in chapter 10. The immediate context (1 Cor 11:24–27) refers to the body and blood of the Lord, and this context should and can be expected to determine the meaning of "the body" in verse 29 as that of the Lord. It is noteworthy in this regard that some early Greek manuscripts added for clarity's sake the words "of the Lord," indicating that already very early on "the body" in verse 29 was understood to be the Lord's. As a result of these two factors, the language used and the context of the text, the vast majority of scholars understand "discerning the body" to refer to Christ's body.[36]

Are children capable of doing the necessary judging and examining of themselves, as well as adequately discerning the body of Christ at the Lord's Supper? The classic Reformed liturgy for this celebration assumes that children are not able to judge and discern in the manner Paul enjoined. The traditional form for the celebration of the Lord's Supper has therefore understood this self-examination as calling upon all participants to consider their sins and accursedness that they may

---

34. The given definition is from BDAG, s.v. "διακρίνω"; similarly, Montanari, *The Brill Dictionary of Ancient Greek*, 492; Liddell and Scott, *A Greek-English Lexicon*, 399; Lampe, *A Patristic Greek Lexicon*, 354; Louw and Nida, *Greek-English Lexicon*, 1:362–64 (§§ 30.99, 109, 113).

35. Thiselton, *First Corinthians*, 891–94; other scholars who are likewise not convinced, as noted by Thiselton, are Barrett, Peter Marshall, Otfried Hofius, Christian Wolff, and Wolfgang Schrage; similarly Garland, 1 *Corinthians*, 552; also see Gentry, "Pauline Communion," 199–202.

36. For scholars in the Reformed tradition and otherwise to understand the body as referring to Christ's body, see, e.g., Calvin, *Institutes* 4.16.30, Hodge, 1 *Corinthians*, 233; Grosheide, 1 *Korinthe*, 314; Kistemaker, 1 *Corinthians*, 402; Morris, 1 *Corinthians*, 164; Ellingworth and Hatton, *A Handbook on Paul's First Letter to the Corinthians*, 266–67; for a possible combination of the two interpretations so that the passage refers in the first instance (due to the context) to the body of Christ and secondarily maybe alludes to the congregation, see Anderson, 1 *Korintiërs*, 167.

humble themselves before God; to examine their hearts whether they believe the sure promise of God that all their sins are forgiven them only for the sake of the suffering and death of Jesus Christ and that the perfect righteousness of Christ is freely given them as their own; and to determine whether they intend gratefully to serve the Lord with their entire life and to live in true love and harmony with their neighbour.[37] Even an author in favour of paedocommunion admits that the assumption of the Reformed liturgical form is that such self-examination implies the exclusion of children.[38] This understanding of the self-examination mandated in 1 Corinthians 11 also resonates in the Reformed and Presbyterian confessions.[39]

It is telling that since the time of the Reformation until midway through the twentieth century, the almost unanimous view among Reformed churches was that children were not able to examine themselves and to discern the body of Christ and thus were barred from the Lord's Supper.[40]

Who Attends the Lord's Table?

We have considered the matter of paedocommunion from the way it is often brought up: its proponents argue that children attended Passover and therefore should attend the Lord's Supper. We have, however, seen that the Lord's Supper is a new sacrament, not a Christian Passover. Indeed, the background of the Lord's Supper is much more than the Passover. Consequently, applying the analogy of those attending the Passover to the Lord's Supper does not hold. Furthermore, Scripture speaks of needed discernment for those attending the table of the Lord, a requirement never mentioned with Passover attendance. At this point, one could start quibbling about what the age of discernment is. It seems that often any discussion on paedocommunion can be quite vague as to exactly which children are in view. Whom are we discussing?

---

37. See the Abbreviated Form for the Celebration of the Lord's Supper in *Book of Praise*, 608–10.
38. Weima, "Children at the Lord's Supper," 7.
39. Belgic Confession, Art. 35; Heidelberg Catechism, LD 30; Larger Catechism, Q&A 171, 173–74; Shorter Catechism, Q&A 97.
40. Sinia, "From the Least to the Greatest," 474–75.

The Central Issue

Peter Leithart has helpfully clarified the underlying issue at stake. The question, he asserts, is not in essence about the age of admission. Some who reject paedocommunion may admit very young children on the supposition that they have the age of discernment. The real question is this: "Does baptism initiate the baptized to the Lord's table, so that all who are baptized have a right to the meal? Paedocommunion advocates for all their differences will answer in the affirmative. Nothing more than the rite of baptism is required for access to the Lord's table."[41] Historically, this position has even meant practising intinction, giving infants bread soaked in wine.[42] Leithart notes that "paedocommunion teaches that baptism ingrafts a child into the body of Christ, and that all members of the body of Christ are welcome at the Lord's table."[43] So, anyone who is baptized has the right to partake of the Lord's Supper. Is this assumption biblical?

Those arguing in favour of paedocommunion reason somewhat as follows. The Lord's Supper speaks of the communion of the saints and the communion with Christ. Since children are part of the congregation, they, too, share in these communions and therefore ought to participate in the Lord's Supper, which expresses this fellowship.[44] However, this approach fails to recognize that although children are certainly part of the congregation and can be reckoned as Christian children, they are so due to God's having embraced them in holy baptism and giving them his promises. They are passive recipients of divine grace and have not yet responded publicly by professing their faith and thus showing the biblically mandated discernment which would qualify them for admission to the table (1 Cor 11:27–29).

In light of these considerations, one can argue that the push for paedocommunion indicates a misunderstanding of what baptism

---

41. Leithart, "A Response," 298; similarly Mathison, *Given for You*, 313.

42. See Scudamore, "Infant Communion," 835–37. It should be noted that "in the remotest antiquity it appears that infant and child communion did not exist." Beckwith, "The Age of Admission," 127. On the nature of the evidence of paedocommunion in the early church, also see Needham, "Children at the Lord's Table."

43. Leithart, "A Response," 298; also see on the need for clarity, Thomas, "'Not a Particle,'" 97, n. 1; 115, n. 45.

44. Keidel, "Is the Lord's Supper for Children?" 336–37; Leithart, "A Response," 299; Rayburn, "Defense of Paedocommunion," 152; Gallant, *Feed My Lambs*, 101.

signifies. Children by virtue of having been baptized are not to be considered regenerated. Their baptism is a sign and seal that God's promises are not just for their parents but also for them (Acts 2:39). They are children of the covenant; they are holy (1 Cor 7:14); they have been received "into grace in Christ."[45] But this identity does not mean that they are automatically going to be believers. God does not promise that all those baptized in the covenant community will embrace his promises (cf. Rom 9:4–7). Life experience confirms this truth. As those baptized grow up, they need to respond to God's gracious promises and make these their own.[46] In this way they gain admission to the table of the Lord. It is, after all, with the mouth of faith that they are to partake of the body and blood of Christ (cf. John 6:47–58; Luke 22:17–20). But it is precisely the need to respond to God's promises with faith that those arguing for paedocommunion deny as being necessary for admission to the table. They may shrink away from the implications of intinction and limit participation in the sacrament to those who can physically take in the elements, yet, crucially, the definition of a child is always someone who has not yet reached "the age of discernment."[47]

But to insist that any baptized member of the church should attend the Lord's Supper overlooks the fact that this is a new sacrament for a new age as part of the new covenant. As mentioned earlier, although all, young and old, participated in the feast of the Passover, remembering the physical exodus out of Egyptian bondage, in the case of the Lord's Supper only those participate who, in full awareness and appreciation of having escaped the spiritual bondage of sin and judgment in the fullness of time, have consciously committed their lives to Christ and are thus able to discern the meaning, seriousness, and glory of the Lord's table. It is the sacrament commemorating *the* exodus from the bondage of sin and judgment. Not all in Israel are of Israel. In the new covenant the standards for admission to the Lord's table are different from those to the Passover. A living faith and discernment of the body of Christ are now needed.[48] Derek Thomas correctly notes the importance of maintaining

---

45. Form for the Baptism of Infants, Book of Praise, 597.

46. On the position of covenant children, see, e.g., J. Douma, Infant Baptism and Regeneration, 35—a booklet originally published in Dutch as a series of articles in De Reformatie (1976). Also, Waters and Duncan, "Where Do We Go from Here?" 181–94.

47. Keidel, "Is the Lord's Supper for Children?" 305–6.

48. See also Beckwith, "The Age of Admission," 128–30.

a credible profession of faith for admission to the Lord's Supper: "The practice of paedocommunion, in the end, leads to an unconverted church, for it removes the very means of ensuring the piety of its covenant membership—the practice of self-examination and profession of faith required before participating in the Supper."[49]

Time or Age of Admission

Scripture does not give any specific age for admittance to the Lord's Supper. God's Word does give some indication of certain important transitory points in the development of a person's maturation.[50] Roger Beckwith has shown that Scripture indicates that the age of discretion "is an age not yet attained by infants or children, and the intertestamental literature takes the same view (Wisdom 12:24-26; 15:14). At this age [of discretion], somewhere between the early teens and the early twenties probably, the new communicant will also be able to make a mature profession of faith; such a profession is implicit in his public use of the sacrament."[51]

Many factors are, of course, involved when evaluating Christian maturity—including clear indications that a covenant child has been born again and has actively embraced the baptismal promises received as an infant. What Herman Bavinck observed over a century ago still holds true today: "During puberty every child goes through a crisis that is of the greatest importance for one's physical and mental development. . . . [T]he years of puberty constitute a period when a boy or girl very often reacts to and loses the deep religious and moral impressions received in childhood." During this critical period, covenant children need to make important decisions. "They have to answer to their baptism and the new obedience to which it obliges and admonishes them." For this reason it is during this period that admission to the Lord's Supper is granted.[52]

---

49. Thomas, "'Not a Particle,'" 116-17; similarly Hendriks, *Kinderen aan de tafel van Christus?* 127-28.

50. See, e.g., the discussion in Wolff, *Anthropology of the Old Testament*, 120-21.

51. Beckwith, "The Age of Admission," 129.

52. Bavinck, *Reformed Dogmatics*, 4:155, 156; Hendriks, *Kinderen aan de tafel van Christus?* 121-23; on adolescence, see also, e.g., Schwab, "Youth/Adolescence," 661-62.

What is considered an appropriate age of discretion has varied somewhat in Reformed churches through the centuries. In Calvin's time the average age of publicly professing one's faith seems to have been about fifteen.[53] Calvin wrote about the necessity of catechizing and noted that "a child of ten would present himself to the church to declare his confession of faith, would be examined in each article [of the catechism], and answer to each; if he were ignorant of anything or insufficiently understood it, he would be taught." Calvin then went on to say that "if this discipline were in effect today, it would certainly arouse some slothful parents, who carelessly neglect the instruction of their children as a matter of no concern to them; for then they would not overlook it without public disgrace."[54] Calvin's point seems to be that children starting at age ten would be catechized and tested publicly in church in an attempt to shame and encourage the parents into assuming their duties in educating their children in the faith at home.[55] Those who conclude that children were actually admitted to the Lord's Supper at age ten overlook the fact that their instruction would continue as needed and that Calvin's reason for having the children answer questions publicly in church was to encourage parents in their parental educational responsibilities. Furthermore, Calvin also mentioned in the same context that the best method for catechizing would be to make use of a manual "summarizing in a simple manner most of the articles of our religion." This manual was in all likelihood Calvin's *Instruction in the Faith* (1537), which has been widely considered far too difficult for a ten-year-old.[56] Whatever the situation, the age

---

53. Van 't Veer, *Catechese*, 310; Plomp, *De kerkelijke tucht bij Calvijn*, 68–69; Hendriks, *Kinderen aan de tafel van Christus?* 121; also see note 56 below. For the broader context of admission to sacraments in this time period see DeMolen, "Childhood and the Sacraments in the Sixteenth Century," 49–71.

54. Calvin, *Institutes* 4.19.13.

55. See Plomp, *De kerkelijke tucht bij Calvijn*, 68–69; also on the age of admittance to the Lord's table in the time of the sixteenth century Reformation, see Hendriks, *Kinderen aan de tafel van Christus?* 120–21; Sinia, "From the Least to the Greatest," 132–33.

56. Calvin, *Instruction in Faith* (1537); for its unsuitability for young children, see De Jong, "Calvin's Contribution," 178. Some years later, Calvin came up with a second catechism which employed a question and answer method. See his Catechism of the Church of Geneva (1545) in Reid, *Calvin: Theological Treatises*, 83–139. It, too, would have been quite daunting for a ten-year-old. Among those who interpret Calvin as admitting ten-year-old children to the Lord's table is Sinia, "From the Least to the Greatest," 110; see also DeJong's contribution elsewhere in this volume, "Growing Up into Christ." On the other hand, Calvin scholars Herman Selderhuis and Elsie McKee put the age for admission to the Lord's table at "the teenage years" and "about eleven or twelve,"

of admission to the Lord's table appears to have been generally lower than it is in our time and in our particular context. This might indicate that the sixteenth century experienced an earlier age of maturity and discernment than we would normally expect today.[57] In any case, catechetical instruction and a public profession of faith preceded admission to the Lord's table. Infants and very young children were not admitted.[58]

Today the average age of admission to the Lord's Supper tends to be higher, around the age of eighteen, in the Canadian Reformed Churches and the Reformed Churches (Liberated) in the Netherlands.[59] This may be due to many different factors, such as greater expectations of not only knowing the essentials of the Reformed religion, but also of giving evidence of a mature conviction of the faith.[60] In this context it is interesting to observe that there are indications that the stage of adolescence is currently extending beyond the teenage years, so that mature discretion takes longer to develop. It will not surprise those who keep a close eye on societal cultural trends that Susan M. Sawyer has recently argued that whereas the time of adolescence used to encompass age ten to nineteen years, it now stretches from age ten to twenty-four years. Transitioning from childhood to adulthood now takes more of a typical life course than ever before. Consequently, there is a significant delay in role transitioning, including completing one's education, entering into marriage, and parenthood.[61] Recent publications have raised justified concerns about this trend. How these developments impact the maturation of one's Christian faith is open to discussion.[62] It

---

respectively; Selderhuis, *John Calvin*, 184; McKee, *The Pastoral Ministry*, 227, n. 135, where McKee also notes "the Consistory's use of catechism as a gauge of age for marriage."

57. Cf. the notion that children were treated as young adults in medieval times (pre-seventeenth century) popularized in Ariès, *Centuries of Childhood*; see the overview of early reactions to Ariès's legacy and further studies in Cunningham, "Review Essay: Histories of Childhood," 1195-208. See also, e.g., Van den Berg, *The Changing Nature of Man*, 25-32 and passim.

58. See further Sinia, "From the Least to the Greatest," 109-16.

59. Hendriks, *Kinderen aan de tafel van Christus?* 121; also for data showing how the age of admission to the Lord's table historically went up in Reformed churches in the Netherlands over the course of the nineteenth century and into the twentieth, see Sinia, "From the Least to the Greatest," 132-33.

60. For some discussion on Calvin's expectations for doctrinal knowledge and religious conviction, see Plomp, *De kerkelijke tucht bij Calvijn*, 69-71.

61. Sawyer, "The Age of Adolescence," 223-28.

62. See, e.g., Berger, *The Juvenilization of American Christianity*; West, *The Death of the Grown-Up*; Sasse, *The Vanishing American Adult*.

is noteworthy that notwithstanding these cultural developments, North American churches such as the Orthodox Presbyterian Church and to a greater extent the Christian Reformed Church have officially made decisions that have opened the door to allow for admittance to the table at a younger age.[63] This trend has also not bypassed Reformed Churches in the Netherlands.[64]

In any case, what is critical for admission to the Lord's Supper is a credible profession of faith—not the biological age as such but the spiritual maturity of the person. The ability of young persons to discern can be evaluated by their parents, who know them best, and by the consistory or session whose responsibility it is to examine and judge their qualifications for admission to the Lord's Supper. There are many factors to consider, but at the heart of it all lies evidence of true faith. The Heidelberg Catechism defines true faith as follows:

> True faith is a sure knowledge whereby I accept as true all that God has revealed to us in his Word. At the same time it is a firm confidence that not only to others, but also to me, God has granted forgiveness of sins, everlasting righteousness, and salvation, out of mere grace, only for the sake of Christ's merits. This faith the Holy Spirit works in my heart by the gospel.[65]

This biblical notion of true faith indicates that a certain level of knowledge is needed.

According to the Church Order (Article 61) adopted by the Synod of Dort (1618–19), one had to confess the Reformed religion in order to be admitted to the table. To that end, catechetical instruction was given to

---

63. For the Orthodox Presbyterian report and decisions taken (a key one being that "not age but a faith that confesses, discerns, remembers, and proclaims the body of Christ" is decisive), see *Minutes of the Fifty-Fifth General Assembly*, 374–421 (the report) and §§209, 212, 251–52. While these decisions have created room for younger members to partake, they do mean that public profession of faith is required prior to partaking of the Lord's Supper (https://www.opc.org/qa.html?question_id=191; accessed April 1, 2019). The Christian Reformed Church decided that "all baptized members who come with age- and ability-appropriate faith in Jesus Christ are welcome to the Lord's Table. . . . A formal public Profession of Faith prior to participation in the Lord's Supper is not required." *Acts of Synod 2010*, Art. 27 (pp. 810–12). A detailed account of the history of the issue in the Christian Reformed Church is found in Sinia, "From the Least to the Greatest," 315–41. For a list of prominent conservative North American Reformed and Presbyterian leaders who advocate paedocommunion and churches that practise it, see https://paedocommunion.com/whoswho (accessed April 1, 2019).

64. E.g., already in 1962 a congregation of the Reformed Churches (Liberated) admitted children to the Lord's Supper, and in 2011 a special edition of *De Reformatie* was dedicated to exploring the issue of paedocommunion with one article promoting it. See, respectively, Sinia, "From the Least to the Greatest," 341, and Roth, "Neem, eet en gedenk," 296–99.

65. Answer 21, *Book of Praise*, 523; Schaff, *The Creeds of Christendom*, 3:313.

the youth of the church. Calvin had set high standards for knowledge with his *Instruction in the Faith* and his subsequent Catechism in question and answer form.[66] Historically the Heidelberg Catechism has been at the centre of instruction in Reformed churches. However, the knowledge that is desired is not only a basic education in the Reformed faith but also a heartfelt acceptance of Scripture as the very Word of God and the spiritual knowledge indicated by one of the Catechism's proof texts: "This is eternal life, that they know you, the only true God, and Jesus Christ whom you have sent" (John 17:3). There needs to be the conviction and confidence that the Lord Jesus Christ is one's personal Saviour. Coupled with that is, of course, the needed testimony of a godly walk of life that is in harmony with this confession.

Consistent with the catechetical instruction received, the classic Reformed Form for the Public Profession of Faith asks: "Do you wholeheartedly believe the doctrine of the Word of God, summarized in the articles of the Christian faith and taught here in this Christian church?" The "articles of the Christian faith" are those comprising the Apostles' Creed, which are explained in the Heidelberg Catechism (Lord's Days 8–22).[67] Subsequent questions for the public profession of faith highlight the need to accept God's baptismal promises, detest and reject sin, and commit one's entire life in holy service to God.

In sum, it is a great privilege to partake of the Lord's Supper. It is not automatically open to everyone who is baptized, but only to those who have consciously accepted the baptismal promises, are able to "discern the body of Christ," and are committed to leading a Christian life. To that end, godly upbringing and example in the parental home and catechetical instruction are important. All members of the church should be encouraged to seek admission to the Lord's Supper and so receive the benefits of this sacrament as well.

---

66. See note 51 above.

67. The Canadian Reformed Churches changed the expression "the articles of the Christian faith" into "the Creeds" (Acts General Synod 1980, Art. 144, and Appendix IV) and into "the confessions" (Acts General Synod 1983, Art. 145, and Appendix V). See the objections noted by J. Faber, "Letter to the Editor," *Clarion* 44, no. 17 (1995): 386, and the discussion in Bouwman, *Gereformeerd Kerkrecht*, 2:381–83.

Concluding Summary

At the time of the exodus, the Passover was celebrated in the homes of the Israelites and the entire household seems to have been involved, including children. However, the norm in the Promised Land was that only mature males needed to celebrate the Passover, and they had to do so at the central place of worship, which for most of history was Jerusalem. In other words, the Passover had been removed from the home setting. This reality shows that participation by women and children was not a high priority for the LORD in Old Testament times. The possible attendance of children at Old Testament Passover meals is therefore hardly a strong argument that they are expected to be or must be present at the Lord's table.

Furthermore, the Lord's Supper is not a New Testament version of the Passover. It is a new sacrament and the fulfilment not only of the Passover but of all the sacrificial laws of the Old Testament. The fact that Christ in instituting the Lord's Supper alluded to the sacrificial meal on Mount Sinai in the presence of God underlines the discontinuity between the Lord's Supper and the Passover. Furthermore, the Lord's Supper fulfils the entire sacrificial service of the Old Testament. It is a new sacrament, and one cannot appeal to the Passover feast to justify the inclusion of children in its celebration. This new sacrament has new rules.

The instructions that the New Testament gives regarding the observance and attendance of the Lord's Supper are normative for us living in the final age before Christ's return. Any possible analogies with the Passover festivities are not normative. We have the new and better covenant (Heb 7:22; 12:24). Now that *the* sacrifice has been made by our Saviour, it is not surprising that more stringent requirements are in place for admission to the table of the Lord. There is the serious need to examine oneself, lest one fail to discern the body of Christ and be guilty of the body and blood of the Lord and so bring judgment on oneself (1 Cor 11:27–32). The historic position of the Reformed and Presbyterian churches has been that children are not capable of this type of self-examination and discernment. This position is biblically justified and should be maintained.

The key factor in determining admission to the table of the Lord is not one's biological age but a sincere and knowledgeable faith in the

Lord Jesus which is also evident from one's walk of life. Parents and office-bearers should be engaged in educating the youth in the faith and encouraging them to profess their faith and commit their lives to Christ and so also benefit from the signs and seals of the Lord's Supper.

Bibliography

Acts of Synod 2010. Grand Rapids: Christian Reformed Church in North America, 2010.

Anderson, R. Dean. 1 Korintiërs: orde op zaken in een jonge stadskerk. Commentaar op het Nieuwe Testament. Kampen: Kok, 2008.

Ariès, Philippe. *Centuries of Childhood: A Social History of Family Life*. Translated by Robert Baldick. New York: Vintage Books, 1962.

Avraham, Nachum. "On the Question of Male Maturity in Israelite Society During Biblical Times." *Journal of Northwest Semitic Languages* 38, no. 1 (2012): 31-44.

Barrett, C. K. *The First Epistle to the Corinthians*. Black's New Testament Commentary. London: Continuum, 1968.

Bauer, Walter, Frederick W. Danker, W. F. Arndt, and F. W. Gingrich. *A Greek-English Lexicon of the New Testament and Other Early Christian Literature*. 3rd ed. (BDAG). Chicago: University of Chicago Press, 2000.

Bavinck, Herman. *Reformed Dogmatics*. 4 vols. Edited by John Bolt. Translated by John Vriend. Grand Rapids: Baker Academic, 2003-8.

Beckwith, Roger T. "The Age of Admission to the Lord's Supper." *Westminster Theological Journal* 38 (1976): 123-51.

Berger, Thomas E. *The Juvenilization of American Christianity*. Grand Rapids: Eerdmans, 2012.

Bock, Darrell L. *Luke 1:1-9:50*. Baker Exegetical Commentary on the New Testament. Grand Rapids: Baker Academic, 1994.

Book of Praise: Anglo-Genevan Psalter. Winnipeg: Premier, 2014.

Bouwman, H. *Gereformeerd kerkrecht*. 2 vols. Kampen: Kok, 1928-1934.

Calvin, John. *Institutes of the Christian Religion*. Edited by John T. McNeill. Translated by Ford Lewis Battles. Library of Christian Classics. Philadelphia: Westminster, 1960.

———. *Instruction in Faith* (1537). Translated and edited by Paul T. Fuhrmann. Philadelphia: Westminster Press, 1949.

Charlesworth, James H., ed. *The Old Testament Pseudepigrapha*. Garden City, NY: Doubleday, 1983.

Coppes, Leonard J. *Daddy, May I Take Communion? Paedocommunion vs. the Bible*. Thornton, CO: Published privately, 1988.

Craigie, Peter C. *The Book of Deuteronomy*. The New International Commentary on the Old Testament. Grand Rapids: Eerdmans, 1976.

Cunningham, Hugh. "Review Essay: Histories of Childhood." *American Historical Review* 103 (1998): 1195-208.

De Jong, Peter Y. "Calvin's Contribution to Christian Education." *Calvin Theological Journal* 2 (1967): 162-201.

DeMolen, Richard L. "Childhood and the Sacraments in the Sixteenth Century." *Archiv für Reformationsgeschichte* 66 (1975): 49-71.

Douma, J. *Infant Baptism and Regeneration*. Translated from the Dutch. Kampen: Privately published, 1976.

Ellingworth, Paul, and Howard Hatton. *A Handbook on Paul's First Letter to the Corinthians*. The United Bible Societies' New Testament Handbook Series. New York: United Bible Societies, 1995.

Faber, J. "Letter to the Editor." *Clarion* 44, no.17 (1995): 386.

Fee, Gordon D. *The First Epistle to the Corinthians*. The New International Commentary on the New Testament. Grand Rapids: Eerdmans, 2014.

Fleishman, Joseph. "The Age of Legal Maturity in Biblical Law." *Journal of the Ancient Near Eastern Society of Columbia University* 21 (1992): 35–48.

Gallant, Tim. *Feed My Lambs: Why the Lord's Table Should Be Restored to Covenant Children*. Grande Prairie, AB: Pactum Reformanda, 2002.

García Martínez, Florentino, and Eibert J. C. Tigchelaar, eds. *The Dead Sea Scrolls: Study Edition*. Leiden/Grand Rapids: Brill/Eerdmans, 1997.

Garland, David E. *1 Corinthians*. Baker Exegetical Commentary on the New Testament. Grand Rapids: Baker Academic, 2003.

Gentry, Kenneth. "Pauline Communion vs. Paedocommunion." In *The Covenant: God's Voluntary Condescension*, edited by Joseph A. Pipa Jr. and C. N. Willborn, 163–210. Taylors, SC: Presbyterian Press, 2005.

Grosheide, F. W. *De eerste brief aan de kerk te Korinthe*. Commentaar op het Nieuwe Testament. Kampen: Kok, 1957.

Hendriks, A. N. *Kinderen aan de tafel van Christus?* Kampen: Van den Berg, 1986.

Hodge, Charles. *An Exposition of the First Epistle to the Corinthians*. 1857. Grand Rapids, Michigan: Eerdmans, 1953.

Instone-Brewer, David. *Traditions of the Rabbis from the Era of the New Testament*. Vol. 2a, *Feasts and Sabbaths: Passover and Atonement*. Grand Rapids: Eerdmans, 2011.

Josephus: Jewish Antiquities, Books 9–11. With an English translation by Ralph Marcus. Vol. 6. Loeb Classical Library 326. Cambridge, MA: Harvard University Press, 1937.

Keidel, Christian L. "Is the Lord's Supper for Children?" *Westminster Theological Journal* 37 (1975): 301–41.

Keil, Carl Friedrich. *Manual of Biblical Archaeology*. 2 vols. Translated by Peter Christie and Alexander Cusin. Edited by Frederick Crombie and Alexander Cusin. Edinburgh: T&T Clark, 1887–88.

Kistemaker, Simon J. *Exposition of the First Epistle to the Corinthians*. New Testament Commentary. Grand Rapids: Baker, 1993.

Klein, Ralph W. *2 Chronicles: A Commentary*. Hermeneia. Minneapolis: Fortress, 2012.

Knight III, George W. "1 Corinthians 11:17–34: The Lord's Supper: Abuses, Words of Institution and Warnings, and the Inferences and Deductions with Respect to Paedocommunion." In *Children and the Lord's Supper*, edited by Guy Waters and Ligon Duncan, 75–95. Fearn, UK: Mentor, 2011.

Lampe, G. W. H. *A Patristic Greek Lexicon*. Oxford: Oxford University Press, 2003.

Lane, William L. *The Gospel According to Mark*. New International Commentary on the New Testament. Grand Rapids: Eerdmans, 1974.

Leithart, Peter J. "A Response to '1 Corinthians 11:17–34: The Lord's Supper.'" In *The Auburn Avenue Theology, Pros and Cons: Debating the Federal Vision*, edited by D. Calvin Beisner, 297–304. Fort Lauderdale, FL: Knox Theological Seminary, 2003.

Liddell, Henry George, and Robert Scott. *A Greek-English Lexicon*. 1940. 9th ed. Revised and augmented by Henry Stuart Jones, with the assistance of Roderick Mckenzie. With a supplement 1968. Oxford: Clarendon, 1978.

Louw, Johannes P., and Eugene A. Nida, eds. *Greek-English Lexicon of the New Testament: Based on Semantic Domains*. 2nd ed. New York: United Bible Societies, 1988.

Mathison, Keith A. *Given for You: Reclaiming Calvin's Doctrine of the Lord's Supper*. Phillipsburg, NJ: P&R, 2002.

McConville, J. G. *Deuteronomy*. Apollos Old Testament Commentary. Leicester, UK/Downers Grove, IL: Apollos/IVP, 2002.

———. *Law and Theology in Deuteronomy*. JSOTSup 33. Sheffield. UK: JSOT Press, 1984.

McKee, Elsie Anne. *The Pastoral Ministry and Worship in Calvin's Geneva*. Travaux d'Humanisme et Renaissance 556. Geneva: Droz, 2016.

Minutes of the Fifty-Fifth General Assembly, May 18-25, 1988, and Yearbook of the Orthodox Presbyterian Church. Philadelphia: Orthodox Presbyterian Church, 1988.

Montanari, Franco. *The Brill Dictionary of Ancient Greek*. Edited by Madeleine Goh and Chad Schroeder. Leiden: Brill, 2015.

Morris, Leon. *The First Epistle of Paul to the Corinthians: An Introduction and Commentary*. Tyndale Bible Commentaries. Vol. 7. Grand Rapids: Eerdmans, 1958.

Needham, Nick. "Children at the Lord's Table in the Patristic Era." In *Children and the Lord's Supper*, edited by Guy Waters and Ligon Duncan, 145-61. Fearn, UK: Mentor, 2011.

Plomp, J. *De kerkelijke tucht bij Calvijn*. Kampen: Kok, 1969.

Rabin, Chaim, ed. and trans. *The Zadokite Documents*. 2nd revised ed. Oxford: Clarendon, 1958.

Rayburn, Robert S. "Defense of Paedocommunion." In *The Covenant: God's Voluntary Condescension*, edited by Joseph A. Pipa Jr. and C. N. Willborn, 147-62. Taylors, SC: Presbyterian Press, 2005.

Reid, J. K. S., ed. *Calvin: Theological Treatises*. The Library of Christian Classics: Ichthus Edition. Philadelphia: Westminster, 1954.

Ridderbos, Herman. *The Coming of the Kingdom*. Edited by Raymond O. Zorn. Translated by H. de Jongste. Philadelphia: P&R, 1962.

Roth, Robert. "Neem, eet en gedenk: de liturgische positie van de kinderen van de kerk." *De Reformatie* 86, no. 14 (2011): 296-99.

Safrai, S. "The Temple." In *The Jewish People in the First Century: Historical Geography, Political History, Social, Cultural and Religious Life and Institutions*, edited by S. Safrai and M. Stern. Compendia Rerum Iudaicarum Ad Novum Testamentum, 865-907. Assen/Amsterdam: Van Gorcum, 1974.

Sasse, Ben. *The Vanishing American Adult: Our Coming-of-Age Crisis and How to Rebuild a Culture of Self-Reliance*. Paperback ed. New York: St. Martin's Griffin, 2018.

Sawyer, Susan M. "The Age of Adolescence." *The Lancet: Child & Adolescent Health* 2, no. 3 (2018): 223-28.

Schaff, Philip. *The Creeds of Christendom*. 1877. Grand Rapids: Baker, 1966.

Schwab, Ulrich. "Youth/Adolescence V. Psychology of Religion." In *Religion Past and Present: Encyclopedia of Theology and Religion*, edited by Hans Dieter Betz, Don S. Browning, Bernd Janowski, and Eberhard Jüngel, 13:661-62. Leiden/Boston: Brill, 2013.

Scudamore, William Edward. "Infant Communion." In *A Dictionary of Christian Antiquities*, edited by William Smith and Samuel Cheetham, 1:835-37. London: John Murray, 1875-80.

Selderhuis, Herman J. *John Calvin: A Pilgrim's Life*. Downers Grove, IL: IVP Academic, 2009.

Sinia, Peter G. "From the Least to the Greatest: Children at the Lord's Supper; Paedocommunion in the Dutch Reformed Tradition." Th.D. diss. published as a book. Kampen: Theologische Universiteit van de Gereformeerde Kerken in Nederland, 2018.

Stek, John H. "Children and the Lord's Supper." *The Banner* 115, no. 48 (1980): 4.

Thiselton, Anthony C. *The First Epistle to the Corinthians: A Commentary on the Greek Text*. New International Greek Testament Commentary. Grand Rapids: Eerdmans, 2000.

Thomas, Derek W. H. "'Not a Particle of Sound Brain'—A Theological Response to Paedocommunion." In *Children and the Lord's Supper*, edited by Guy Waters and Ligon Duncan, 97–117. Fearn, UK: Mentor, 2011.

Van Bruggen, Jakob. *Lucas: het evangelie als voorgeschiedenis*. Commentaar op het Nieuwe Testament, derde serie. Kampen: Kok, 1993.

Van den Berg, J. H. *The Changing Nature of Man: Introduction to a Historical Psychology*. Translated by H. F. Croes. New York: Dell, 1975.

VanderKam, James C. "Jubilees, Book of." In *Encyclopedia of the Dead Sea Scrolls*, edited by Lawrence H. Schiffman and James C. VanderKam, 434–38. New York: Oxford University Press, 2000.

Van 't Veer, M. B. *Catechese en catechetische stof bij Calvijn*. Kampen: Kok, 1942.

Venema, Cornelis P. *Children at the Lord's Table? Assessing the Case for Paedocommunion*. Grand Rapids: Reformation Heritage Books, 2009.

Versteeg, J. P. "Het avondmaal volgens het Nieuwe Testament." In *Bij brood en beker: leer en gebruik van het heilig avondmaal in het Nieuwe Testament en in de geschiedenis van de westerse kerk*, edited by W. van 't Spijker, W. Balke, K. Exalto, and L. van Driel, 9–64. Goudriaan: De Groot, 1980.

Waters, Guy Prentiss, and J. Ligon Duncan III. "Where Do We Go from Here? Some Pastoral Reflections on the Covenant of Grace, the Children of the Church, and the Lord's Supper." In *Children and the Lord's Supper*, edited by Guy Waters and Ligon Duncan, 181–215. Fearn, UK: Mentor, 2011.

Waters, Guy, and Ligon Duncan, eds. *Children and the Lord's Supper*. Fearn, UK: Mentor, 2011.

Weima, Jeffrey A. D. "Children at the Lord's Supper and the Key Text of 1 Corinthians 11:17–34." *Calvin Theological Seminary Forum* 14, no. 2 (2007): 7–8.

West, Diana. *The Death of the Grown-Up: How America's Arrested Development Is Bringing Down Western Civilization*. New York: St. Martin's Griffin, 2007.

Wilson, M. R. "Passover." In *The International Standard Bible Encyclopedia*, edited by Geoffrey W. Bromiley, 675–79. Revised edition. Vol. 3. Grand Rapids: Eerdmans, 1986.

Wolff, Hans Walter. *Anthropology of the Old Testament*. Translated by Margaret Kohl. Philadelphia: Fortress, 1974.

Let the Children Receive the Sign of the Covenant

Jason Van Vliet

Already in the days of Abraham, children had an integral place in God's covenant. They belonged to one of the *parties* of the covenant. The LORD said to Abraham, "I will establish my covenant between me and you and your offspring after you" (Gen 17:7). The LORD also made children part of the *promise* of the covenant when he spoke to our spiritual forefather: "Look toward heaven, and number the stars . . . . So shall your offspring be" (Gen 15:5). Finally, male children received the *sign* of the covenant, that is, circumcision, already when they were just eight days old (Gen 17:12).

So whether we are reading about the parties or the promises or the sign of the covenant, children are consistently in focus. With this in mind, shouldn't the whole matter be rather straightforward? If children are included in the covenant, then they should also receive the sign of that covenant. Case closed, wouldn't you say?

Historically speaking, this has been clear, at least to the Reformed mind. For example, take some of the well-known words of the Heidelberg Catechism in Q&A 74:

> Should infants, too, be baptized? Yes. Infants as well as adults belong to God's covenant and congregation. Through Christ's blood the redemption from sin and the Holy Spirit, who works faith, are promised to them no less than to adults. Therefore, by baptism, as sign of the covenant, they must be incorporated into the Christian church and distinguished from the children of unbelievers. This was done in the old covenant by circumcision, in place of which baptism was instituted in the new covenant.[1]

To the Baptist mind, though, this answer from the Catechism is objectionable for at least three reasons. In the first place, even though some Baptists have embraced covenant theology, they would still question whether we can draw such a straight line from circumcision

---

1. The text for the Heidelberg Catechism is taken from the translation in *Book of Praise: Anglo-Genevan Psalter*, 541–42.

in the Old Testament to baptism in the New.[2] Ultimately, then, this becomes a question of *hermeneutics* and how we interpret the New in light of the Old. Secondly, they would ask whether infants belong to God's congregation in the same way that adults do because they hold to the idea of a pure church consisting of only the regenerate.[3] This is a matter of *ecclesiology* or the doctrine of the church. Thirdly, Baptists refuse to administer baptism to children because many of them have a different view of both the purpose and the direction of God's covenant sign. This involves the doctrine of the *sacraments*, and it is the specific topic we will concentrate on in this chapter.

According to the Reformed confessions the purpose of the sacraments is to focus us on God's *promises*.[4] In this way God uses his sacraments to declare and seal something *to us*. In other words, the direction is downwards—heaven to earth, God to us (↓). The Belgic Confession sums up both aspects very succinctly when it says that the sacraments "seal [God's] promises to us" (Art. 33).

This is markedly different from the common Baptist position, in which the sacrament or ordinance, as some prefer to call it,[5] predominantly testifies to the believer's faith in God. For instance, a common statement of faith, the *Baptist Faith and Message* (2000) explains that baptism is an "act of obedience symbolizing *the believer's faith* in a crucified, buried, and risen Saviour, the believer's death to sin, the burial of the old life, and the resurrection to walk in newness of life in Christ Jesus. It is a testimony to *his faith* in the final resurrection of the dead" (Art. 7).[6] This

---

2. For example, see Wellum and Parker, *Progressive Covenantalism*. Elsewhere Stephen Wellum clarifies that it is not a matter of whether covenant theology is central but a question of whether covenant theology includes one overarching covenant of grace with two dispensations or various distinct covenants with one overarching divine plan. See "Baptism and the Relationship Between the Covenants," 102. Also important in this discussion are Malone, *The Baptism of Disciples Alone*; Kingdon, *Children of Abraham*. For a Reformed response to Kingdon's position, see Douma, *Infant Baptism and Conversion*.

3. Wellum emphasizes the importance of pure church ecclesiology when he asks, "What does this have to do with infant baptism? Everything." See "Baptism and the Relationship Between the Covenants," 113.

4. Heidelberg Catechism, LD 25, Q&A 66.

5. Regarding the difference between sacrament and ordinance, see Brownson, *The Promise of Baptism*, 24–25. Also, historically speaking, Baptists have given different answers to the crucial question whether baptism is a sacrament and therefore a means of grace or not. See Tull, "The Ordinances/Sacraments in Baptist Thought"; Brewer, "'Signs of the Covenant.'"

6. "Southern Baptist Convention > The Baptist Faith and Message." This understanding of baptism is also found in a recent and well-researched publication on the topic: Schreiner and Wright, eds., *Believer's Baptism: Sign of the New Covenant in Christ*. For example, on page 7 of this book

could be represented by an upward arrow, as our faith reaches up and rests in him who is enthroned above the heavens (↑).

To make matters more perplexing, though, a Reformed catechism, the *New City Catechism* (2012), includes both directions when speaking of baptism. In Q&A 44 we read, "It signifies and seals our adoption into Christ (↓), our cleansing from sin (↓), and our commitment to belong to the Lord (↑) and to his church (↔)."[7]

So, what is it now? Does the sacramental sign of baptism point to God's redemptive promises to us, or to the believer's faith in God, or ... to both? Clearly, the last option holds out the attractive potential that it might bridge the historic gap between Baptists and the Reformed. But the question must be decided on the basis of Scripture and not, in the first place, on the potential benefits it may have for ecumenical discussions. Our goal, then, will be to survey the Old and New Testaments on this topic and then to integrate those findings into a doctrinal synopsis that pays particular attention to how children do belong to God's covenant and therefore should also receive the sign of his covenant.

The Old Testament and the Sign of the Covenant

As a complete phrase, "the sign of the covenant" (*'ôt bryt*), only occurs four times in the Old Testament. Three times the LORD designates the rainbow as the sign of his covenant with Noah and every living creature (Gen 9:12, 13, 17), and once he uses it to describe circumcision (Gen 17:11). Looking more broadly, Moses and the prophets spoke about the sign of the Sabbath within the conceptual framework of the covenant in Exodus 31:13 and Ezekiel 20:12, 20.[8] To uncover the full significance of this relatively infrequent but nonetheless important phrase,[9] we will look

---

baptism is simply called "the sign of faith" and the argument is made that since infants have not exercised faith, they should not receive the sign of faith.

7. "The New City Catechism."

8. Although the exact phrase "the sign of the covenant" is not found in Exod 31 or Ezek 20, the word "covenant" by itself does appear in Exod 31:16 and Ezek 20:37. Also, Exod 31:13 and Ezek 20:12, 20 contain phrases that correspond closely to the covenantal language in Genesis 17: "between me and you" (vv. 7, 10, 11) and "throughout your generations" (vv. 7, 9, 12).

9. Beckwith and Stott, *This Is the Day*, 13.

at each kind of occurrence in turn; however, to begin with, a few general observations will help set this matter in its broader OT context.

Observations from the OT about Signs in General

Many astonishing signs (ʼōtōt) appear on the pages of the OT. Here is a representative, but incomplete, list: turning a staff into a serpent and a healthy hand into a leprous one (Exod 4:8, 9, 17, 28, 30), the ten plagues (Exod 7:3; 8:19; 10:1–2), the miracles performed during the wilderness wanderings (Num 14:11, 22), fire springing from a rock to consume the food that Gideon brought out (Judg 6:17), and the prophecy of a virgin who will conceive and bear a son (Isa 7:10, 14). Each one of these signs is performed directly by the LORD himself or by one of the LORD's servants, such as Moses, acting on his behalf.[10] This also means that the people of Israel themselves do *not* perform signs, with the exception of observing the Sabbath (Exod 31:13), which will be explained below.

Another noteworthy feature of these signs is that, generally speaking, the LORD gives them to help people overcome doubt. The people questioned if Moses had indeed been sent by the LORD. Pharaoh procrastinated as long as he could before fully submitting to the LORD's command to let his people go. On various occasions Israel became skeptical that the LORD would actually take them into the promised land. Every time the key issue was the same: a failure to fully trust that God *will* follow through on his word. To deal with this hesitation God puts striking, visible signs before human eyes to assure all involved that if he says it, he will do it.

However, the signs themselves do not always or automatically accomplish what they are intended to do. The first nine signs did not fully persuade Pharaoh to let God's people go. The tenth one finally did. More to the point, in Numbers 14:11 the Lord says to Moses, "How long will this people despise me? And how long will they not believe in me, in spite of all *the signs* that I have done among them?"

All of this substantiates one central theme: God, or one of his appointed servants, performs signs to call people "to take his words seriously,"[11] either in saving faith (e.g., Israel) or at least in submission to

---

10. Helfmeyer, "oth," 1.188.

11. Helfmeyer, 1.171.

his will (e.g., Pharaoh). The direction in which the sign functions, though, is clear: from God to people (↓).

Rainbow: The Sign of God's Covenant in the Days of Noah

Turning more specifically to the signs *of the covenant*, we begin in the time of Noah. Because the wickedness of humanity had become so great, the Lord "blotted out *every* living thing that was on the face of the ground .... *Only* Noah was left, and those who were with him in the ark" (Gen 7:23; emphasis added). Devastation on such a massive scale must have left Noah feeling anxious, despite the fact that he and his loved ones were floating safely in the ark. When the waters subsided and Noah stepped out onto dry ground again, the Lord promised that he would never again destroy all living creatures with a flood (Gen 8:21). This promise applied both to the present and to the future, both to Noah's family and to all future generations (Gen 9:9, 12). To solemnize and reinforce his promise, God even wrapped it within an everlasting covenant (Gen 9:11, 16). The timing here is noteworthy: God's promise refers to what he *will* do, not to what he has already done.

In and of itself, receiving God's promise within an everlasting covenant was sufficient for Noah, and for us too, to trust that the Lord will fulfil his word. Yet the God of all grace also added a visible sign to his covenant, the rainbow (Gen 9:12–13).[12] This rainbow was also an eminently suitable sign, for, as F. J. Helfmeyer observes, "A 'sign' by its very nature points to something."[13] In the case of the rainbow, the water droplets of this shimmering, polychromatic arch assure Noah and his posterity that the watery deluge of cataclysmic wrath will never flow again.

In this connection we should note that only God can produce and administer this particular covenantal sign. It takes very specific meteorological conditions—a combination of rain clouds and sunshine in a certain configuration and at just the right angle—for a rainbow to appear.[14] Only the most sovereign God controls these factors, as he

---

12. Victor Hamilton says it well when he writes, "God's promise about no more floods would have been sufficient for Noah and his posterity. But to that promise he appends a covenant, and to that covenant he attaches a sign—a bow in the sky." See *The Book of Genesis 1–17*, 316.
13. Helfmeyer, "oth," 1.169.
14. "How Do Rainbows Form?"

reminds Noah when he says, "I have set *my* bow in the cloud . . . [and] When I bring clouds over the earth and the bow is seen in the clouds" (Gen 9:13–14; emphasis added). What, then, is Noah's role in all of this? Clearly he is on the receiving end. With this sign Noah and his children receive *visual* assurance that both in the present and the future God will always remember[15] his promise, even if—or more accurately *when*—the human race becomes as corrupt as it was in the days of Noah (Gen 8:21; Matt 24:37–38).

Circumcision: The Sign of God's Covenant in the Days of Abraham

In Genesis 15 the LORD came to Abram in a vision and made, or literally cut (*krt*), a covenant with him. The LORD also solemnized this covenant in a dramatic fashion. With a smoking fire pot and a flaming torch representing his glorious presence, God passed between the slaughtered halves of a heifer, a female goat, a ram, a turtledove, and a young pigeon. Much could be said about this unforgettable ceremony, but for our purposes it will suffice to highlight two points.

In the first place, as part of this covenant, Abram received three things: (1) the promise of a son who, in turn, will give Abram many more descendants (vv. 2–5); (2) the promise of possessing the land of Canaan (vv. 7, 18–21); (3) God-reckoned[16] righteousness by faith (v. 6). The last of these three promises was distinct from the first two. Chronologically speaking, Abram received the righteousness immediately, while he would have to wait for the fulfilment of the other promises. He waited about fourteen years (16:16; 17:1, 21) before God gave him and his wife a baby boy. And, in fact, he never took possession of the land, and his descendants waited more than four centuries before God fulfilled his word (15:13). Also, cognitively speaking, Abram knew about the promises of posterity and land, whereas the text gives no indication that God

---

15. It may sound as if God is the beneficiary of the rainbow sign as it seems to help him remember his promise (Gen 9:16). In this respect Hamilton even speaks of a "conspicuous anthropomorphism." See *The Book of Genesis 1—17*, 318. However, the point of the passage is that Noah and his descendants *are assured* that God will remember his promise, not that God needs a rainbow lest he forget what he said. After all, he is omniscient!

16. One central meaning of this verb, *ḥšb*, is to compute financial accounts in economic transactions. See Seybold, "ḥsb," 231. In this spiritual context the word "reckon" adequately captures the meaning.

told Abram about the gift of righteousness. He may well have received it *without* knowing it.

In the second place, and remarkably so, although the covenant is made "with Abram" (v. 18), he himself does not walk through the halves of the slaughtered animals. This would have been the expected custom when a covenant was made between two parties.[17] Instead, by passing solo through the animals, the Lord indicates that he, *and he alone*, will be the one who ultimately accomplishes *all* the promises and commitments within this covenant, whether sooner or later. From the very beginning it is clear that when it comes to covenant theology God's incomparable sovereignty must hold centre stage.

Next, let us carry these special features of God's covenant in Genesis 15 forward into a more detailed consideration of Genesis 17.[18] The LORD uses two verbs, "confirm" (v. 2) and "establish" (vv. 7, 19, 21), which indicate that he is reaffirming and expanding the covenant relationship which he began with Abram in Genesis 15.[19] The LORD also highlights his sovereignty in this relationship when he calls this covenant "my covenant" no fewer than eight times in this chapter.[20] Indeed, it was *his* covenant, for he was the only one who passed through the animals.

At the same time, as God Almighty speaks to Abraham a second time, we also expect that he has something more to say about his covenant:

1. In Genesis 15 the LORD only spoke about his covenant promises. Here in Genesis 17, the LORD immediately announces that his covenant also includes an obligation that Abraham must fulfil: "Walk before me and be blameless" (v. 1).
2. In Genesis 15 the LORD made a covenant "with Abram" (v. 18), and he spoke about Abram's offspring as a *promise within the covenant*

---

17. Lipiński, "Etymological and Exegetical Notes on the Meša' Inscription," 337.

18. Working with the JEDP theory of authorship for Genesis, some critical scholars suggest that Genesis 17 is an entirely different, Priestly, account of the covenant initiation as compared to the Yahwist account in Genesis 15. For example, see Von Rad, *Genesis*, 192–93. This view ignores the redemptive-historical progression from God's appearance to Abram when he was 86 years old (Gen 16:16) to his subsequent appearance when he was 99 years old (Gen 17:1).

19. Particularly the first verb, *ntn*, is fascinating because its standard meaning is simply "to give." If nothing else, this highlights the fact that the covenant is a *gift* from God to Abraham, and not an arrangement that was reached by mutual desire or consent. For more on the use of this verb in this context, see Deenick, *Righteous by Promise*, 16–17.

20. Gen 17:2, 4, 9, 10, 13, 14, 19, 21. More broadly, in the entire Scriptures God speaks of *"my* covenant" fifty-five times, "the covenant *of the Lord"* forty-one times, and "the covenant *of God"* five times, but never once refers to *our* covenant.

(vv. 4–5), but in Genesis 17 the LORD clarifies that these promised children will also be *participants in the covenant*. He speaks repeatedly of his everlasting covenant "with you [Abraham] *and your offspring after you*" (vv. 7, 8, 9, 10).
3. Genesis 15 clearly outlines God's promises of descendants and land, but Genesis 17 reveals that these gifts come within the overarching promise that truly encompasses all of life, namely, having a relationship with God. The heart of the covenant is this: I will "be God to you and your offspring after you" (vv. 7–8). It is striking that the relationship which God has with Abram is exactly the same for Abram's children, even those not yet born.
4. In Genesis 15 there is a ceremony that initiates the covenant, but in Genesis 17 God gives a sign, circumcision, that must be administered—also to the children of the covenant (vv. 10, 12, 14).

Yet even as the LORD adds certain elements to his covenant, the promises involved remain the same . . . or do they? As expected, the promise of many descendants reappears (Gen 17:4, 6, 16), as does the promise of the land (Gen 17:8), but is the promise of God-given righteousness by faith also still in the covenantal picture? Karl Deenick convincingly claims that it is, although it appears in a different guise. Here is the core of his argument:

> Perhaps most significant for our purposes, though, is that even before Abraham is called to be blameless in Genesis 17:1, the two notions of blamelessness and righteousness have been connected in the person of Noah: 'Noah was a righteous [*ṣaddîq*] man; he was blameless [*tāmîm*] in his generation' (Gen. 6:9, my tr.). The parallelism between the first two clauses suggests that the phrase 'he was blameless in his generation' is explanatory of the first, 'Noah was a righteous man.' . . . For the reader of Genesis, 17:1 may easily be rephrased as 'walk before me and be righteous.'[21]

However, isn't there a fundamental leap in logic here? How can the *gift* of God-reckoned righteousness of Genesis 15 suddenly become the *command* to be righteous (or blameless) in Genesis 17? Also, considering our present focus, doesn't the direction change then? The gift of righteousness is from God to us (↓), while the command calls us to return our obedience unto God (↑). Yes, there is some cognitive tension here,

---

21. Deenick, *Righteous by Promise*, 30–31.

but in a very real sense that is precisely the point. Neither Abraham nor any other mere human being can be totally blameless in God's sight. After the Fall into sin, that standard is unattainable; yet it still stands, by God's explicit decree in Genesis 17:1. How, then, can sinful Abraham ever fulfil his covenant obligation? There is only one way. He must believe that somehow *the sovereign* LORD —who passed solo through the halves of the animals—will provide the way.

But how would God do this? The path forward is not entirely clear in Genesis 17, but the general direction is indicated. It will be through *a* child—not descendants but a certain descendant. Earlier, while delineating the differences between Genesis 15 and 17, we left one off the list. In both chapters the LORD uses the word "offspring" (*zera'*). On the first occasion he emphasizes the *collective* sense: the offspring will be as many as the stars in the sky (Gen 15:5). On the second occasion, though, while maintaining the vast number of Abraham's descendants (Gen 17:4), the LORD turns his attention to the *singular* sense of the word: one particular covenant child. God *included* Ishmael and the children of Abraham's servants within his covenant, but he *established* his covenant through one special, promised, miracle-baby, named Isaac (Gen 17:20–21).[22]

This was no mere coincidence. As the Holy Spirit indicates in Galatians 3, the distinction between the collective and the singular sense of "offspring" in Genesis is much more than an intriguing lexical detail; it actually reveals the heart of the gospel message (vv. 15–18). How can blameless righteousness be both a promise and an obligation within God's covenant? Only through the miracle Child, whose name is not Isaac but Jesus. Through this Descendant, God graciously reckoned righteousness to Abraham and will also reckon it to all those who share Abraham's faith (Rom 4:1–8, 16).

In this way the significance and pedagogical suitability of circumcision becomes clearer. Of all the different signs that the LORD could have chosen for his everlasting covenant, why did he opt for circumcision? As a *sign* it is hardly visible because it is covered with clothing almost all the time. Beyond that, it can only be administered to males, but surely female Israelites belong to the covenant as well.[23] The answer to this

---

22. Bernat, *Sign of the Covenant*, 32–34.
23. For example, the inclusion of female children within the covenant is evident from the fact

question goes back to the collective and singular senses of the word "offspring." Circumcision, as a sign of the covenant, is a small surgery on the "very instrument of procreation"[24] because one of the key promises in that covenant is the blessing of many descendants (Gen 17:2), from whom, one day, a special Child will be born, the One in whom all the covenant promises will be fulfilled.[25] To teach all God's children—male *and* female—to focus on him, the Lord puts the sign of his covenant on the *male* reproductive organ.

It is also worth noting that the LORD insists that the sign of the covenant be administered also to babies who are only eight days old, when at least some of the covenant promises are not yet fulfilled. It is true, at the time of infant circumcision the LORD has already graciously fulfilled his promise to "be God" also to those newborn children (Gen 17:7), but there are other covenant promises that God will only fulfil years later, and some perhaps not even in their own lifetime. However, this is not a problem. The sign of the covenant does not inform us that God *has already* fulfilled his word. Rather, it powerfully assures us that, as a faithful God, the LORD *most certainly* keeps all his promises, whether in the past, present, or future. Moreover, part of receiving the sign is also receiving the ongoing call and obligation to believe wholeheartedly in all the covenant promises to which the sign points.

Evidently, then, God never intended circumcision to be a quick surgery that had no deeper implications for ethical living and spiritual devotion. Far from it! In fact, as the LORD continues to reveal more about the sign of his covenant, he goes on to teach that the *hearts* of his people—both male and female—must also be circumcised. This God-ordained sign in the instrument of physical *procreation* shows the need for spiritual *re*-creation, involving "the whole human self in a transformation of the mind, will, affections, desires, motivations, and actions."[26] The heart of rebellion must be cut off and replaced with a heart of love.

---

that the portion of the promised land allotted to Zelophehad had to be kept within the family through his daughters (Num 36). If his five daughters were not even covenant members, it is hard to see how they could have retained rights to the inherited land, which was ultimately a matter of covenant promise (Gen 15:7).

24. Deenick, *Righteous by Promise*, 49.

25. Ibid., 50.

26. Lemke, "Circumcision of the Heart," 319.

Interestingly, circumcision of the heart appears first in Deuteronomy 10:16 as a divine command, as the Lord says, "Circumcise therefore the foreskin of your heart, and be no longer stubborn." However, later in the same speech, Moses adds a divine promise that is also extended—let us not fail to notice—to the children of the covenant: "And the Lord your God will circumcise your heart *and the heart of your offspring*, so that you will love the Lord your God with all your heart and with all your soul, that you may live" (Deut 30:6; emphasis added). Once more, how can the Lord promise what he commands and command what he promises? What may seem incongruent to the logical mind is resolved by faith in the covenant-fulfilling God who supplies not only the reckoned righteousness but also the regeneration of the heart.

Sabbath: The Sign of God's Covenant in the Days of Moses

The sign of the Sabbath is different from the previous two. The rainbow is something that only God can put in the sky, and circumcision is a small surgery that is done to the male involved. In both cases the one benefiting from the sign is *passive*, that is to say, he is the one receiving the blessing, not the one performing it. With the sign of the Sabbath, though, things change. Observing the Sabbath is something that all of God's people must perform (Exod 20:8–11; Deut 5:12–15). In line with this, we might think that in this particular sign the roles are reversed, and that God is the one receiving regular, concrete, and visible evidence that his people are devoted to him. Surprisingly, though, that is not how Scripture speaks about the *sign* of the Sabbath. Consider each of the following verses that share a strikingly similar structure:

> Exodus 31:13
> You are to speak to the people of Israel and say, "Above all you shall keep my Sabbaths, for this is a sign between me and you throughout your generations
>   *that you may know that I, the* Lord, *sanctify you.*"

> Ezekiel 20:12
> Moreover, I gave them my Sabbaths, as a sign between me and them,
>   *that they might know that I am the* Lord *who sanctifies them.*

> Ezekiel 20:20
> Keep my Sabbaths holy that they may be a sign between me and you,
>   *that you may know that I am the* Lord *your God.*

As the final, italicized phrase in each verse demonstrates, the ultimate beneficiary of the Sabbath sign is not God but his people. Even as they observe the Sabbath, the LORD is busy reassuring them that they may know for certain[27] that, among all the nations, the LORD holds them as special (Exod 31:13; Ezek 20:12) and commits himself to them as *their* God (Ezek 20:20). John Durham states the matter concisely when he writes:

> The intention of this sign and the reason it must be kept so regularly and so conscientiously is that Israel might know Yahweh's Presence by experience, in every generation, and be reminded constantly that only by that Presence are they a people set apart.[28]

Dan Block makes the same basic point as he comments on Ezekiel 20:12:

> For him [Ezekiel] the Sabbaths served two functions. First, they were a perpetual reminder of Yahweh's covenant with them. What the rainbow was to the Noachian covenant (Gen. 9:8-17), the Sabbath was to Yahweh's covenant with Israel—an attesting sign of Israel's relationship with him. Second, they had a didactic function: to remind the nation that their special status derives from Yahweh's action alone.[29]

Here, then, a subtle yet crucial distinction comes into view. The Sabbath, *as a commandment obeyed by the people*, expresses appropriate gratitude to the God of redeeming grace. The direction of this observance is from man to God (↑). But the Sabbath, *as a sign ordained by God*, repeatedly reassures the people that, despite their many weaknesses, they are still the apple of God's holy eye (Deut 32:10).[30] The direction of this sign is from God to man (↓). Also, in this way the character of the sign, a sanctified day, makes a suitable and understandable connection with the promise being signified, a sanctified people.[31]

Before leaving this topic, we should carefully observe that in Scripture sanctification has two related meanings. It can refer to the blessing

---

27. It is striking that in each of the verses the same verb, yd ', is used. Especially when it is used in conjunction with signs, 'ōt, this word refers to much more than a mere intellectual awareness. It also includes a deep sense of recognizing the majesty of the LORD, who also realizes his promises through his insuperable power. See Botterweck and Bergman, "yda," 5.472-43.

28. Durham, *Exodus*, 412-13.

29. Block, *The Book of Ezekiel*, 632.

30. Drudge, "Living by the Sign of the Sabbath," 7-8.

31. "In a clever departure from the decalogic Sabbath, which called on Israel to sanctify the day, here the Sabbaths are perceived as gifts that declare that Yahweh had sanctified them." Block, *The Book of Ezekiel*, 632.

that God sets his people apart from the nations and makes them his own special people (Deut 7:6; 14:2). Theologians sometimes called this *positional* or *definitive* sanctification. At the same time, this word can specify a growing walk in godliness according to the commands of God (Num 15:40). Another term for this is *progressive* sanctification.[32] Under God's blessing the first leads to the second: the people whom God makes special are also the ones whom he will transform from stubborn rebels into obedient children. At the same time, these two senses of sanctification ought to be distinguished lest confusion, or even heresy, ensue.

In summary, then, the Sabbath sign ordained, and the Sabbath command obeyed are distinct, even though they are wrapped up in one and the same event. It would be easy to confuse or conflate these two aspects; however, to blur them together would be to lose the special quality of each.[33]

Sacrifices and Vows in the OT

Some may fear that this strong emphasis on the sign of the covenant confirming God's word of promise leaves little or no room for human response. But such is definitely not the case. The covenant is bilateral in its administration, even if it is unilateral in its initiation.[34] After all, God's covenant is compared to marriage (Jer 31:32), and marriage is a two-way street, as they say.

In our marriages today, the husband and the wife both symbolize their loving commitment to each other with the same sign: each gives the other a ring. However, within the OT covenant things were different. God gave various signs (e.g., rainbow, circumcision, Sabbath) to solemnly symbolize his unwavering loyalty to his covenant promises, but his people expressed their devotion in different ways. On the one hand, they did so simply through a holy lifestyle. Those who adhered to the

---

32. Hoekema, "The Reformed Perspective," 72–77.

33. As further evidence that these aspects are truly distinct, we can mention that there are solid arguments in favour of the position that the Sabbath day was also observed, albeit inconsistently, in the patriarchal era. During this time, although the Sabbath was a special day, it had not yet become a God-given sign of the covenant. That only occurred at Mt. Sinai when the Sabbath commandment was "re-enacted" and also made to be "a token or sign of the Sinaitic covenant between God and Israel." See Beckwith and Stott, *This Is the Day*, 13.

34. Geertsema, ed., *Always Obedient: Essays on the Teachings of Dr. Klaas Schilder*, 25–27.

LORD also heeded his instructions. On the other hand, if they wanted to express their devotion to God in a more solemn or ceremonial way, two options were readily available to them: the whole burnt offering (Lev 1) and the voluntary vows (Lev 27; Num 6, 30). As Cornelis Van Dam points out, the motivation behind the whole burnt offering was "to give a gift to God,"[35] not merely of something but indeed of one's whole life.[36] Later Van Dam adds, "The sacrifices of the burnt offering are pictures of the dedication that God expected from his people and which he received in the Lord Jesus Christ. In Christ we may do the same."[37] Similarly, vows and votive offerings expressed, in a concrete and tangible way, "a promise to dedicate persons or property to God."[38]

As such, God did not need these offerings or vows to know if his people were truly dedicated to him. With his omniscient eye the LORD could look straight into their hearts and discern between those who truly loved him and those who did not, regardless of how many sacrifices they offered (1 Sam 15:22–23). Yet, from their side, when God's people wanted to show their commitment to the LORD of the covenant, then the God-ordained way to do so was through sacrifices and vows, not by (re-)administering the covenant signs.

Summary

At this point we should pause and gather together what we have learned from Scripture. The table below summarizes the visible and cognitively suitable connection between the signs and the covenant promises that they signify. In each case the direction of the sign is consistently from God to his people. Following the table, a diagram takes this a step further and demonstrates how one of these signs, circumcision, assures God's people that he keeps the promises he makes, whether that fulfilment has already happened, is presently happening, or will as yet happen. In fact, as the diagram demonstrates, whether it was Abraham when he was 86 years old (Gen 16:16), or God's people when they were a large nation (Exod 1:7), all of God's people lived with a mixture of already fulfilled

---

35. Van Dam, "The Burnt Offering in Its Biblical Context," 198.
36. Ibid., 199.
37. Ibid., 206.
38. Hyman, "Four Acts of Vowing in the Bible," 231.

and yet-to-be-fulfilled promises from God. To be precise, then, covenant signs do not *report* what God has done. Rather, they visibly *confirm* what he has spoken in his promissory word. This also means that so far as the covenant sign is concerned, the exact timing of the fulfilment is, one might almost say, irrelevant. Rather it is the dependability of the promise-making God that holds centre stage.

Table 1

Sign	Promise Signified	Connection	From Whom	To Whom	Direction
Rainbow	God will not punish the world again with a flood	A pleasant sight made with water replaces the catastrophic punishment with water	God	Noah and his descendants	↓
Circumcision	God will bless his people in many ways through a particular, promised child	Surgery on the male reproductive organ points to the male Descendant in whom all covenant promises are fulfilled	God through Abraham and future fathers in the covenant	Abraham and his household	↓
Sabbath	God's promise to sanctify his people	The sanctified day reminds his people of their graciously sanctified status	God through Israel	All Israel	↓

Figure 1

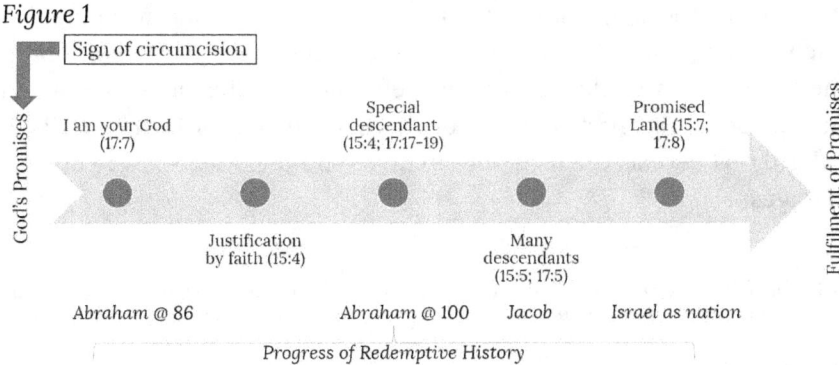

The New Testament and the Sign of the Covenant

As soon as we turn from the Old to the New Testament, we immediately appear to run stuck. There is no verse in the NT that uses the phrase "the sign of the covenant." To be sure, there are many passages that speak about signs (*sēmeia*) and there are enough sections that refer to God's covenant, but we search in vain for a verse that explicitly brings the two together. However, to halt the investigation here would be to overlook a crucial truth. In the language of Holy Scripture, the sign can refer, almost directly, to the thing signified.[39] This appears already in Genesis 17 when the Lord says, "This is my covenant . . . : Every male among you shall be circumcised" (v. 10). Of course, the covenant itself is much more than the external sign of circumcision. Yet, in a manner of speaking, the sign can stand in the place of the thing signified. A similar thing happens in the New Testament when Stephen refers to "the covenant of circumcision" (Acts 7:8). Keeping this in mind, we will again begin with a few observations about how signs in general are used in the NT and then move on to how the sign of the OT covenant, circumcision, is fulfilled in the NT and replaced with a new sign, baptism.

Observations from the NT about Signs in General

Many people were eager for signs in the days that our Saviour walked on this earth. The Jews demanded that Jesus perform mighty signs (Matt 12:38–39; 1 Cor 1:22). Often they did so to test him, and Jesus did not always give in to their tactics (Matt 16:1–4). By the same token, at the time of his own choosing, Jesus did perform mighty signs and wonders—so much, in fact, that it became a dominant theme in the Gospel of John.[40] There are no fewer than seventeen references to the signs of Jesus in this Gospel.[41] The first and last of those occurrences form a striking *inclusio* that reveals the main intention behind these signs. Here are the passages:

---

39. In this regard also see Lord's Day 29 of the Heidelberg Catechism, which reminds us that the bread of the Lord's Supper can be "called Christ's body *in keeping with the nature and usage of sacraments*."

40. Johns and Miller, "The Signs as Witnesses in the Fourth Gospel," 519.

41. John 2:11, 18, 23; 3:2; 4:48, 54; 6:2, 14, 26, 30; 7:31; 9:16; 10:41; 11:47; 12:18, 37; 20:30.

John 2:11
This, the first of his signs, Jesus did at Cana in Galilee, and manifested his glory. And his disciples *believed in him*.

John 20:30–31
Now Jesus did many other signs in the presence of the disciplines, which are not written in this book; but these are written *so that you may believe that Jesus is the Christ*, the Son of God, and that by believing you may have life in his name.

The italicized phrases indicate a link between the performance of signs and the call to, and cultivation of, faith in Christ.[42] Similarly, when the apostles of our Lord performed special signs, they did so to substantiate the power of the gospel and bring both Jew and Gentile to faith in Christ, the only foundation of salvation (Rom 15:18–21).

We observe, then, a remarkably close correlation between the OT and the NT concerning signs in general.[43] Just as signs in the OT were performed by the Lord himself or one of his special servants, so also in the NT they are performed by either Jesus Christ or his apostles. They establish the credibility of the one who does the sign and are intended to generate and reinforce faith in the recipients of the sign. This also establishes an important connection between these miraculous signs in general and, more particularly, the signs of the covenant. The *source* and *purpose* of both kinds of signs are essentially the same: they come from God and they call people to trust in God.

The Promise of Salvation in the NT

One of the key passages concerning the place of children in the new covenant is Acts 2:38–39. All the right ingredients appear to be there: baptism (v. 38), children (v. 39), and promise (v. 39), as well as a close, linguistic parallel to the formulaic, covenantal language of the OT (vv. 38–39).[44] Since these verses receive further attention in another chapter in this book,[45] we will focus on only one element here and that is the

---

42. As Johns and Miller argue, "the signs consistently play a positive role for faith in the Fourth Gospel." See "The Signs as Witnesses in the Fourth Gospel," 521.

43. See the section regarding the Sabbath above.

44. Bruce, *The Acts of the Apostles*, 130.

45. See the contribution in this volume by Visscher, "Peter, Paul, and the Promises of God to the Children of Believers."

significance of the word "promise" in verse 39, when the apostle Peter says, "For the promise is for you and for your children and for all who are far off, everyone whom the Lord our God calls to himself."

Contextually speaking, "the promise" refers most directly to the gift of the Holy Spirit (1:4; 2:33, 38) but also includes the forgiveness of sins (v. 38).[46] In this way the apostle Peter links together the same key redemptive blessings that the apostle Paul also frequently connects: justification and sanctification (e.g., Rom 5—6; Col 2:11-15). Closely related to this, the promised gift of the Holy Spirit is not limited to speaking in other languages but, as Ned Stonehouse convincingly argues, includes all "the saving benefits of Christ's work as applied to the believer by the Spirit."[47]

Next, it is striking that this promise is given *in the same way* to those who cried out, "Brothers, what shall we do?" and their children. To put a finer point on this, in the broad category of "your children," which could even include grandchildren and more distant descendants,[48] there were undoubtedly people in many different stages and statuses: children who were physically present with their parent(s), listening to Peter's sermon, and those who were not; children who were young infants and those who were much older; children who had reached the age at which they could understand and agree with what Peter was saying and those who could not; children who were mentally handicapped and those who were not; children who were born and those who were still in the womb. Yet regardless of how many differences might be found within this category of "your children," God's promise to them all remained the same. Without qualification, limitation, or differentiation, Peter says in a most straightforward fashion, "The promise is to you and to your children."

This language is even more surprising when we consider that it is precisely on Pentecost that God takes his people one significant step further into the age of *fulfilment*. For centuries God's people had been waiting for God's redemptive promises to be fulfilled: the birth of the long-expected Messiah (Isa 7:14), the atoning death of the suffering

---

46. Longenecker, Acts, 751.

47. Stonehouse, "Repentance, Baptism and the Gift of the Holy Spirit." See also Bruce, *The Book of the Acts*, 71.

48. The Greek word used here for children, *teknon*, can refer more generally to descendants; BDAG, s.v. "τέκνον." For this usage, see Acts 13:33.

Servant (Isa 53), and the outpouring of the Holy Spirit on all of God's people (Joel 2:28–29). Now, as of Pentecost day, every one of those promises has all been fulfilled. So, why is the apostle Peter still speaking about an ongoing promise that still reaches forward for generations to come? Is it not time to stop speaking of promises and to start speaking of fulfilment? No, because even though these promises have been fulfilled so far as redemptive history is concerned, they have not yet been redemptively applied with saving benefit by the power of the Spirit in the lives of those listening; *in that sense*, they remain promises. With this in mind the apostle Peter says, "The promise (of God's salvation now fulfilled in the work of Christ and the outpouring of the Holy Spirit) is for you and your children (so that the salvation gained may become the salvation given)."

This promissory language also re-appears, in a remarkable way, throughout the rest of the NT. Even in the new age of fulfilment, God's people are still called "children of *promise*" (Gal 4:28), participants in "covenants of *promise*" (Eph 2:12–13), "partakers of the *promise* in Christ Jesus" (Eph 3:6), heirs of "the *promises*" (Heb 6:12), and those who enjoy a covenant relationship that contains "better *promises*" (Heb 8:6). At this juncture, then, a decisive question comes into focus. Does the sign of baptism point to the fact that *God has promised* to give these saving benefits to his people or to the fact that *his people have already received*, through faith, such benefits from God? In other words, does the sign report a *fait accompli* or confirm a promise given? The connection between verses 38 and 39 in Acts 2 makes it clear that the call to repentance and baptism is grounded in *the promise which God makes to his people*.[49] This also means that the direction is clearly downwards (↓).

The Circumcision of Abraham and the NT Church

Another key prooftext in the NT for sacramental theology is Romans 4:11. There the apostle Paul writes, "He [Abraham] received the *sign* of

---

49. Verses 38 and 39 are connected with a Greek conjunction, *gar*, which indicates that verse 39 supplies the underlying reason, or perhaps even assurance, for what precedes it. See Lenski, *The Interpretation of the Acts of the Apostles*, 109. The grounding reason therefore is the promise that God makes. Also, at this point those inquiring of the apostle Peter have not yet received the promised Spirit, for he says, "You *will* receive the Holy Spirit" (v. 38). So again, the promise made, not the fulfilment experienced, is in view.

circumcision as a *seal* of the righteousness that he had by faith while he was still uncircumcised." In large measure, the classic description of sacraments as "holy, visible, signs and seals" takes its cue from this verse.[50] However, since the apostle Paul speaks so emphatically in Romans 4 about faith,[51] couldn't someone argue that he is affirming that circumcision is a sign of Abram's faith in God, thereby turning the direction of the sign from downwards (↓) to upwards (↑)? Indeed, Thomas Schreiner does precisely that:

> Circumcision in Romans 4 is a seal, ratification, or authentication of a faith and righteousness Abraham already had. How such an argument supports infant baptism is mystifying since faith precedes circumcision; it does not follow it. Circumcision functions as a seal because it documents and ratifies a faith and therefore a right-standing with God that already exists. If this verse is introduced into the debate on infant baptism, it clearly supports the Baptist view.[52]

Although it may sound convincing, there are two fundamental flaws in this argument. In the first place, concerning Abraham it is true: *his* faith preceded *his* circumcision. But this did not apply generally to all circumcisions, and it certainly did not apply to the other patriarchs, Isaac and Jacob. They were both circumcised on the eighth day, long before they believed, let alone made a credible profession of their faith. And surely God intended circumcision to have the same meaning for Abraham as it did for his son Isaac and the rest of his descendants in the line of the covenant.

Secondly, there is a subtle shift in Schreiner's argument that drifts away from what Scripture actually says. Romans 4:11 reads as follows, "[Abraham] received the sign of circumcision as a seal of the righteousness that he had by faith." There is a crucial distinction here: the *object* that is signified is the righteousness that comes from God and the *instrument* by which this righteousness became Abraham's own possession is faith.[53] Schreiner blurs object and instrument together,

---

50. Heidelberg Catechism, LD 25; Belgic Confession, Art. 33; Westminster Confession of Faith, Ch. 27.

51. Either the verb "to believe" (*pisteuō*) or the noun "faith" (*pistis*) occurs 17x in this chapter alone.

52. Schreiner, "Baptism in the Epistles: An Initiation Rite for Believers," 87.

53. A very literal translation of this phrase would be "a seal of the righteousness of faith" (*sphragida tēs dikaiosynēs tēs pisteōs*). The use of two genitives in a row does not offer a clear grammatical distinction between the two words, but, contextually speaking, the apostle has already explained this distinction quite clearly in Romans 3:22-25.

even reversing the revealed order, when he says that circumcision is "a seal . . . of a faith *and* righteousness." Scripture puts faith in a different position than righteousness, one that is subordinate rather than coordinate. Two distinct questions will hopefully bring the matter into sharper focus. What is signified and sealed in circumcision? *The righteousness of God*, which is clearly a gift that comes down from God, in Christ, to us (Rom 3:21–26). How can we make this gift our own? *Through faith*, which trusts in the promises of God. In Abraham's case some of those promises were already fulfilled (e.g., righteousness; Rom 4:9) while others were yet to be fulfilled (e.g., being the father of many nations; Rom 4:16–21).

One more thing needs to be mentioned. Romans 4 is not about infant baptism; in fact, it is not even about baptism per se. It is about righteousness by faith, not by works of the law (vv. 2–8, 13–15), and about the inclusion of uncircumcised Gentiles among the children of Abraham (vv. 9–12, 16–17). However, there is an important lesson about covenant continuity here. As the apostle makes clear in the verses 13–17, whether someone lives in the Old Testament or in the New, one thing certainly remains the same: the righteousness of God is imputed only to those who believe in *the promises of God*. And obviously the promise of God comes before faith. After all, if there were no divine promise, in what would we believe?

For some, like Abraham, faith precedes the administration of the sign, just as today adults are baptized after they have been converted. However, since the sign is linked to God's promise, there is another possibility: the administration of that sign can also precede faith. To say it in other words, just as it was for Isaac and Jacob—God's promise and its sign were *before* faith—so it can also be for us in the NT, particularly for the little ones in God's household. In fact, the very reason the administration of the covenant sign can precede faith is that it is not reporting the presence of faith *in us* but it is confirming the reliability of God's promises *to us*.

The Circumcision of Christ and Baptism

Turning next to Colossians 2:11–15 we find two remarkable phrases: the "circumcision made without hands" and the "circumcision of Christ" (v. 11). The apostle connects these phrases to the twofold blessing of being united with Christ's death and resurrection (v. 12).[54] The circumcision of Christ is the circumcision *done by* Christ, through his Holy Spirit, and therefore it is done without human hands.[55] In physical circumcision human hands cut off a small piece of flesh, the foreskin. However, when Christ circumcises us, the entire body of our flesh, that is, our sinful nature, is cut away and replaced by a new life (vv. 11-12), which is focused on seeking the things that are above (3:1-17). Today we call this sanctification or, more precisely, progressive sanctification.

At the same time, justification is also in the picture. The apostle goes on to say that just as surely as Christ has overcome the uncircumcision of our hearts by uniting us to his own resurrection (v. 13), so surely has he also ensured that our "record of debt," with all its legal demands, was cut off and "cancelled" by nailing it to the cross (v. 14). We also call this justification, the other promised blessing that has been included in the covenant since the days of Abram (Gen 15:6).

In short, then, we encounter a most fascinating development here in Colossians 2. In the OT *circumcision* was the *sign* of the covenant. Yet as we enter the NT era, the shadows are replaced by the substance in Christ (v. 17). In fact, the circumcision *of Christ*, done without hands, is no longer the *sign* of the covenant but now becomes the substance of what was previously signified, namely, God's promise to bless his covenant people with justification and sanctification.[56] Since the substance of circumcision done by Christ has arrived, the old shadow of circumcision done by a pair of human hands is now decidedly obsolete (Gal 5:2; Col 3:11).

---

54. The concept of union comes out strongly in two words, both containing the prefix "with" (Gk: syn): *syntaphentes* and *synēgerthēte*.

55. David Pao argues extensively that the circumcision of Christ refers to his crucifixion. See *Colossians & Philemon*, 165-66. But Jerry Sumney posits persuasively that it must refer to the act of God that "brings one into the covenant established in Christ." See *Colossians*, 137-38. From a grammatical point of view, the circumcision *of Christ* could mean either the circumcision which Christ himself underwent, that is, his crucifixion (objective genitive) or the circumcision which was done by Christ (subjective genitive). In this case, though, since Christ's crucifixion was obviously done by human hands and this circumcision is done without hands, this phrase must refer to the circumcision done by Christ.

56. Schreiner is correct in stating that we must not make quick and easy connections between physical circumcision and baptism since Colossians 2 has spiritual circumcision in view. See "Baptism in the Epistles," 78. By the same token, there is a connection between physical circumcision and the spiritual circumcision done by Christ, which, in turn, links to baptism. In short, the connection is far more Christo-centric than some defenders of infant baptism suggest, but there is still a connection.

This advance in redemptive history, though, did not make covenantal signs *as such* obsolete. In the new covenant, no less than in the old, God's people often struggle with the weakness of their faith. They still need some visible, tangible sign to reassure them. Not surprisingly, then, right in the middle of this passage about *circumcision done without hands* the apostle mentions something else, namely, *baptism done with hands*.

How is this new sign, water baptism, linked to the old one, circumcision? In short, it symbolizes, even more clearly, what God was already portraying in the OT sign of the covenant: his gracious promises of justification and sanctification.[57] Water is such a suitable symbol for both. In justification our sins are washed away (Acts 22:16). But spiritual re-birth can also be represented by water. As the baby is born from his mother's fluid-filled womb, so too the child of God is born again of water and Spirit (John 3:5). Later the apostle Paul even describes this as "the washing of regeneration" (Titus 3:5).

At the same time, unlike most of the washing we do, this sacramental washing is something that is done *to us*, not done *by us*. There is no hint of self-washing in baptism. In this way *the sign and the redemptive realities that it signifies* are aligned in the same direction, and both are downwards (↓). Concerning the redemptive realities, burial and resurrection with Christ are done *to us*, not *by us*. After all, people who are dead in their trespasses (v. 13) can neither bury nor raise themselves; in fact, they cannot even lift a finger to help in the process.[58] In line with this, the sign of baptism is also something that is done *to us*. In the entire NT, and still to this day, no one ever self-baptizes; rather, it happens to us. In the NT people were baptized by the apostles and today we are baptized by ordained ministers.

It is true, of course, that believing adults actively consent to being baptized. Their consent may seem to change the direction of the sign from downwards to upwards. However, that is not the case. The connection is between water and spiritual washing, not water and consent. After all, how would water symbolize consent in a readily

---

57. For more detail on the connection and continuity between the OT sign of circumcision and the NT sign of baptism, see Salter, "Does Baptism Replace Circumcision?" and Gibson, "Sacramental Supersessionism Revisited."

58. In this respect there is no room for the "double agency" for which Jeffrey Peterson argues. See "'The Circumcision of the Christ,'" 74, n. 25. In both physical and spiritual resurrection the one being raised is clearly not an agent but a recipient.

understandable way? Instead, whether it is adults or children who receive the waters of baptism, the downward direction remains unchanged: it is always God who does the washing and we who receive the cleansing (↓).

Before finishing this section, one more thing needs to be emphasized. The administration of circumcision or baptism, *in and of itself*, does not justify, sanctify, or eternally save a person.[59] As Abraham had to trust in God for the fulfilment of the redemptive promises, so do all the spiritual children of Abraham, whether Gentile or Jew (Rom 4:16). For this reason the apostle Paul also adds "through faith" in Colossians 2:12. However, as we discovered in Romans 4, a careful distinction must be made here. The sign of baptism *does not point* to the faith by which a person receives the saving benefits of Christ's death and resurrection, nor does baptism express his or her allegiance to Christ. The water of baptism points to the same promise that Peter spoke about on Pentecost day, God's promise to perform a double, spiritual washing. We must not blur the God-given object to which the sign points, namely, God's promises, and the God-given instrument by which the promised blessings become ours, namely, faith. Object and instrument should be related, *not* equated.

Summary

Once more our findings can be pulled together. The table below highlights the continuity, but also the progression, between the covenant signs of the OT and NT. With the coming of Christ, the sign changes but essentially the promised blessings do not, other than the fact that the shadows of the OT become the substance of the NT. Following this table there is another diagram that illustrates that what was true in redemptive history is also true, to a large degree, in the personal application of Christ's saving benefits to us. That is to say, all of God's covenant people live with a mixture of already fulfilled and yet-to-be-fulfilled promises of God. Regardless of age, mental capacity, or spiritual maturity, all of God's covenant people benefit from God's promise to be God to us and our children after us. For the rest there are

---

59. For an interesting discussion on how this important distinction is embedded right within the syntax of Colossians 2:11–12, see Gardner, "'Circumcised in Baptism–Raised Through Faith.'"

many differences. The Lord may work faith in someone's heart sooner or later; the Holy Spirit may sanctify a person more dramatically or more gradually; a person may be baptized before he believes (cf. Isaac's circumcision) or he may be baptized after he believes (cf. Abraham's circumcision); however, one thing remains the same: the sign of baptism points to God's promises and seals their reliability.

Table 2

			Promised blessings	Doctrinal equivalents
Redemptive Historical Progress	OT Sign & Shadow	Circumcision with hands	Many descendants & one Descendant (Gen 15:5; 17:6, 8; Gal 3:15-16)	Incarnation
			The land of Canaan	Eschatology; new creation
			God-reckoned righteousness (Gen 15:6; Rom 4:3-12)	Justification
			Heart circumcision, as obligation and promise (Deut 10:16; 30:6)	Sanctification
	NT Substance	Circumcision of Christ / circumcision without hands	Union with the death of Christ, the Descendant (Col 2:12a, 14)	Justification
			Union with the resurrection of Christ, the Descendant (Col 2:12b-13; 3:1-17)	Sanctification
	NT Sign	Baptism with hands	Washing of forgiveness (Acts 22:16)	Justification
			Washing of regeneration, as obligation and promise (John 3:7,8; Titus 3:5)	Sanctification

Figure 2

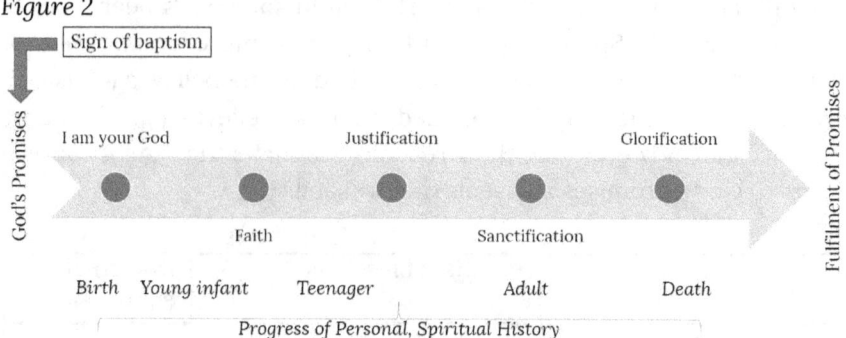

Doctrinal Synopsis

We have now come to the point that we can organize our scriptural study into a doctrinal synopsis. We will do this in a series of paragraphs that build successively upon each other. Along the way we hope to address some of the key theological and pastoral questions that arise, especially with a view to children and the sign of the covenant.

1. The covenant has two parties: God and his people. At the same time, in the days of Abram the LORD passed solo through the halves of the animals (Gen 15:17) in order to reveal that in the final analysis he retains possession of, and responsibility for, his covenant. The covenant is unilateral in its initiation, bilateral in its administration, *and* ultimately unilateral in its fulfilment. Therefore, from the start all considerations concerning the covenant need to acknowledge God's comprehensive sovereignty over this precious relationship. For example, when it comes to covenant membership, all too easily the discussion begins with an analysis of the persons involved: have they made a credible profession of faith or not? However, if we start there, then not only infants but also mentally challenged persons are excluded since they cannot (yet) do this. The picture changes dramatically, though, if we begin with God's sovereignty. If God Almighty wants to include them within *his* covenant, who are we to suggest otherwise?

2. In the Old and New Testaments, God and his ordained servants administer signs to help doubt-prone people take divine words seriously. This holds true for signs in general and signs of the

covenant in particular. Some of these signs, such as circumcision and baptism, double as sacraments. A sacrament is a visible, divine word. When God speaks, he speaks *to us*. Likewise, when he gives a sign, he shows something *to us*. In each case the direction is from God to us (↓). Even though very young children cannot understand everything that is said or shown to them, that never stops their earthly parents from talking to them or visually demonstrating something to them. Parents know that, over time and under the Lord's blessing, the children will understand one day. Fundamentally it is the same with their heavenly Father. Through the preached Word and the administered sacraments, God speaks, also to the little ones. With his blessing, in due time, they will learn, understand, and believe.

3. Circumcision and baptism, as signs of the covenant, both point to the redemptive promises that God makes to his people. These promises centre around justification and sanctification (Gen 15:6; Rom 4:11; Col 2:11–14), culminate in the LORD's commitment to be our God (Gen 17:7; Rev 21:3), and find their fulfilment in Christ, the special Offspring of the covenant (Gen 17:7; Gal 3:16). Therefore, baptism is neither a public "expression" of an internal faith[60] nor a visible report or ratification of a faith that "already exists";[61] instead, it is a visible sign and seal by which God assures his people that what he has promised, he will do. This promissory character of the sacraments, summarized so superbly in the Heidelberg Catechism,[62] is absolutely crucial to understanding baptism correctly, including the baptism of infants.[63] Since the eternal God makes his promises as part of an everlasting covenant, the time at which the sign is

---

60. Wellum, "Baptism and the Relationship between the Covenants," 114, 151. Schreiner also states that baptism "documents and ratifies a faith . . . that already exists." See "Baptism in the Epistles," 87.

61. Schreiner, "Baptism in the Epistles," 87.

62. Notice the repeated use of the word "promise" in LD 25, 26, 27, and 28.

63. This is the key flaw in an essay by Shawn D. Wright. He accurately summarizes John Calvin's understanding of the sacraments by highlighting the centrality of the promise, but then when he goes on to evaluate this position, the entire aspect of the promise virtually drops off the map, and baptism is only about the realities of salvation already experienced by believers. See "Baptism and the Logic of Reformed Paedobaptists," 209, 237–40. It is not enough for Baptists to embrace the sovereignty of God and covenant theology. They must also come to terms with the promissory character of the sacraments before they will understand the scriptural support for infant baptism.

administered does *not* need to be tied to a particular moment in the spiritual development of a believer (e.g., *after* regeneration or *after* a credible profession of faith). Rather the sign is anchored to the time-transcending promises of God. Furthermore, the sign is linked to promises *made*, not necessarily promises *already fulfilled*. Both in redemptive history and personal salvation, God fulfils many of his promises *after* the covenant sign is administered. In this way, newborn children of believing parents can also receive the sign of the covenant, while prayers request and faith anticipates the fulfilment of those promises according to the schedule of God's eternal counsel.

4. Within the two-way relationship of the covenant we have obligations just as certainly as God has made promises. By fulfilling our obligations we express our loyalty and commitment to our God. However, this aspect of covenant life is not done through administering signs but through giving sacrifices and making vows. Symbolizing loyalty within the covenant is asymmetrical: God uses signs, but his people used whole burnt and votive offerings in the Old Covenant (Lev 1, 27) and now use living sacrifices (Rom 12:1–2) and vows (1 Tim 6:12) in the New. This asymmetry in symbols corresponds well with the asymmetrical nature of the covenant itself. God and his people are both parties of the covenant, but they are certainly not standing face-to-face, on the same level. This asymmetry also extends to chronology. In his sovereignty God can give his loyalty symbol *first* and his people can respond with their vow *later*. There is nothing inherently inappropriate about that.

5. Baptism replaces circumcision. In many respects this simple statement lies at the heart of the dispute between the Reformed and Baptists. However, as our present survey of Scripture demonstrates, at their core circumcision and baptism are visible signs that both point to precisely the same divine promise: the twofold blessing of justification and sanctification. To be sure, *if* the sign of circumcision merely marks people as belonging to the Jewish nation[64] and *if* the sign of baptism is recast as a visible expression of one's faith,[65] then it is hard to see how latter replaces the former.

---

64. Wellum, "Baptism and the Relationship between the Covenants," 157.
65. Ibid., 151.

However, those understandings misrepresent the true meaning of God's covenant signs. If we look closely at what the apostle Paul says about new-covenant circumcision, that is, circumcision done by Christ and without hands, then the connection between circumcision and baptism is not merely plausible but it becomes undeniable: both point to the promise of justification and sanctification worked by God in Christ. Moreover, once this proper connection is clear, it follows that also children should receive the sign of the covenant, for this twofold blessing of the covenant is promised to them no less than to adults.

6. There is a link between the signs of the covenant and faith, but this connection needs to be carefully circumscribed. Faith is the God-given instrument by which the promises are personally appropriated, but it is not the God-ordained object to which the sign points. Moreover, the LORD uses the signs of the covenant to call his people to faith and to strengthen the same within them. To be more specific, the LORD did not give Abraham the sign of circumcision as a public testimony of his faith but rather as a divine reassurance to bolster his faith in the promises he had just received. Abraham was a genuine believer (Gen 15:6), but he still had a hard time trusting that God would give him a child through his wife Sarah. In fact, sadly he laughed at God's pledge (Gen 17:17–18). Therefore, he needed that covenantal sign of circumcision *to strengthen* his faith, not to show his faith. In much the same way baptism summons us to trust wholeheartedly in God's verbal promises, while at the same time helping us to do this very thing with its powerful visual confirmation. This obligation to trust in God rests on *all* God's covenant people, older and younger alike.

7. For a sacrament to make sense to God's people, there needs to be a simple, obvious coherence between the character of the sign and the content of the promise signified. The summary tables 1 and 2 sketch those lines of coherence. But if baptism symbolizes the believer's faith, where is the obvious connection? How does water visibly portray trust? It does not, at least not in any simple, obvious way. By contrast, the connection between water and the two-fold washing of forgiveness and regeneration is so simple that even children can readily understand it.

8. Just because God administers his covenant sign to his people, this

does not mean that each and every one of them will automatically receive the blessings signified therein. Scripture clearly says that the Lord gave his people signs through Moses, but some did not believe and received divine punishment instead of blessings (Num 14:11–12). In this respect we need to remember that, according to God's own word, his covenant involves not only two parties and two parts, but also two *outcomes*: blessings and curses (Deut 28:1—29:1; Heb 10:29). With sincere love and age-appropriate clarity, we also need to teach God's covenant children about these two outcomes.

9. When an adult is baptized, he receives the visible sign and seal of God's covenant promises to him. On that same occasion he also publicly professes his faith before God and many witnesses. Even though both things happen at the same time, we should not conflate them. As with Sabbath day observance in the old covenant, so also with adult baptism two distinct actions can happen on one and the same occasion, even if those two actions have different directions. In the case of adult baptism, the covenant sign is from God to the believer (↓), while the profession of faith is from the believer to God (↑). Let us be clear though: chronological proximity does not mean that the two actions are fused into one. In the case of adult baptism, God's administration of his covenant sign is *accompanied* by faith, but it does not metamorphosize into a symbol of faith.

10. Confessions and catechisms should echo these scriptural truths, distinctly and accurately. Concerning the doctrine of baptism, it would be most helpful if the *New City Catechism* were to be improved. Although it correctly states that this sacramental sign symbolizes the manifold blessings that God promises us in Christ (e.g., adoption, regeneration, forgiveness, and resurrection of the dead), it confuses the matter by including "our commitment to belong to the Lord" in that list. To do so is to conflate what should be distinguished. From a historical viewpoint this formulation is perhaps somewhat understandable. The *New City Catechism* relies heavily upon the Westminster Confession of Faith, which lists "his giving up unto God, through Jesus Christ, to walk in the newness of life" (Chapter 28.1) in connection with baptism, and the Westminster Shorter Catechism, which includes "our engagement to be the Lord's" (Q&A 94). However, a close study of these confessional documents, and especially their underlying scriptural support,

reveals that the Westminster divines used these phrases to describe how God takes his people out of their slavery to sin and joins them unto his Son instead (Rom 6:1–14, esp. v. 13).[66] This certainly leaves God's covenant people with a *call and duty* to be committed to the Lord and walk in newness of life, but the sign of baptism *as such* points to God's promise, not to our commitment. The *New City Catechism* could therefore be corrected to state that baptism "signifies and seals God's promises to us, namely, our adoption into Christ, our cleansing from sin, and our incorporation into the Lord's covenant and church." Alternatively, it could also say that baptism "signifies and seals . . . our obligation to be loyal to the Lord and to his church."[67]

Confessing all of these doctrinal truths compels us in one direction: to exclude children from baptism is wrong. Admittedly, it does not answer all the questions concerning infant baptism. As stated in the introduction, there are also crucial questions concerning hermeneutics and ecclesiology that have not been addressed in this essay.

However, as the scriptural survey demonstrates, excluding the little ones, or those who are non-verbal due to mental incapacity, from the sign of God's covenant reveals a misunderstanding of the basic purpose and direction of all signs of the covenant. These signs reassure us of God's promises to us (↓), not our commitment to him (↑). Refusing to baptize children also obscures the simple clarity of God's sign: baptism is all about washing, and children, too, need washing. In fact, already from birth sinful children need to be washed by the blood and Spirit of Christ just as much as sinful adults do. So, also in the new and better covenant (Heb 7:22), let the children come and receive the sign of God's covenant.

---

66. Concerning baptism, and particularly the phrases about "giving up unto God" and "our engagement to be the Lord's," the Westminster Standards reference Romans 6. In the first half of that chapter it is clear that it is God who unites us to Christ and thus brings us from death into life, from slavery to sin into service to God. As a result of God's redemptive action, we are also called to walk in newness of life (v. 4). However, to be precise, baptism indicates that *God calls us* to this new life, not that we have already decided to make the commitment to pursue this new life. Even if the latter is true, it is not what baptism is pointing towards.

67. In this regard the commentary of Chad Van Dixhoorn on Chapter 28 of the Westminster Confession is helpful: "It [baptism] includes a call to be what we are in Christ: it *calls us* to surrender our lives to God, through Christ" (emphasis mine). Van Dixhoorn, *Confessing the Faith*, 368.

Bibliography

Bauer, Walter, Frederick W. Danker, W. F. Arndt, and F. W. Gingrich. A *Greek-English Lexicon of the New Testament and Other Early Christian Literature*. 3rd ed. (BDAG). Chicago: University of Chicago Press, 2000.

Beckwith, Roger T., and Wilfrid Stott. *This Is the Day: The Biblical Doctrine of the Christian Sunday in Its Jewish and Early Church Setting*. London: Marshall, Morgan & Scott, 1978.

Bernat, David A. *Sign of the Covenant: Circumcision in the Priestly Tradition*. Ancient Israel and Its Literature 3. Atlanta, GA: Society of Biblical Literature, 2009.

Block, Daniel Isaac. *The Book of Ezekiel*. The New International Commentary on the Old Testament. Grand Rapids: Eerdmans, 2007.

Book of Praise: Anglo-Genevan Psalter. Winnipeg: Premier, 2014.

Botterweck, G. J., and J. Bergman. "yda." In *Theological Dictionary of the Old Testament*, edited by G. Johannes Botterweck, Helmer Ringgren, and Geoffrey W. Bromiley. Grand Rapids: Eerdmans, 1974.

Brewer, Brian C. "'Signs of the Covenant': The Development of Sacramental Thought in Baptist Circles." *Perspectives in Religious Studies* 36, no. 4 (2009): 407–20.

Brownson, James V. *The Promise of Baptism: An Introduction to Baptism in Scripture and the Reformed Tradition*. Grand Rapids: Eerdmans, 2007.

Bruce, F. F. *The Acts of the Apostles: The Greek Text with Introduction and Commentary*. 3rd ed. Grand Rapids: Eerdmans, 1990.

———. *The Book of the Acts*. Rev. ed. The New International Commentary on the New Testament. Grand Rapids: Eerdmans, 2008.

Deenick, Karl. *Righteous by Promise: A Biblical Theology of Circumcision*. New Studies in Biblical Theology 45. Downers Grove, IL: Apollos, 2018.

Douma, Jochem. *Infant Baptism and Conversion*. Winnipeg: Premier, 1979.

Drudge, Kevin R. "Living by the Sign of the Sabbath." *Vision* 6, no. 2 (2005): 6–13.

Durham, John I. *Exodus*. Word Biblical Commentary. Waco, TX: Word Books, 1987.

Gardner, Paul D. "'Circumcised in Baptism–Raised Through Faith': A Note on Col 2:11-12." *The Westminster Theological Journal* 45, no. 1 (1983): 172–77.

Geertsema, J., ed. *Always Obedient: Essays on the Teachings of Dr. Klaas Schilder*. Phillipsburg, NJ: P&R, 1995.

Gibson, David. "Sacramental Supersessionism Revisited: A Response to Martin Salter on the Relationship Between Circumcision and Baptism." *Themelios* 37, no. 2 (2012): 191–208.

Hamilton, Victor P. *The Book of Genesis 1—17*. The New International Commentary on the Old Testament. Grand Rapids: Eerdmans, 1990.

Helfmeyer, F. J. "oth." In *Theological Dictionary of the Old Testament*, edited by G. Johannes Botterweck, Helmer Ringgren, and Geoffrey W. Bromiley. Grand Rapids: Eerdmans, 1974.

Hoekema, Anthony A. "The Reformed Perspective." In *Five Views on Sanctification*, edited by Melvin Easterday Dieter, 59–90. Grand Rapids: Academie Books, 1987.

"How Do Rainbows Form?" Social Media Blog. Bureau of Meteorology. http://media.bom.gov.au/social/blog/899/how-do-rainbows-form/. Accessed August 31, 2018.

Hyman, Ronald T. "Four Acts of Vowing in the Bible." *Jewish Bible Quarterly* 37, no. 4 (2009): 231–38.

Johns, Loren L., and Douglas B. Miller. "The Signs as Witnesses in the Fourth Gospel: Reexamining the Evidence." *The Catholic Biblical Quarterly* 56, no. 3 (1994): 519–35.

Kingdon, David. *Children of Abraham*. Sussex: Carey, 1973.

Lemke, Werner E. "Circumcision of the Heart: The Journey of a Biblical Metaphor." In *A God So Near: Essays on Old Testament Theology in Honor of Patrick D. Miller*, edited by Brent A. Strawn and Nancy R. Bowen, 299–319. Winona Lake, IN: Eisenbrauns, 2003.

Lenski, R. C. H. *The Interpretation of the Acts of the Apostles*. Minneapolis: Augsburg, 1961.

Lipiński, Edward. "Etymological and Exegetical Notes on the Meša' Inscription." *Orientalia* 40, no. 3 (1971): 325–40.

Longenecker, Richard N. *Acts*. Edited by Tremper Longman III and David E Garland. The Expositor's Bible Commentary. Grand Rapids: Zondervan, 2007.

Malone, Fred A. *The Baptism of Disciples Alone: A Covenantal Argument for Credobaptism versus Paedobaptism*. Cape Coral, FL: Founders, 2003.

"The New City Catechism." http://newcitycatechism.com/. Accessed August 31, 2018.

Pao, David W. *Colossians & Philemon*. Zondervan Exegetical Commentary on the New Testament. Vol. 12. Grand Rapids: Zondervan, 2012.

Peterson, Jeffrey. "'The Circumcision of the Christ': The Significance of Baptism in Colossians and the Churches of the Restoration." *Restoration Quarterly* 43, no. 2 (2001): 65–77.

Rad, Gerhard von. *Genesis: A Commentary*. The Old Testament Library. Philadelphia: Westminster Press, 1961.

Salter, Martin C. "Does Baptism Replace Circumcision? An Examination of the Relationship Between Circumcision and Baptism in Colossians 2:11-12." *Themelios* 35, no. 1 (2010): 15–29.

Schreiner, Thomas R. "Baptism in the Epistles: An Initiation Rite for Believers." In *Believer's Baptism: Sign of the New Covenant in Christ*, edited by Thomas R. Schreiner and Shawn D. Wright, 67–96. NAC Studies in Bible & Theology. Nashville, TN: B & H Academic, 2006.

———, and Shawn D. Wright, eds. *Believer's Baptism: Sign of the New Covenant in Christ*. NAC Studies in Bible & Theology. Nashville, TN: B&H Academic, 2006.

Seybold, K. "ḥsb." In *Theological Dictionary of the Old Testament*, edited by G. Johannes Botterweck, Helmer Ringgren, and Geoffrey W. Bromiley. Grand Rapids: Eerdmans, 1974.

"Southern Baptist Convention > The Baptist Faith and Message." http://www.sbc.net/bfm2000/bfm2000.asp. Accessed August 31, 2018.

Stonehouse, Ned B. "Repentance, Baptism and the Gift of the Holy Spirit." *The Westminster Theological Journal* 13, no. 1 (1950): 1–18.

Sumney, Jerry L. *Colossians: A Commentary*. The New Testament Library. Louisville, KY: Westminster John Knox, 2008.

Tull, James E. "The Ordinances/Sacraments in Baptist Thought." *American Baptist Quarterly* 1, no. 2 (1982): 187–96.

Van Dam, Cornelis. "The Burnt Offering in Its Biblical Context." *Mid-America Journal of Theology* 7, no. 2 (1991): 195–206.

Van Dixhoorn, Chad B. *Confessing the Faith: A Reader's Guide to the Westminster Confession of Faith*. Edinburgh: The Banner of Truth Trust, 2016.

Wellum, Stephen J. "Baptism and the Relationship Between the Covenants." In *Believer's Baptism: Sign of the New Covenant in Christ*, edited by Thomas R. Schreiner and Shawn D. Wright, 97–162. NAC Studies in Bible & Theology. Nashville, TN: B&H Academic, 2006.

———, and Brent E. Parker, eds. *Progressive Covenantalism: Charting a Mediating Position Between Dispensational and Covenant Theologies*. Nashville, TN: B&H Academic, 2016.

Wright, Shawn D. "Baptism and the Logic of Reformed Paedobaptists." In *Believer's Baptism: Sign of the New Covenant in Christ*, edited by Thomas R. Schreiner and Shawn D. Wright, 207–56. NAC Studies in Bible & Theology. Nashville, TN: B&H Academic, 2006.

Pearls, Gifts, and Beggars: Infant Baptism in the Early Church

Tyler J. Vandergaag

Nobody would deny it. Pearls are precious, valuable, and ought to be treated with the greatest respect and care. As it is with pearls, so it was with baptism in the early church. Baptism was considered a precious pearl and treated with great care and respect. On this point all the Church Fathers would agree. However, just as not everyone will agree on who should receive a precious pearl, so there was not complete agreement in the early church on who should receive baptism. As I will argue in this article, the literature of the early church (at least from the third century until the early mid-fifth century) reveals a diverse picture when it comes to who can receive the precious pearl of baptism. To demonstrate this, I have chosen to focus on the writings of three Fathers: Tertullian's *On Baptism*, Gregory of Nazianzus' *On Baptism*, and Augustine's *The Punishment and Forgiveness of Sins and the Baptism of Little Ones*. Their arguments for infant baptism (Augustine), against it (Tertullian), and somewhere in between (Gregory) allow us to recognize this diversity, but also help us to consider the theological rationale they have put forward for each of their respective views. In turn, this allows us to learn from some of the weaknesses in their baptismal theologies and consider some of the challenges they present us with when it comes to the implications of our own understanding of baptism. I pray that in this way greater unity will result when it comes to this precious pearl that Christ has given to his Church.

Giving Pearls to Pigs: Tertullian

Around AD 200, Tertullian wrote *On Baptism* to deal with a variety of doctrinal and practical aspects relating to baptism. Of particular interest for our purposes are his discussions of how many water baptisms there are and whether children ought to be baptized.

In regard to the first issue, Tertullian is adamant that there is "one baptism, and one only" (*On Baptism* 15). According to Tertullian, the baptism of heretics is no baptism at all because they are outsiders and not united in fellowship to the Church. This allows him to deny the validity of heretical baptisms and still maintain, especially on the basis of Ephesians 4:5, that "we enter into the bath once only, once only are our sins washed away, because these ought not to be committed a second time" (*On Baptism* 15).

After pointing out that there is also a baptism of blood (*On Baptism* 16; cf. 1 John 5:6), and discussing who can and cannot perform the rite of baptism (*On Baptism* 17), Tertullian moves on to discuss who should receive the sacrament of baptism. He begins by stating that those who know the function of baptism know that it "ought not to be rashly granted" (*On Baptism* 18). The reason for this is two-fold. First, baptizing in haste is reckless and dangerous, both to the person being baptized and to those who present a child for baptism (whom Tertullian calls "sponsors"). For this he appeals especially to Matthew 7:6 ("Do not throw your pearls before pigs, lest they trample them underfoot and turn to attack you") and 1 Timothy 5:22 ("Do not be hasty in the laying on of hands").[1] Tertullian does not elaborate on how these texts support his view, but they seem to be applied to baptism by analogy. Baptism is like a precious pearl and so should not be given to those who are not yet ready for it. Similarly, baptism is like the laying on of hands and so should not be administered hastily.

The second aspect of Tertullian's argument has to do with the connection between baptism and faith. Tertullian is aware of instances where baptism was done in haste: the Ethiopian eunuch (Acts 8:26–40) and the apostle Paul (Acts 9:1–19). According to Tertullian, their baptisms were done in haste but were not irresponsible, because the Lord made it clear to the ones baptizing them that faith was evident in their lives. Tertullian goes on to argue that both of these examples prove that faith precedes baptism (cf. *On Baptism* 13).

These two aspects of his argument form the basis of his famous statement against infant baptism:

> It follows that deferment of baptism is more profitable, in accordance with each person's character and attitude, and even age: and especially so as regards children. For what need is there, if there really is no need, for even their sponsors to be brought into peril, seeing they may possibly themselves

---

1. All Scripture quotations are taken from the English Standard Version.

> fail of their promises by death, or be deceived by the subsequent development of an evil disposition? It is true our Lord says, *Forbid them not to come to me*. So let them come, when they are growing up, when they are learning, when they are being taught what they are coming to: let them be made Christians when they have become competent to know Christ. Why should innocent infancy come with haste to the remission of sins? Shall we take less cautious action in this than we take in worldly matters? Shall one who is not trusted with earthly property be entrusted with heavenly? Let them first learn how to ask for salvation, so that you may be seen to have given to one that asketh. (*On Baptism* 18)

According to Tertullian, baptism is precious *and* is preceded by faith. Therefore, it is better to wait for clarity of faith than baptize in haste. This is especially true when it comes to children. Of all people it is most difficult to discern true faith in *their* hearts, especially when they are still unable to speak. So, if they cannot express their faith or show the fruits of faith, they should not be baptized—plain and simple. To baptize infants is to give them something they have not asked for and are not prepared for. It is like giving pearls to pigs.

At first glance the Anabaptist position seems identical to Tertullian's, but as A. N. S. Lane points out, Tertullian was not a "proto-Baptist."[2] The Anabaptist tradition is in full agreement that faith must precede baptism. The mainstream Anabaptist position goes further, however, by denying the validity of infant baptism on the basis that true baptism requires "profession of faith and repentance."[3] The question here is whether Tertullian agrees. Here we need to exercise some historical caution. Tertullian does not speak to this issue directly. He never expressly rejects infant baptism, nor does he ever say such baptisms are valid. However, as noted above, Tertullian openly rejects the baptism of heretics in connection with his affirmation of one baptism, but he never once does so when it comes to infant baptism. Perhaps he did not feel the need to express his rejection of infant baptism so directly, but this seems unlikely. It seems more likely, as Peter Leithart argues, that Tertullian "cautioned against infant baptism."[4] Even though he thought baptism was rashly granted to infants and finds it dangerous, Tertullian does not appear to be willing to reject and deny its validity.

---

2. Lane, "Did the Apostolic Church Baptise Babies?" 114.
3. Dever, "Baptism in the Context of the Local Church," 343.
4. Leithart, "Infant Baptism in History," 246; cf. Ferguson, *Baptism in the Early Church*, 366.

Scholars continue to debate how widespread and established the practice of infant baptism was prior to and during Tertullian's lifetime.[5] But regardless of how widespread and established it was (or was not), one thing is clear: Tertullian's warning against infant baptism indicates this practice was not so firmly established that it could not be questioned without the risk of being declared unorthodox. His willingness to address the issue also suggests that there were enough opponents to infant baptism who felt that the Church should follow in the footsteps of what they believed to be the pattern of the New Testament, where they thought faith precedes baptism. In addition, Tertullian's warning seems to have made an impact. By the mid-third century and on into the fourth, the delay of baptism was trending (at least to some degree). Among a larger number of Christians, Gregory of Nazianzus and Augustine of Hippo were born into Christian homes but not baptized as infants.[6] What is surprising, however, is that in their own ministry neither of these men advocated for the delay of baptism in the way Tertullian suggested. They bucked against this trend. They belonged to a different generation that no longer viewed the delay of baptism as beneficial but considered it harmful and dangerous.

Ruining the Gift: Gregory of Nazianzus

On January 6, AD 381, Gregory of Nazianzus preached a brief sermon (brief at least in his opinion) on baptism in Constantinople. From the content of the sermon it appears that his listeners were hesitant to be baptized. They were afraid, unsure, and uncommitted. This was a great concern for Gregory. He frequently urged his listeners to be baptized. One of his most memorable pleas comes near the end of his lengthy sermon:

> What need do I have for long speeches? For it is the time for teachings, not controversies. "I testify before God and the elect angels," that you must be baptized with this faith. If anyone has written in you a way other than my

---

5. See Ferguson, *Baptism in the Early Church*, 362–79; Strange, *Children in the Early Church*, 85–92; Leithart, "Infant Baptism in History," 246–50; Lane, "Did the Apostolic Church Baptise Babies?"

6. Some notable others include Basil the Great, Gregory of Nyssa, John Chrysostom, Ephraim the Syrian, Jerome, and Rufinus. Ferguson, *Baptism in the Early Church*, 582.

discourse demands, come and have the writing changed. (*On Baptism* 44; cf. 1 Timothy 5:21)

The reason for Gregory's frequent exhortation is that delaying baptism robs a person of the most precious gift and the greatest good anyone can receive:

> Yet do you fear ruining the gift, and because of this postpone the purification, since you do not have a second chance? But why? Do you fear ... being deprived of the greatest good you have, Christ? So it is because of this that you avoid becoming a Christian? Forget it! (*On Baptism* 16)

If a person dies without being baptized, he will have ruined the gift of baptism, which is intended to unite people to Christ, and make them Christians. What is more, Gregory goes on to explain that all the unbaptized will be subject to judgment, though depending on the circumstances some will receive greater punishment than others. Those who despise baptism completely will "pay a penalty, both for their wickedness and also for despising the bath." Those who "honour the gift" but put it off due to heedlessness or greed will also have to "pay, but less, since they brought about their failure to attain it through stupidity rather than evil." Finally, those who "do not have the power to receive it ... will neither be glorified nor punished by the just judge" (*On Baptism* 23).

Gregory does not leave his listeners in the dark as to how this applies to infants. Unbaptized children who die in infancy fall into this last group. In fact, Gregory explicitly includes them in this group (*On Baptism* 23). They will be neither "glorified nor punished." Even though this place between glory and punishment is not the worst place to be, it is clearly not ideal. A bit later in the sermon Gregory returns to infants once again. In answer to the question, "Should we baptize [infants] also?" Gregory is clear: "Absolutely" (*On Baptism* 28). He goes on, however, to clarify exactly what his position on this matter is: "Absolutely, if indeed there is some immediate danger. For it is better to be sanctified without perceiving it than to depart unsealed and uninitiated" (*On Baptism* 28). Gregory is here advocating emergency baptisms for children who are near death's door but have not yet been baptized. In support of these emergency baptisms at such a young age and without the child's awareness, Gregory appeals to two Old Testament examples. First, like these baptisms, circumcision "is conferred on those who still lack reason" (*On Baptism* 28). Second, he compares a child, who is still unconscious of grace, to the doorposts that were anointed with blood to preserve the firstborn son (Exod 12:22): "And likewise the anointing of the doorposts which guarded the firstborn by means of inert things" (*On Baptism* 28). The point here seems to be that even though the doorposts were unconscious, their being anointed with blood nonetheless had saving power for the firstborn. In the same way, even though children are unconscious of baptism, it still has saving power for them.

Even though Gregory has found scriptural support for baptizing infants while they are still unaware of grace, this is his advice only when it comes to emergency situations. If no pressing danger exists, his regular, preferred advice on infant baptism is this:

> But as for the rest, I give my recommendation to wait for the third year, or a little more or a little less, when they can also hear something of the mystery and respond, so even if they do not understand completely, at any rate they are imprinted. And then sanctify them in both body and soul by the great mystery of initiation. For indeed the situation is as follows. They begin to be responsible for their lives at the time when their reason is matured and they learn the mystery. And it is more useful in every respect to be fortified by the bath because the sudden assaults of danger that befall us are beyond help. (*On Baptism* 40.28)

Maybe we wonder if Gregory had any children himself, but notice that what a child needs to know is limited. They do not need to "understand completely." They just need enough understanding to be able to confess something of the mystery of the faith, something even a toddler should be able to do. In any case, like Tertullian, Gregory wants to follow the pattern of faith preceding baptism. He would also agree that baptism is like a precious pearl, but precisely because it is so precious, Gregory is convinced that baptism must not be withheld for long. The dangers are too great. Therefore, young children ought to receive baptism, be united to Christ, and so become Christians as soon as they can express their faith, be it ever so childlike, lest the gift of baptism be ruined.

Begging for Baptism: Augustine

What Gregory feared, Augustine nearly experienced. In his *Confessions* (ca. AD 397–400), Augustine recounts how, as a young unbaptized boy near death's door, he begged for baptism (*Confessions* 1.17). As a result, preparations for an emergency baptism were made by his natural mother

(Monica) and his spiritual mother (the Church), but suddenly Augustine recovered and his baptismal cleansing was delayed. Augustine laments this delay because it meant that the restraints to sin were "relaxed" for him and other unbaptized youths and that he was not granted the protection of the Lord. He concludes that it would certainly have been "much better" for him to have been baptized as a child (*Confessions* 1.18). Some of Augustine's views regarding baptism changed over time.[7] However, his view that infant baptism is preferred, remained constant. This is clear in *The Punishment and Forgiveness of Sins and the Baptism of Little Ones* (AD 412). In this work (the title of which is abbreviated below as *Baptism*), Augustine responds to "the new Pelagian heresy" (*Revisions* 2.33), especially as it relates to infant baptism.

On the basis of Jesus' words in John 3:5 ("Truly, truly, I say to you, unless one is born of water and the Spirit, he cannot enter the kingdom of God"), both Augustine and the Pelagians agreed that entrance into the kingdom requires baptism. For Augustine, however, entrance into the kingdom implies and necessitates the need for the forgiveness of sins. Christ came to save sinners, not the righteous: "And thus, just as he did not come to call them, if they are righteous, so he did not come to call them, if they are not sinners" (*Baptism* 1.19, 24). Applying this to infants, Augustine points out that if they are innocent of all sin (as the Pelagians claim), they have no need to be born again, no right to be baptized, and no right to come to Christ. He goes so far as to say that baptizing and giving access to the kingdom of heaven to sinless, innocent children would be both "pointless" and "wrong" (*Baptism* 1.19, 24). Augustine is certainly pressing the issue here, but his point is to show the inconsistency of the Pelagian position.[8] It is not possible to grant children admission into the kingdom via baptism *and* maintain their innocence. Admission to the kingdom *necessitates* a declaration of a child's need for the forgiveness of sin (cf. *Baptism* 1.30, 58).

Although even the youngest of children require the forgiveness of sin, Augustine believes these same children are innocent of actual sin. He even says that "words or proofs are superfluous for establishing the innocence of infants in the life which they live in their own persons immediately after their birth" (*Baptism* 1.17, 22). Yet, forgiveness is

---

7. Wright, "Augustine and the Transformation of Baptism."
8. Ferguson, *Baptism in the Early Church*, 811.

required because of the guilt they share in the condemnation of original sin (*Baptism* 1.17, 22). This is why they must be baptized: "Since they are not yet held guilty of any sins from their own lives, the illness stemming from their origin is healed in them by the grace of him who saves them through the bath of rebirth" (*Baptism* 1. 19, 24; cf. 1.17, 22). Once children are baptized and the guilt of original sin has been removed from them, they are "correctly called believers" even though they are "not capable of believing" (*Baptism* 1.19, 25). This is because "they in some sense profess the faith by the words of their parents" (*Baptism* 1.19, 25). And if such children should die before "coming to the age of reason," Augustine has no difficulty in affirming that by virtue of baptism their original sin "has been removed, and they will be made perfect in that light of the truth" (*Baptism* 1.19, 25). A few chapters later Augustine defends this by appealing to two classes of people described in John 3:35–36: (1) those who do not believe in the Son and as such will not have life; and (2) those who do believe in the Son and so have eternal life. Augustine then asks: "In which of these classes, then, are we to put infants?" Some would say neither, but this, Augustine says, is "not what the rule of the Church indicates, for it includes baptized infants among the faithful," and they are "counted among the faithful" (*Baptism* 1.20, 28; cf. 1.24, 35; 1.33, 62).

Augustine's position on children who die in infancy at first glance appears similar to that of the Canons of Dort 1.17. Both Augustine and the Canons agree that children of believers can be made perfect and receive eternal life if they die before they reach the age of reason (whatever that age may be), but on slightly different grounds. According to Augustine, if children die unbaptized, they have no life, no remission of original sin: "Those who lack the sacrament should be regarded as among those who do not believe in the Son" (*Baptism* 1.18, 28; cf. 1.24, 34). Even though Augustine refuses to accept that unbaptized children have access to the kingdom of heaven, salvation, and eternal life, he is not prepared to say that they will suffer the full wrath of God's judgment: "Little ones who leave the body without baptism will be under the mildest condemnation of all" (*Baptism* 1.16, 21). It is the "mildest" punishment because they are still innocent of actual or voluntary sins and therefore will be punished only for the original sin they "contracted through birth in the flesh" (*Baptism* 1.15, 20).[9]

---

9. As Christopher A. Hall points out, however, Augustine does make clear in *Against Julian* 5.44

It should be noted that nowhere in this discussion does Augustine make a distinction between children born of believers and those of unbelievers. This mild condemnation applies to *all* unbaptized children. Anyone who thinks otherwise "misleads others very much" and is "very mistaken" (*Baptism* 1.16, 21). On this point, Augustine goes further than Gregory, who considered such children to be neither glorified nor punished. This, too, is where Augustine and the Canons of Dort diverge. According to the Canons, it is not by virtue of their baptism that they are counted among the faithful, but "by virtue of the covenant of grace" (Canons 1.17). Unlike Augustine, the Canons of Dort are convinced that unbaptized children of believers are counted among the faithful.[10]

There is one other important aspect of Augustine's baptismal theology that we need to address. For Augustine, baptism provides access to the Lord's Supper, which is also necessary for salvation and eternal life: "If . . . no one can hope for either salvation or eternal life without baptism and the body and blood of the Lord, there is no reason to promise either salvation or eternal life to little ones without these" (*Baptism* 1.24, 34).[11] Augustine supports this by appealing to John 6:54 ("Whoever feeds on my flesh and drinks my blood has eternal life"), which he takes to be a reference to the Lord's Supper: "Accordingly, his flesh, which was given for the life of the world, was also given for the life of the little ones, and if they have not eaten the flesh of the Son of Man, they will not have life either" (*Baptism* 1.20, 27). At this point, we may wonder how and why Augustine has moved from infant baptism to the Lord's Supper. The logic, for Augustine, is simple. John 6:54 makes clear that a person cannot receive eternal life without first participating in the Lord's Supper. Only those who are baptized can participate in the Lord's Supper. Therefore, it must follow that unbaptized children cannot receive eternal life (as the Pelagians claim). Such children have not eaten the flesh of Christ. In turn, this also means that every baptized person—even little children—must participate in the Lord's Supper to receive eternal life. This, then, also heightens the importance of baptism for Augustine. It is not only an entrance into the kingdom of heaven but

---

that this condemnation will be so mild that it would still be better for a child to suffer this condemnation than never to have been born at all. Hall, *Worshipping with the Church Fathers*, 49.

10. Feenstra, *Unspeakable Comfort*, 56.

11. "The body and blood of the Lord" is clearly a reference to the Lord's Supper, which Augustine just referred to as "the Lord's table." *Baptism* 1.24, 34.

also the gateway to the Lord's Supper, and ultimately the gateway to eternal life and salvation.[12]

In many ways Augustine finds himself in agreement with Tertullian and Gregory. He, too, considers baptism to be a precious pearl (to use Tertullian's expression) and fears (along with Gregory) that delaying baptism will ruin this gift. However, Augustine goes further. Baptism is so precious a pearl that the pattern of faith preceding baptism is trumped by a child's need to receive the forgiveness of sins and eternal life through baptism (and, by extension, the Lord's Supper). Similarly, baptism is too great a gift to put off for even a few years until a child can express faith, for should a child die unbaptized, the gift of baptism would be ruined and the child punished eternally. For Augustine, children of believers should never have to beg for baptism or the Lord's Supper as he did. Instead, he begs that the precious gifts of baptism and the Lord's Supper be given even to the youngest of children.

Conclusions and Implications

Tertullian, Gregory, and Augustine (and the early Christian tradition more generally) have a deep respect for baptism. All agree that it is a precious pearl, but the question became who can handle such a precious gift. As we have seen, the different answers to this question lead to a diversity of practice in the early Christian tradition. Some followed Tertullian, others followed Gregory, and still others followed Augustine. Tertullian was willing to challenge infant baptism and argue for a practice of baptism that he believed to be more in line with the New Testament. This sentiment appears to have been shared by a number of believing parents (especially in the third and fourth centuries) who did not present their infant children for baptism (unless an emergency required it). In addition, there would also have been those who, like Gregory, took a middle position on this issue by delaying baptism for a few years until the child was able to express its faith, albeit in a childlike manner.

---

12. The close link between baptism and the Lord's Supper is already present in Augustine's *Confessions*. Although he begged only for the sacrament of baptism, preparations for both sacraments were made by his mother: "She hastily made arrangements for me to be initiated and washed in the sacraments of salvation, confessing you, Lord Jesus, for the remission of sins." *Confessions* 1.17.

In many respects the Christian tradition (broadly speaking) today finds itself in a similar situation to that of the early church. All agree that baptism is a precious pearl, but the question of who can handle this pearl remains. While a good many in the Christian tradition affirm infant baptism (i.e., Roman Catholic, Eastern Orthodox, Anglican, Reformed, and Presbyterian), those in the Anabaptist tradition generally reject it (i.e., Baptists, Mennonites, and some evangelicals).

The reality of this diversity of practice in the early church and still today does raise an interesting question: should we allow and even promote the same kind of diversity of practice that existed in the early Christian tradition? Lane suggests such diversity be promoted and argues that this is precisely what happened in the early Christian tradition.[13] Now although there is no denying the reality of diversity of practice in the early Christian tradition, there is also no evidence to indicate that such diversity was considered acceptable, encouraged, or even promoted. Both Tertullian's appeal not to baptize infants and Gregory's and Augustine's position that failure to baptize a child puts that child's very salvation in jeopardy, show that none of them thought other positions were equally acceptable to their own. In the words of Sinclair Ferguson, the "middle-Lane position" is too relative for the early church.[14]

Rather than argue that this diversity was promoted in the early Christian tradition, it is better to say there was toleration (for lack of a better word). Tertullian never cries "heresy" at those who promoted infant baptism, and neither do Gregory or Augustine the other way around. This is, I believe, how it should be today. Anabaptists should tolerate us; we should tolerate them. Here the Belgic Confession is helpful. It speaks of "the heresy of the Anabaptists" when it comes to their denial of Christ's taking on the "human flesh of his mother" (Art. 18). And, indeed, to deny the full humanity of Christ is heresy. But when it comes to the Anabaptists' condemnation of infant baptism, the Belgic Confession does not refer to this as a heresy but as an "error of the Anabaptists" (Art. 34). That's how we ought to view those who deny infant baptism: they are not heretics; they are mistaken and in error. At the same time, too much is at stake to simply leave the issue alone. Baptism

---

13. Lane, "Dual-Practice Baptism View," 163–71.
14. Ferguson, "Dual-Practice Baptism View: Infant Baptism Response," 181.

is too precious a pearl to agree to disagree. The way forward is to settle the issue on biblical and theological grounds (which is precisely what Tertullian, Gregory, and Augustine attempted to do).

There are three theological/biblical issues in particular that arise from the writings of these three men that ought to be kept in mind when it comes to promoting greater unity regarding the precious gift of baptism. First, Tertullian (and to a lesser degree Gregory) promotes a delay in baptism because of the New Testament examples of faith preceding baptism. However, neither Tertullian nor Gregory takes into consideration that the context surrounding baptism in the New Testament was different from their own context. Faith precedes baptism when it comes to those converted to the Christian faith, but what should we do when these converts have children of their own? Does this same pattern apply? Here there is no New Testament precedent. We do not have a direct and explicit New Testament example of a couple coming to faith, having a child some time later, and then either immediately presenting that child for baptism or withholding the child from baptism until faith is evident. What this means is that whatever position one takes with regard to the children of believers and baptism, it will be a "modification" of the pattern found in the New Testament.[15] One can only wonder whether Tertullian (and Gregory to a lesser extent), had he recognized this difference, would have been so insistent on following the pattern of faith preceding baptism when it comes to the children of believers. In any case, this contextual difference must be recognized and dealt with openly and honestly.

Second, what is noticeably absent in Tertullian, Gregory, and Augustine when it comes to infant baptism and the fate of the unbaptized is the place of the covenant. Although there is an awareness of "sponsors" who answer on behalf of infant children in Tertullian and a positive acceptance of this in Augustine, this is not explicitly tied to children of believers and their place in the covenant. The same is also true in the case of Gregory. Although he provides Old Testament support for baptizing infants prior to faith, he does not connect this with the covenant God made with Abraham and his descendants in Genesis 17 (cf. Acts 2:39). This neglect, it seems to me, leads to Gregory's and

---

15. Lane, "Dual-Practice Baptism View," 143; cf. Motyer, "Baptism in the Book of Common Prayer," 49, n. 21.

Augustine's troubling conclusion that unbaptized infants of believers are not granted access to eternal life. Any discussion on baptism today, therefore, must take into account the place of children in the covenant.

Third, as the debates surrounding paedocommunion continue to swirl in the broader Reformed tradition, it is helpful to know that this is not a foreign practice.[16] It was alive and well in the early church. We would do well to acknowledge this and to wrestle with the theological basis on which Augustine (and others) defend this practice, as well as his view that baptism is the gateway to the Lord's Supper.[17] This will help us to consider if we are, as Peter Leithart claims, "compromised paedobaptists who shrink from the full implications of their position and fail to embody their theology in practice," or if there are good biblical and theological reasons to withhold children from the Lord's table.[18]

Ultimately, of course, it is not Tertullian, Gregory, or Augustine that we follow or seek to please, but together their voices encourage us to cherish the precious pearl and gift of baptism and motivate us to continue to seek biblical and theological unity when it comes to the practice and implications of baptism.[19]

---

16. For the various positions on paedocommunion in the Reformed tradition, see Waters and Duncan, *Children and the Lord's Supper*; Cornelis Venema, *Children at the Lord's Table?*; Tim Gallant, *Feed My Lambs*; Gregg Strawbridge, *The Case for Covenant Communion*; Keith Mathison, *Given For You*, 313–24.

17. It would also be helpful to understand some of the reasons why the Church of the Middle Ages shifted away from paedocommunion. Strange argues that the movement away from it was partly due to a shift away from Augustine's application of John 6:53–54 to every believer (including infants) and a greater emphasis on the importance of self-examination in 1 Corinthians 11:27–29. Strange, *Children in the Early Church*, 106.

18. Leithart, "Infant Baptism in History," 262. For arguments against paedocommunion, see the contribution of Van Dam in this volume, "Children, Passover, and Lord's Supper."

19. I want to thank Hans Boersma for his comments on an earlier draft of this article.

Bibliography

Augustine. *Confessions*. Translated by Henry Chadwick. Oxford World's Classics. Oxford: Oxford University Press, 1991.

———. "Punishment and Forgiveness of Sins and the Baptism of Little Ones." In *Answer to the Pelagians, The Works of Augustine: A Translation for the 21st Century I/23*, translated by Roland J. Teske; edited by John E. Rotelle, 34–137. Hyde Park, NY: New City, 1997.

Dever, Mark E. "Baptism in the Context of the Local Church." In *Believer's Baptism: Sign of the New Covenant in Christ*, edited by Thomas R. Schreiner and Shawn D. Wright, 329–52. NAC Studies in Bible and Theology. Nashville, TN: B&H Academic, 2006.

Feenstra, Peter G. *Unspeakable Comfort: A Commentary on the Canons of Dort*. Winnipeg: Premier, 1997.

Ferguson, Everett. *Baptism in the Early Church: History, Theology, and Liturgy in the First Five Centuries*. Grand Rapids: Eerdmans, 2009.

Ferguson, Sinclair B. "Dual-Practice Baptism View: Infant Baptism Response." In *Baptism: Three Views*, edited by David F. Wright, 177–86. Downers Grove, IL: IVP Academic, 2009.

Gallant, Tim. *Feed My Lambs: Why the Lord's Table Should Be Restored to Covenant Children*. Grande Prairie, AB: Pactum Reformanda, 2002.

Gregory. "Oration 40: On Baptism." In *Festal Orations*, translated by Nonna V. Harrison, 99–142. Popular Patristics Series. Crestwood, NY: St. Vladimir's Seminary Press, 2008.

Hall, Christopher A. *Worshipping with the Church Fathers*. Downers Grover, IL: IVP Academic, 2009.

Lane, Anthony N. S. "Did the Apostolic Church Baptise Babies? A Seismological Approach." *Tyndale Bulletin* 55, no. 1 (2004): 109–30.

———. "Dual-Practice Baptism View." In *Baptism: Three Views*, edited by David F. Wright, 139–71. Downers Grove, IL: IVP Academic, 2009.

Jeremias, Joachim. *The Origins of Infant Baptism: A Further Study in Reply to Kurt Aland*. Translated by Dorothea M. Barton. London: SCM, 1962. Repr., Eugene. OR: Wipf & Stock, 2004.

Leithart, Peter J. "Infant Baptism in History: An Unfinished Tragicomedy." In *The Case for Covenantal Infant Baptism*, edited by Gregg Strawbridge, 246–62. Phillipsburg, NJ: P&R, 2003.

Mathison, Keith A. *Given for You: Reclaiming Calvin's Doctrine of the Lord's Supper*. Phillipsburg, NJ: P&R, 2002.

McKinion, Steven A. "Baptism in the Patristic Writings." In *Believer's Baptism: Sign of the New Covenant in Christ*, edited by Thomas R. Schreiner and Shawn D. Wright, 163–88. NAC Studies in Bible and Theology. Nashville: B&H Academic, 2006.

Strawbridge, Gregg, ed. *The Case for Covenant Communion*. West Monroe, LA: Athanasius, 2006.

Strange, W. A. *Children in the Early Church: Children in the Ancient World, New Testament and the Early Church*. Milton Keynes, UK: Paternoster, 1996. Repr., Eugene, OR: Wipf & Stock, 2004.

Tertullian. *Homily on Baptism*. Translated by Ernest Evans. London: SPCK, 1964. Repr., Eugene, OR: Wipf & Stock, 2016.

Waters, Guy, and Ligon Duncan, eds. *Children and the Lord's Supper: Let a Man Examine Himself*. Fearn, Ross-shire, UK: Mentor, 2011.

Wright, David F. "Augustine and the Transformation of Baptism." In *The Origins of Christendom in the West*, edited by Alan Kreider, 287–31. New York: T&T Clark, 2001.

"Whoever Is of God Has the Spirit of God": Children in the Reformation Documents, with Particular Reference to Heinrich Bullinger and Guido de Brès

Theodore G. Van Raalte

Debate with Anabaptists

Special attention fell upon the place of the child in the communities of the Reformation already in the 1520s, particularly as Zwingli, Bucer, and Bullinger sought to counter the Anabaptist charges that by baptizing their infants they were inconsequential in their reforming ideals. The Reformed response has been traced in careful and accurate detail by Hughes Oliphant Old in his seminal work of 1992 on the shaping of the Reformed baptismal rite.[1] One of his remarkable conclusions is that the Reformed continued baptizing the infant children of believers not because they unwittingly maintained medieval tradition (as the Anabaptists charged) but rather because they carefully worked through the biblical data, particularly tracing out a new theme—covenant. Indeed, Old argues, they baptized their infants precisely because they *were* consequential in their reforming theology. Baptizing these children exemplified salvation by grace alone and, especially with its accompanying prayers, conformed well to the prominent place of the Holy Spirit in the Reformed liturgy.[2]

---

1. Old, *The Shaping of the Reformed Baptismal Rite in the Sixteenth Century*.
2. Old, *Reformed Baptismal Rite*, 143–4; 59, 155, 230, 242, 284–5. Old came to the study of baptism through his work on the history of liturgy. See Old, *The Patristic Roots of Reformed Worship*. He calls attention to the frequent epicletic sections of the Reformed baptism services, especially where the church prays for the Holy Spirit before the baptism. For comparison, note the comment of Bastiaan Wielenga about the Reformed baptism prayer asking God to incorporate the child by his Holy Spirit into his Son Jesus Christ: "This is the central petition on which everything depends." Wielenga, *The Reformed Baptismal Form*, 217.

Medieval Background

Old makes the argument that for all the apparent radicality of the Anabaptists, they were actually continuing late medieval German mystical teachings and leaning upon a particular strand of late medieval theology, namely nominalism.[3] The mystical background helps explain their emphasis on the imitation of Christ and on personal experience—both largely in contrast to the Reformed emphasis on justification—and their nominalism helps explain the important role they gave to the human will (voluntarism) and the need for faith before baptism.[4] Jonathan Rainbow, in an essay against paedobaptism, similarly states that the late medieval tie between baptism and faith was actually maintained by the Anabaptists, though instead of claiming faith for the infants as the medievals did, they denied baptism until they could ascertain faith (as evidenced by outward regeneration or holy living).[5] According to Old—and Guido de Brès—the Anabaptists claimed that infants could not receive the Holy Spirit until they had developed their own power of reason.[6]

The need for faith to be present in order to proceed to the administration of baptism had led the medieval church to argue for baptism on the basis of the faith of the child—if not, then of the parent; if not, then of the godparent; if not, then of the church on earth; if not, then of the church triumphant. The faith of another (*fides aliena*) became

---

3. Nominalism describes a philosophical position that says that universals exist only in name, not in reality. Only particulars are real. More pertinent to the point at hand, medieval nominalist theologians held that there are no innate laws written into the structure of things; rather, God created the world entirely freely and made it as he did entirely freely (e.g., so that trees grow upwards and grass is green and murder is evil). God could have made it otherwise, but now that he has made it as he has, he is faithful to himself and has covenanted to maintain this world according to his ordained will. Nominalist theologians also taught that the fall into sin had done very little damage to man. See the summary in Steinmetz, "Scholasticism and Radical Reform: Nominalist Motifs in the Theology of Balthasar Hubmaier," 126–27.

4. Old, *Reformed Baptismal Rite*, 22, 53, 83, 92–93, 97, 108, 178. Old refers at this point to Steinmetz, "Nominalist Motifs," 123–44.

5. He refers to Hubmaier in particular. Rainbow, "'Confessor Baptism': The Baptismal Doctrine of the Early Anabaptists," 202.

6. Old, *Reformed Baptismal Rite*, 134–35. Guido de Brès, *La racine, source, et fondement des Anabaptistes*, 655–56, 662. See also Steinmetz, "Nominalist Motifs," 142. For an example of an Anabaptist insisting that the children are unable to reason and therefore cannot be regenerated, see Dirk Philips' frequent use of Deut 1:39, "Your children who do not yet know good from bad," in *Vander doop onses Heeren Iesu Christi, bekentenisse*, 75, 80, 81, 85, 98, 135. This work contains Philips' explanation of baptism, with the response of the Reformed theologian Jacob Kimedoncius.

the basis for the baptism of infants. In time, the medieval church began to speak of baptism itself infusing the virtue or power of faith (*fides infusa*).[7] All of this the Reformed churches rejected.

The Reformed agreed with the medieval theologians in distinguishing essential and non-essential elements in baptism, and in agreeing that the mode of baptism was non-essential.[8] But, because the Reformed did not think that baptism itself secured forgiveness of sins and because they thought that its administration by an ordained man was of the essence, they strove hard to eliminate midwife baptism.[9] Especially Zwingli distinguished the inner and outer realities in order to counter the medieval ascription of forgiving and regenerating power to the water.[10] The Reformers also sought to end private baptisms, on the grounds that the sacraments belonged to the *church* and thus were to be administered within the congregation. The use of the godparents was retained for quite some time by the Reformed, but the understanding of their role changed: the godparents at the baptism, instead of undertaking the vow *in place of* the child or confessing faith in place of the child, simply agreed to oversee the instruction of the child in Christian truth.[11]

Finally, according to Old, one ought to view the Reformed requirement of the reciting of the catechism by the older child before the church (or answering the questions as a profession of faith) as the child's utterance of the baptismal vows.[12] This ought not, he argues, to be viewed as a "confirmation" of anyone's earlier vows or the completion of baptism, for baptism was never to be regarded as something one completed; rather, baptism was the sign "under which the whole of the Christian life was to be lived."[13] The completion of catechesis, not of baptism, was in view when the youth recited the catechism for admission to the Lord's Supper.

---

7. Rainbow, "'Confessor Baptism,'" 191.
8. Old, *Reformed Baptismal Rite*, 53, 250, 264–71.
9. Ibid., 53.
10. Ibid., 197–98.
11. Ibid., 201–6.
12. Ibid., 207, 209, 221.
13. Ibid., 221-25 (see p. 225 for the quote).

Early Reformed Arguments in Defence of Infant Baptism

By the mid-sixteenth century Calvin, Beza, De Brès and others would pick up the various arguments for infant baptism, but already in the 1520s Oecolampadius, Zwingli, Bucer, and Bullinger were freshly studying the Scriptures regarding baptism. Old summarizes their defence of infant baptism under six points:

- First, they argued that the command of Christ and the example of the apostles required baptizing their infants, for one can most certainly make disciples of children by baptizing and teaching them, per Matthew 28:18-20.
- Second, they noticed that the apostles followed the patterns and principles of the Old Testament and appealed to the Old Testament for authority, and that God followed orderly and consistent patterns when he dealt with his people: here Old (the author) included the argument from circumcision to baptism.
- Third, the typology of circumcision led them into the argument which in time became a major Reformed theme: covenant theology.
- Fourth, the admonitions to parents in the Scriptures, including Ephesians 6:4, entailed that the children were to be brought up *inside* the church.
- Fifth, they argued that the Holy Spirit is at work in the children of believers even before they have the power of reason.[14]
- Sixth, they asserted that the primacy of grace was properly upheld when God's promises were sealed in baptism to their infants, before the infants were even able to respond.[15]

The Work of the Holy Spirit in the Children

The present essay will pursue in particular the fifth argument identified by Old: the work of the Holy Spirit in the children, according to the Reformers. In connection with this, the Reformers did not want to separate the Holy Spirit from the Father and the Son. Thus, when they asserted that the Spirit was at work in the church's children, they also

---

14. Ibid., 133-35.
15. Ibid., 114-44.

believed that these children were adopted by the Father and washed in the blood of the Son; indeed, these latter realities logically preceded the work of the Spirit. Study of their claims about the Spirit's work must therefore remain tied to study of their claims about the Son's work.

To keep the present essay to a reasonable scope, we will study the views of two Reformers who interacted closely with Anabaptists: first, Heinrich Bullinger (1504–1575), whose writings can be probed for details that Old does not supply; second, Guido de Brès (1522–1567), who wrote at a time subsequent to the era studied by Old and who was responsible for the Belgic Confession (1561).

The arguments of these men reflect the views held by the Reformed at the very time that the Reformed liturgical forms for baptism were written. These forms say some very positive things about the children of believers, such as that they are "sanctified in Christ,"[16] that Christ "promises" them that he "washes them from all their sins in his precious blood," that the Holy Spirit "assures" them that "he will dwell in them," and so forth. In the prayer after either an adult or an infant baptism, the church thanks God that he has "forgiven us and our children all our sins." The meaning of these phrases will surely be more appreciated when the context around them has been elucidated.[17]

One of De Brès's arguments is particularly noteworthy for its uniqueness. Since it appears in Article 34 of the Belgic Confession, it ought to be well known, but in fact almost all commentaries on the Belgic Confession avoid it, and one in particular argues that its placement is inappropriate.[18] De Brès appealed to the old covenant requirement found in Leviticus 12:6 that a lamb was to be offered shortly after Israelite children were born, stating that this offering was "a sacrament of Jesus Christ" and was evidence that the children were "made partakers of the sacrament of Christ's suffering and death." Thus, Christ shed his blood "no less for the washing of the children of the faithful than for adult persons."[19] We will study this argument in more detail and will see that while it is unique and may even be original to

---

16. Regarding this phrase, see elsewhere in this volume the contribution of Vreugdenhil, "'Sanctified in Christ.'"
17. See *Book of Praise: Anglo-Genevan Psalter*, 599, 602.
18. Vonk, *De Voorzeide Leer IIIb: De Nederlandse Geloofsbelijdenis*, 391.
19. Schaff, *Creeds of Christendom*, 3:437.

De Brès, it is completely in agreement with Bullinger's and De Brès's approach to the work of the Son for the children, and what they considered its corollary, the work of the Spirit in the children.

Heinrich Bullinger's Arguments (The Children Possess the Holy Spirit)

Heinrich Bullinger was not merely the successor of Ulrich Zwingli in the city of Zurich, but an independent thinker who was leading reform as early as 1523 and had perhaps the widest influence of all the reformers between the 1530s and his death in 1575. His printed works, especially his *Decades* (five sets of ten sermons, covering most of theology), were available in English translation before Calvin's and much more widely used in England during the sixteenth century.[20] His correspondence exceeded in number that of any other reformer.[21] In 1534 he wrote the first extant treatise on the biblical theme that was to become a trademark Reformed emphasis—God's one, eternal covenant with his people.[22] He was intimately familiar with Zwingli's arguments against the Anabaptists. In fact, Bullinger's work of 1531 against the Anabaptists uses its last twenty pages or so to recast in dialogue form part of Zwingli's work against the "Catabaptists," first written in 1527.[23] Later Bullinger wrote another work against the Anabaptists, but its arguments advance only a little beyond his work of 1531, so we will make use of it sparingly.[24]

---

20. George Ella has written a number of essays and a full-length biography on Bullinger, emphasizing Bullinger's independence of thought, mature diplomacy and wisdom, and his role as leader among the Swiss Reformers. Ella's work combines a commendable depth of research with sometimes tendentious defences of Bullinger. He correctly states, "An average of four editions of his works per year were printed in Switzerland alone for a hundred years and over fifty printers in other European countries were turning out countless editions. Reformers such as Miles Coverdale translated Bullinger into English from the 1530s on." Ella, "Henry Bullinger: Shepherd of the Churches." His monograph-length biography goes by the same title: *Henry Bullinger: Shepherd of the Churches*.

21. The official figure is around 12,000 letters altogether, counting those to and from Bullinger. See Letters, https://www.irg.uzh.ch/en/hbbw/datenbank.html (accessed September 20, 2018).

22. Bullinger, *De testamento seu foedere dei unico & aeterno Heinrychi Bullingeri brevis expositio*.

23. Bullinger, *Von dem unverschampten Fräfel, ergerlichem Verwyrren unnd unwarhafftem Leeren der selbsgesandten Widerrtöuffern: vier Gespräch Bücher*. I am using an English translation from 1551, updating it without further explanation, and consulting the original German as needed. Bullinger, *A moste sure and strong defence of the baptisme of children, against the pestiferous secte of the Anabaptistes*. Zwingli's work of 1527 was *In catabaptisarum strophas elenchus*. This work is also available in English translation in Zwingli, *Selected Works of Huldreich Zwingli*, 123–75.

24. *Adversus Anabaptistas Libri VI*.

Bullinger's treatise against the Anabaptists, just mentioned, is written as a dialogue between Joiada (Reformed) and Simon (Anabaptist) and argues three main points. First, Bullinger, through the person of Joiada, insists that rebaptizing is wrong, because Scripture teaches only one baptism. He spends some time trying to prove that the baptism administered by John the Baptist and that administered by Jesus' disciples were really one and the same, in order to deny the Anabaptist claim that rebaptism occurred in the New Testament—for instance, in Acts 19, where some men had known only the baptism of John and were then baptized into the name of Jesus. Some of the argumentation feels tendentious, as when Bullinger argues that the first "baptism" in Acts 19—the baptism into John—did not involve the sign, but only the signified thing—the teaching—of John.[25] Here Bullinger follows Zwingli; later Bullinger would change his exegesis of Acts 19.[26]

Second, Bullinger argues for infant baptism on the basis of the typology of circumcision. He makes the point that the children of believers were not counted as children of God by virtue of their physical descent from their parents, but by virtue of God's promise.[27] The covenant that God made with Abraham in Genesis 17 is his starting point, to show that when God included the children, he made himself their God even though they were then incapable of a confession of faith. Joiada says, "From the standpoint, therefore, of grace and of the promise of God they ought to be included in the number of believers."[28]

Pushing back against the Anabaptist ideal of a pure church of the elect—one of the factors in their insistence on confessor baptism—he argues that one's outward confession is sufficient for receiving baptism, since only God knows a person's heart and the identity of his elect.[29] Bullinger argues similarly in his *Decades*: if we baptize adults upon profession of faith even though we do not know the secrets of their

---

25. *Strong Defence*, a6r–c2v.

26. See Stephens, "Bullinger's Defence of Infant Baptism in Debate with the Anabaptists," 168, 188. In his later work of 1560, Bullinger changed his exegesis of Acts 19. Bullinger, *Adversus Anabaptistas*, 225r–v. See also Stephens, "Bullinger's Defence," 179, 186–87. Bullinger's later way of interpreting the passage noted the progress of Christ's redeeming work in Acts 19, noticing that the new thing received by the men at Ephesus was the gift of the Holy Spirit, the event being a smaller version repetition of the events on the day of Pentecost.

27. *Strong Defence*, c6r.

28. Old, *Reformed Baptismal Rite*, 126 (*Von dem Fräfel*, 55v).

29. *Strong Defence*, c6v–c7v. On confessor baptism, see Rainbow's essay, cited above.

hearts, then we may the more baptize believers' infants whose hearts we do not know, for God has made his promise to them.[30] In his *Strong Defence*, he takes note of both Ishmael and Esau being circumcised, members of the people of God, and yet not among the number of the elect, arguing,

> [Ishmael and Esau] were circumcised by the commandment of God: circumcision was the sign of the people of God; ergo, in their infancy they were the children of God and also they were of the people of God, yea, though they were not elected . . . . Children, though they cannot confess their faith, are reckoned [*verrächnet werdend*] among the faithful. Or is God only the God of them that are of age, and not also of the children? Or did Christ suffer only for them that are of age, and not also for the children? . . . Since Paul says that whatsoever was fallen by Adam, the same was restored by Christ, and since not only they that be of age, but also children, be lost in Adam, it follows that children are restored again in Christ.[31]

The first thing today's Reformed reader may notice is Bullinger's sensitivity for the tension between God's secret election by which a circumcised or baptized person might turn out not to show the fruits of faith, and God's revealed command by which the children of believers ought to receive the sign of the covenant. But this tension does not to lead him to say that the promise is only for the elect children, nor that those baptized but not elect were, as infants, actually not God's children. He uses a legal or accounting term, specifying that they are "counted, reckoned, or accounted" (*verrächnet*) as God's children.[32] In his *Decades* Bullinger adds that faith itself is imputed or counted to these children of believers.[33]

But equally important is Bullinger's argument that God is the God of every age group (just as he is of every race). Christ died for all, in the sense that no age group (or race) was excluded from the benefits of his death and resurrection. Whatever group was lost in Adam—whether Jew or Gentile, slave or free, male or female, old or young—that same

---

30. *Sermons on the Sacraments*, 173–74.

31. *Strong Defence*, c7v–c8r (*Von dem Fräfel*, 57r).

32. Bullinger says the same in the *Decades*. "Infants, therefore, are numbered and counted of the Lord himself among the faithful . . . . Yet most certain is that saying, that the Lord counts infants among his, that is, among the faithful." *Sermons on the Sacraments*, 132–33.

33. "They are . . . baptized in . . . their own [faith] . . . which it pleases the Lord to impute to them." *Sermons on the Sacraments*, 133.

group is included in the restoration in Christ. According to Bullinger, the Anabaptists deny the benefits of Christ to a certain age group.

When Bullinger writes that the children are "reckoned" among the faithful, he does not mean to imply some kind of "legal fiction," for next he turns to the Book of Acts, chapter 10, where the Holy Spirit was given to Gentiles while Peter preached (evident by a manifestation similar to Pentecost), and Peter asked rhetorically who could forbid baptism for those who had received the Holy Spirit. Joiada's interlocutor, Simon, objects, "But children have not received the Holy Spirit." Bullinger's Joiada replies,

> In this passage to receive the Holy Spirit is to receive a witness that we are of God, who receives us, and that we are cleansed and purged by God. This may be proved by the chapters 10, 11, and 15 of Acts. Children are cleansed and purged by God; ergo, they have the Spirit of God. If they have the Spirit of God, they belong to God and baptism is due unto them, as is sufficiently proved by the Old and New Testament.[34]

Clearly Bullinger reaches his key conclusions by the exercise of reason, putting Scripture texts side by side and arriving at conclusions by good and necessary consequence. Basically he has three times affirmed the antecedent of what are in effect hypothetical syllogisms (*modus ponens*).[35]

When Simon raises the text of Matthew 19, where Christ says the kingdom of heaven belongs not to "these" children but to "such as these," Joiada answers that Christ does not thereby exclude those children themselves, for they were of such a kind, else they could not have been commended. Bullinger then has Simon request an "express testimony" of Scripture that teaches that the children have the Spirit of God. In reply, Joiada presents a categorical syllogism, "Paul says in Romans 8 that whoever does not have the Spirit of God does not belong to him. Whereby it follows that whoever is of God has the Spirit of God; the children are of God [as he has earlier sought to prove]; ergo, they have

---

34. *Strong Defence*, c8v (*Von dem Fräfel*, 57v). Compare Old, *Baptismal Rite*, 134, and Bullinger, *Sermons on the Sacraments*, 133.

35. The first hypothetical syllogism would be, "If children are cleansed by God, they have the Spirit of God," and the second would be, "If they have the Spirit, they belong to God," and the third, "If they belong to God, baptism is due unto them." Notice that Bullinger did not argue that if children are baptized, they must have the Spirit. To argue thus would seriously misrepresent his views.

the Spirit of God."[36] He follows this by reasoning from the thing itself to its sign, from the greater to the lesser, "If they have the Spirit of God, then they ought by good right to be baptized. For Peter says, 'Who can forbid them who have received the Holy Spirit from being baptized?'"[37]

These arguments are remarkable for the matter-of-fact way in which Bullinger speaks of the Holy Spirit being given to the children of believers. He does not specify that they have undergone the kind of regeneration that belongs only to the elect nor that they are fully justified. However, assuming the truth of his earlier arguments that the children of believers belong to the covenant and people of God, he regards them to be "cleansed and purged"—one would assume, by the blood of Christ—and therefore also in possession of the Spirit of God. The argument at this point is probably also assuming the unity of the work of the Son and the Spirit. Whoever possesses the one, possesses the other. Bullinger puts together the texts of Romans 8:9 (those who belong to God have his Spirit) and Acts 10:47 (if they have his Spirit, they should be baptized).

In subsequent dialogue, Joiada points out that the infant is not baptized in order that he or she might become a child of God, but because they already are such, "and are saved through the grace and promise of God, by the force and strength of the covenant, by the satisfaction of Jesus Christ, that he made on the cross for all mankind. In the generality of mankind, not only they that are of age are included, but also children."[38] Bullinger's point here, as above, is that the efficacy of Christ's work for the human race does not exclude certain categories of people, such as children. His language in the *Decades* is on this point the same, and includes the critical term "*we believe* that God . . . has cleansed and adopted them."[39] All these positive things about the children were to

---

36. This reasoning is by way of *modus tollens*, denying the consequent.

37. *Strong Defence*, d1r–d1v (*Von dem Fräfel*, 58r). Cf. *Sermons on the Sacraments*, 133: "Inasmuch as they are of God, they have the Spirit of God, 'And whoso have not, they are not of God' (Rom 8:9)."

38. *Strong Defence*, d2v (*Von dem Fräfel*, 59r).

39. "Do we not therefore baptize them, because God has commanded them to be brought unto him? Because he has promised that he will be our God, and the God of our seed after us? To be short: because we believe that God of his mere grace and mercy, in the blood of Jesus Christ, has cleansed and adopted them, and appointed them to be heirs of eternal life? We, therefore, baptizing infants for these causes, do abundantly testify that there is not first given unto them in baptism, but that there is sealed and confirmed what they had before." Bullinger, *Sermons on the Sacraments*, 96.

be regarded as points of faith, to be believed by the church on the basis of the Word of God.

Shortly after this point, Joiada agrees that the water itself does not purge or renew since it is "plain and manifest" that such men as Simon the Sorcerer, Judas, Hymenaus, and Philetus in Scripture, though baptized outwardly, were not purged inwardly, were not the children of God, but of the devil.[40] This, argues Joiada, shows that the positive things Scripture says about baptism are not about the mere sign, but the sign in unity with the thing signified. The fact that some baptized people turn out not be children of God does not make the meaning of baptism for believers' children dubious, for the action of pouring the water signifies "that the one on whom the water is sprinkled belongs to the church and the people of God, that just as water washes away the smudges and stains of our bodies, so also the one upon whom there is this outpouring, being received by grace, is washed with the blood of Jesus and pledged to a new life."[41] A bit further on we read of "the children whom Christ has washed with his blood."[42]

This entire second section of Bullinger's treatise speaks very positively about the benefits of God's covenant for the children of believers. Bullinger emphasizes two things: first, the work of the Son and Spirit must be for children also, since Christ died for all people generally; second, because the children belong to God, they must have undergone a cleansing from sin and must have the Spirit of God. He does not go into detail about the senses in which the children of believers might or might not have the Spirit of God, for he takes the general rule to be that the children belong to God and are saved by his grace. Though some children turn out not to be elect, this does not lead Bullinger to posit some sort of two-stage salvation as if all the children have their salvation only temporarily or partially or as an unclaimed inheritance until they come of age and show signs of faith—perhaps characterized as positional

---

40. *Strong Defence*, d3v (*Von dem Fräfel*, 59v).

41. Old, *Reformed Baptismal Rite*, 278 (Bullinger, *Von dem Fräfel*, 59v–60r). I have used Old's translation here because the sixteenth-century translator expanded the text significantly at this point, for instance, by adding that the baptized one is cleansed inwardly by the Holy Spirit (*Strong Defence*, d3v–d4r).

42. *Strong Defence*, d7r (*Von dem Fräfel*, 62v). In the *Decades* Bullinger states, perhaps with a slightly different view, that circumcised infants in the OT and baptized infants in the NT eras who wickedly transgress God's commands "fall from grace," but when they repent they are received back into that same grace. *Sermons on the Sacraments*, 108.

sanctification and then possessive sanctification, or as legal and then experiential, or as having the rights and only later the possession, or as covenantal sanctification and then full sanctification. None of that, probably because such terms and definitions awaited later developments in the history of dogma. Rather, he reasons by way of what ought to be the normal pattern—God encompasses the children in his covenant and they are his, possessing salvation.[43]

Similarly, when in his *Decades* Bullinger faces the question, "Who are the people of God who have forgiveness?" he admits that the answer could become a disputation about God's secret election, but he avoids this by pointing out that the church can only judge who belongs to the people of God by two things: men's profession and God's promises. The hearts of the hypocrites are for the Lord to judge. His starting point is God's covenant, not God's secret election.

In the third section of Bullinger's treatise he provides seven arguments from Scripture to show that the apostles did in fact baptize children. After this he casts much of the early work of Zwingli against the Anabaptists (1527) into dialogue form.

Several of the seven arguments reinforce Bullinger's earlier contentions that the children have the Holy Spirit. In the second of these he argues categorically that whomever God counts (*verrächnet*) as among the believers (*glöubigen*) are such. Here he appeals to God's words to Peter in Acts 10 in the vision of the sheet let down from heaven with unclean animals, of which Peter was called to rise, kill, and eat. When Peter objected, he was told not to call impure or common what God had determined was now clean (Acts 10:15). Bullinger then states that since God counts the children as among the number of the believers or faithful, no one should call them unclean.[44]

The third argument returns to Peter's words that baptism could not be forbidden for those who had received the Holy Spirit.[45] In the fifth and sixth arguments synecdoche begins to function in the argument: that is, when the whole is mentioned and the parts are to be inferred, or a part is mentioned but the whole is actually in view. Thus when "all

---

43. *Sermons on the Sacraments*, 173.

44. *Strong Defence*, d8v (*Von dem Fräfel*, 63v). As far as I know, this text was used against the Anabaptists also in regards to their views of the Christian's role in civil government, oath-taking, the military, and more.

45. *Strong Defence*, e1r (*Von dem Fräfel*, 63v–64r).

were under the cloud and went through the sea" (1 Cor 10), the children were included.[46] With the same use of synecdochical language, whole "households" underwent baptism in the New Testament, and, though some may have lacked children, if they had them, they would have been baptized.[47]

Of some significance to the way in which the Anabaptists argued and the way in which the Reformed argued, Bullinger's Joiada objects several times to an Anabaptist hermeneutic that would conclude that because no explicit scriptural positive command to baptize children occurs, baptizing them was strictly forbidden, and that because the words of Scripture do not specify that an actual child was baptized by the apostles, it would be unlawful to do so.[48] The Reformed objected that these arguments were fallacious; the first being an argument from silence and the making of a universal negative out of the absence of a positive, the second a changing of genus from example to norm. Old makes this point several times in his work as well, that the Reformed did not hold to the view that whatever was not commanded was forbidden.[49] De Brès says the same.[50] Rather, what is commanded ought to be done, and what is forbidden ought to be avoided, and beyond this one must develop biblical principles by good and necessary consequence. Besides these fallacies, the Anabaptists "expounded all things by the letter" instead of recognizing figures of speech such as synecdoche.[51]

In conclusion, Bullinger's arguments for the baptism of the infant children of believers clearly included the commitment that they are washed by the blood of Christ and in possession of the Spirit of God. He recognized that ultimately this is not true for some who undergo water baptism, such as Simon the Sorcerer. Nevertheless, it is the general pattern, and is in accordance with the promises of God. Baptism as such

---

46. Bullinger here makes the point that it is the custom in Scripture and among all nations to denominate the women and children under the name of the father, a thing he finds comforting for the women inasmuch as they were not personally circumcised in the Old Testament but were included under the sign that their menfolk underwent. *Strong Defence*, e1v.

47. *Strong Defence*, e2r–e2v. The emphasis on synecdoche appears to have begun with Zwingli.

48. *Strong Defence*, d7r, e3v, e4v, f2v–f3r.

49. Old, *Reformed Baptismal Rite*, 283; cf. 89, 102, 119.

50. De Brès, *Racine*, 702–10.

51. Bullinger, *Strong Defence*, f3v. One ought to note the humanist influences upon Zwingli, Bullinger, and other reformers in their recognition of these figures of speech. This part of Bullinger's treatise is a recasting of Zwingli's work against the Catabaptists.

did not effect these benefits, but was conferred in order to confirm and seal them to the recipient—whether infant or adult. He urges us to speak of the children in line with God's word: Let no one call unclean what God has declared clean.

Guido de Brès's Arguments (A Lamb Offered for the Children)

Like many other Reformers of the time, the dates of Guido de Brès's life (1522–1567) were framed by Bullinger's (1504–1575). De Brès seems to have encountered a good number of Anabaptists in the regions of his ministry, especially in the Southern Netherlands, present-day Belgium. In his day these groups were benefitting from the more settled and learned ministry of Menno Simons (1496–1561) and Dirk Philips (1504–1568), whose writings began to appear in the 1540s. In 1565 De Brès published a lengthy work entitled, *The Root, Source, and Foundation of the Anabaptists or Rebaptizers of our Time*.[52] In three parts he treats the history of the Anabaptists, their views on the human nature of Christ, and their views on baptism. This latter section is divided into twenty-nine chapters, of which the chapters 12–14 deserve our attention. Chapter 12 is entitled, "Anabaptists say baptism ought not to be imparted to little children because they cannot be regenerated;" chapter 13, "The Anabaptists hold the opinion that one ought not to baptize little children because they cannot demonstrate the fruit of their faith by works;" and chapter 14, "It follows to refute the arguments which the Anabaptists use to deny baptism." In fact, De Brès refutes their arguments throughout all three chapters.

In chapter 12, De Brés first sets out to show that God does not make his covenant with all people but leaves much of the world under his wrath. However, believers and their children receive the privilege to be chosen by him. Although they share the sin and corruption of all people in Adam, "nevertheless the children of believers, by the grace of God and by the truth of the promises of the covenant, are delivered from this perdition

---

52. *La racine, source, et fondement des Anabaptistes ou Rebaptisez de nostre temps* ([Rouen]: Abel Clémence, 1565). On Rouen as the likely place of printing, see Clutton, "'Abel Clémence' of 'Rouen': A Sixteenth-Century Secret Press," 136–52; Valkema Blouw, *Dutch Typography in the Sixteenth Century*, 148. Interestingly, another printing of this book, by Pierre de St. André of Geneva in 1595, is virtually identical, with even the same corrections page at the end (only the title page and fourteen-page dedication letter differ). Perhaps André obtained unsold copies of the Clémence printing?

and are sanctified and regenerated . . . by the pure goodness and mercy of God in Jesus Christ."[53] This raises the question that De Brès found in the writings of the Anabaptist Dirk Philips, namely, how can children who do not understand good or evil be regenerated? De Brès replies: "The Lord regenerates the little children and makes them new creatures; I say, of those whom he saves . . . this regeneration is done according to the spirit, in the inside."[54] Although the wording of De Brès's reply seems to posit a distinction between elect and non-elect baptized children, this is not what he pursues next; rather, his focus falls on the manner of regeneration. De Brès never makes election an operative assumption, much less a hermeneutical tool by which to sort out all the promises in Scripture.

De Brès defends his view about this regeneration by pointing out that although Scripture says in 1 Pet 1:23 that sinners are born again by the preaching of the Word, this can, properly speaking, only be attributed to the Holy Spirit. The Spirit is the one who does the work and is able to regenerate when and where it seems good to him, while the Word is the instrument he uses.[55] He then parades in quick succession some six arguments from Scripture to show that it is possible for the Spirit to regenerate infants: John the Baptist was filled with the Spirit from his mother's womb; Jeremiah was set apart for God from his mother's womb; Paul calls the children of believers holy; Christ said the kingdom belongs to them; the Lord promised to circumcise his people's hearts and their children's hearts in Deut 30:6; and the Lord would not desire to leave the children of the new covenant more miserable than those of the old.[56] Rhetorically, he asks why the children would be less able to be renewed than to be corrupted, when both of these lie outside of their understanding. Appealing to 1 Cor 15:50 and Heb 2:9, he adds that

---

53. De Brès, *Anabaptistes*, 659 (translations are my own).

54. Ibid., 661.

55. Ibid., 662.

56. Ibid., 662–3. For an Anabaptist response to the arguments about Jeremiah and John the Baptist, see Philips, *Vander doope*, 77–83. See also Philips, *Enchiridion: Oft hant boecxken van de Christelijcke leere*, 25r, 26v–27r. For a version that is easier to read, consult *Enchiridion: oder handbüchlein von der Christlichen lehre*, 39, or find one of the two twentieth-century English translations (I cannot speak to these, as I have not seen copies). For a similar in-house Reformed critique of the Reformed use of these texts, see Gootjes, "The Promises of Baptism," 191.

in Christ the last Adam and the life-giving spirit, all are made alive, for Christ tasted death for everyone.[57]

These arguments set the stage for the first mention of the lamb offered for the children, similar to what De Brès had included in the Belgic Confession, Article 34, some four years prior. In the Confession he had written, "And, indeed, Christ shed his blood no less for the washing of the children of the faithful than for adult persons; and, therefore, they ought to receive the sign and sacrament of that which Christ has done for them; as the Lord commanded in the law, that they should be made partakers of the sacrament of Christ's suffering and death shortly after they were born, by offering for them a lamb which was a sacrament of Jesus Christ."[58] In 1565, in *Racine*, De Brès writes,

> If one died for all, then all died. The little children thus have the mortification and annulment of their sins in Christ, like the adults. As in a figure the Lord shows us this in Leviticus, commanding that the woman who had a male or female child present to the priest a lamb a year old, etc. This lamb was a figure of Christ, the true lamb of God who takes away the sins of the world. [The Anabaptists] think they can avoid the force of this passage by saying that the woman offered the lamb only for herself and not for the little child, but our St. Luke is a good and faithful expositor, saying that this lamb suffered as much for the mother as for the child, for he says this, "When the days of their purification were completed according to the law," etc. He does not say, "When the days of her purification," but he expressly says "their." It appears then that the child was counted with its mother, and thus Christ has been offered and sacrificed for the children of his people as much as for the adults.[59]

It is of some interest to us that De Brès stated that the Anabaptists had a reply to this argument, saying that the sacrifice covered only the mother, not the child. He does not reference any of their writings, but it could

---

57. If I understand De Brès correctly, his appeal to 1 Cor 15 is not merely to verse 50 but to the verses 45–49, where the apostle speaks of Christ as the life-giving spirit and uses the present tense: "so are those who are of heaven." De Brès writes in a very compact way, "Why can [the infants] not, by the same reason, inherit and possess the regeneration and renewal that we obtain by Christ the second Adam, in his spirit? For just as we all die in Adam, so we are all made alive in Christ, who is the life." *Anabaptistes*, 663.

58. Schaff, *Creeds of Christendom*, 3:437.

59. De Brès, *Anabaptistes*, 663–4. For the same arguments repeated, see p. 675. The biblical texts from which De Brès argues are Lev 12:6 and Luke 2:22. The article of Leonard Verduin, which dismisses chapter three of De Brès's *Racine* as following "the usual line of argument" cannot be considered a serious historical study. Leonard Verduin, "Guido de Bres and the Anabaptists," 262.

also be that he had encountered this objection in personal discussions with Anabaptists.[60]

As a brief excursus, I would like to consider De Brès's argument. As noted earlier, almost every commentary on the Belgic Confession avoids discussion of this argument. In addition, the Scripture commentaries on Luke's Gospel by De Brés's Reformed predecessors and contemporaries that I perused do not make any connection between the purification offering for Mary and Jesus and the practice of infant baptism.[61] Nor do we, as far as I know, find this argument in other confessions of faith.[62] Commentators differ on whether the sacrifice was for Mary only (a textual variant uses the singular, "her" purification rather than "their"), or whether it was for Mary and Joseph or for Mary and Jesus, but it seems that De Brès is on safe ground to assume that Luke is referring to both Mary and Jesus when he speaks of the days of "their" purification being completed. From what did they need purification? Uncleanness is about fitness for temple worship, about admission to the presence of God, not sin as such. A mother who had borne a child committed no sin by virtue of this act, but actually fulfilled a God-given task. Vonk comments helpfully,

> Of course, such a woman would not have committed a sin by bringing a child into the world. On the contrary, such is the task of women, and obedience of this task is even part of her way of salvation (Gen 1:28, 1 Tim 2:15). But with every new birth the fact of the depravity of our human race was again placed before God's eyes, and everything and everyone who comes into contact with it must simply displease him. Therefore it will certainly have been God's will for such a mother that a purification offering be brought, of which we now know that it did not itself bring redemption, but served to signify and to seal the atonement which would be brought about by the Messiah in the fullness of time. Thanks to that atonement through Christ, such a woman could appear

---

60. De Brès interacts with Philips a number of times in *Racine*. My perusal of two key writings of Dirk Philips did not encounter any discussion of these Scripture texts.

61. I consulted commentaries on Luke by Jacques Lefèvre d'Étaples, Johannes Oecolampadius, Ulrich Zwingli, Leo Jud, and John Calvin. Most of them emphasize that the doctrine of original sin is supported by the sacrifice being offered in Luke 2. They usually add that Jesus did not need this sacrifice offered for him but came under the law, just as he willingly submitted to the Torah as he grew up. They did not make connections to infant baptism. A more thorough search could be made of the Church Fathers, whose writings De Brès knew well, but it seems likely that if De Brès had such a source known to him, he would have referenced it.

62. For this essay I especially consulted the Gallican Confession of 1559, Beza's Confession of 1559, the Scots Confession of 1560, and the Heidelberg Catechism of 1561. But from my wider reading of Dennison, *Reformed Confessions of the 16th & 17th Centuries in English Translation*, I am not aware of any other confession using this argument.

again in the meeting of the holy people of the Lord. She was cleansed again by the blood of Christ. That was good for her and pleasing to God.[63]

Thomas Becon (1512–1567), an English reformer, pointed the way to a very positive approach regarding this requirement of a sacrifice: "God constituted this law among his people for a particular purpose, so that the mother . . . would come to the temple."[64] As would the child. And thus our Lord, having undergone circumcision on the eighth day and having been brought to the temple on the fortieth day, with an offering made for his purification, came under the law for our sakes. He was brought into the presence of God as an infant, thereby also opening the way for believers' infants to be brought into God's presence.

Vonk criticized De Brès's argument not so much for its content as for its placement amongst the three main arguments that De Brès made for infant baptism.

> But however well meant and rightly advanced, considered in itself, the *placement* of this argument seems to us unfortunate. For whoever thinks that he still has to posit in his argument an argument for the argument, gives the impression of not being convinced of the truth of the first. And De Brès ought to have been convinced anyway. Indeed, he was.
>
> Even without its further proof by means of a reference to the little lamb for the Hebrew children, the argument of [Christ shedding his blood for the children] is powerful enough: Christ also shed his blood for the children of the church, just as much as for the adults.[65]

Vonk has a point that the wording of the confession becomes a bit awkward here, but as far as the function of the argument is concerned, it seems that it is a good support for the statement that Christ shed his blood as much for the children as for the adults. The argument from the lamb that was offered makes the dimension of forgiveness of sins and fitness for worship more obvious than does the argument from circumcision. It seems to me that De Brès offers a very valuable argument here: God's people received the assurance that the child came under the promise of the forgiveness of sins. This was a message to be received by the church in faith. The parents, in particular, had to hold on to this promise of the Lord in faith, and they promised before the church

---

63. Vonk, *De Voorzeide Leer IIIb: De Nederlandse Geloofsbelijdenis*, 389–90 (translation mine).
64. Kreitzer, ed., *Luke*, 59.
65. Vonk, *De Nederlandse Geloofsbelijdenis*, 391 (italics added).

that this was their view of their child and that they would instruct him or her accordingly.

De Brès could have added that the firstborn male child in particular needed to be brought before the Lord at the temple and redeemed, since these first of all belonged to him as firstfruits of each marriage, being originally destined for the priesthood (Exod 13:2, 12; 22:29; Num 3:11–13). Such Old Testament regulations underlined how fully the children belonged to the Lord. If the Lord had discontinued the special place of the children in the New Testament, he would have needed to make that clear, especially to the Jews. Thus far the excursus.

Immediately following his assertion that the lamb offered for the child was a sign that Christ died for them, De Brès brings up the fact that Dirk Philips would agree that the little children were washed, cleansed, and baptized in Christ's blood, but he would not agree that they were regenerated (Philips may or may not represent other Anabaptists in this view). To this De Brès replies that Philips thinks of regeneration only as the outward change of works, which of course one could not observe in the infants, but "Christ shows us in Saint John that regeneration is nothing else but the washing and interior purging of the water, and, moreover, he speaks of the rebirth by the water and the Spirit and makes express mention of the water to signify that the Spirit in the regenerate person washes the sins, just as water washes bodily impurities." Further, De Brès presses the point that washing in Christ and regeneration by the Spirit belong together—whoever denies the one loses the other; indeed, he well illustrates this unity when he writes of the *Holy Spirit* washing away the child's sins.[66]

De Brès also highlights Jesus' own sanctification from his infancy as the assurance for believers that all ages are sanctified in him.[67]

The case of believers' children dying in infancy—with or without baptism—presented a case for both Bullinger and De Brès to argue that their place in God's covenant ensured their salvation. De Brès is consequent in saying that God regenerates these children: "They are elect of the Lord; he regenerates and renews them by his Spirit as he pleases, according to his hidden and incomprehensible power for us."[68]

---

66. *Anabaptistes*, 664.
67. Ibid., 665.
68. Ibid., 667.

Evidently, such regeneration would not be by means of the Word, but in some other secret way. And such regeneration is necessary since without it no one can enter God's kingdom (John 3), for all are conceived and born in sin.[69]

God himself might well be understood to have told all believers' children at their baptism what Jesus told Peter when he washed his feet, "You do not understand now what I have done for you, but you will understand later."[70] In the same way, the little children brought to Jesus by their mothers did not understand the significance of his prayers and hands (and the Anabaptists, says De Brès, act like the disciples of Jesus did at that time).[71] According to De Brès the Reformed are not concerned that the children's lack of understanding might preclude their baptism; to the contrary,

> seeing that God deigns happily to wash our children in the blood of his Son and seeing that by this means they have forgiveness of their sins, and that baptism is the seal and pledge of the free forgiveness of sins and the adoption by which God receives us to himself, we say [that they should be baptized].... For, as we have already said above, the children are also renewed by the Spirit of God, according to the measure and capacity of their age. And this divine power which is hidden in them grows by degrees and shows itself clearly in its time.[72]

The case of the deaf and the mute who have believing parents provides De Brès with a case similar to that of the infants. He argues that the Anabaptist theology of faith and baptism leaves such persons without salvation, but the Reformed believe that God regenerates such persons before they die: "God works inside such persons in a manner unknown to men."[73] De Brès then argues from the lesser to the greater, positing that if the Anabaptists will baptize deaf or mute persons when they can discern but small signs of faith in them, how much more ought they to baptize their infants, who are far more likely to understand and show signs of faith in time.[74]

---

69. Ibid., 682.
70. Ibid., 676.
71. Ibid., 678.
72. Ibid., 680.
73. Ibid., 682–83.
74. Ibid., 684.

In conclusion, De Brès agreed with Bullinger in insisting that the children of believers are renewed by the Holy Spirit, but he added that this is age-appropriate, or according to the measure and capacity of their age. De Brès's use of Leviticus 12:6 and Luke 2:22 seems to be a unique contribution on his part. Perhaps he found this in one of the church fathers that he was so fond of reading, though if he had, he would likely have provided the reference. Unique or not, the argument was quite in keeping with the rest of the arguments and views of the Bullinger and De Brès.

Conclusions

Today, after a whole series of debates about baptism, election, and covenant in the twentieth century, we are first of all tempted to read our debates into the sixteenth-century material. A reader from the Protestant Reformed churches might emphasize that De Brès wrote in one place that he seemed to have in mind only those children that God saves.[75] A reader from the Canadian Reformed churches might emphasize that Bullinger and De Brès wrote so positively about the promises of God for all the children, even the non-elect. Kuyper no doubt would have emphasized the frequency and intensity of both authors' insistence that the children receive the Holy Spirit, and he would have insisted that this is the proper ground for baptism. But all such later readers would be reading their own concerns into the text, asking earlier authors to address questions which had not yet been or were only beginning to be asked. And it may well be that we would make greater progress by going back to an earlier time in the discussions in order to ascertain whether or not the further developments and refinements have been helpful.

The Reformed Forms for Baptism come from the era of Bullinger and De Brès. They speak of the children of believers being conceived and born in sin and subject to all sorts of misery, even to condemnation

---

75. The editor's footnotes in the translation of Wielenga's *Reformed Baptism Form* are a great example of a tendentious reading of the form, wherein every promise of God, indeed, every statement in the form, is understood and subsumed under the rubric of divine election. See esp. 122, n. 40; 125, n. 42; 177–78, n. 15; 215–16. n. 14; 385, n. 1; 390, n. 2; 395, n. 6; 396, n. 7; 400, n. 9. The added footnotes certainly help clarify the views of the Protestant Reformed Churches and make reading the book more interesting.

itself, and yet being sanctified in Christ.[76] If the positive statements about the children of believers in the Form for the Baptism of Infants are to be understood in the way that Bullinger and De Brès thought of the children, it would seem that they speak *in general* of the normal pattern of salvation, and do so because they speak according to the Word of God about the children, particularly the promises extended to them in the covenant. The parents are to *believe* God the Father when he *promises* that he forgives and accepts and renews not only them but also their children. If they have taught their children God's ways, then from the earliest age, when they ask their children whether they belong to God, the children will say yes. If they follow up by asking their children whether they have the Holy Spirit, the children will again affirm. Then the children will also be holding on to God's Word *in faith*. As they grow up, their understanding will increase, but fundamentally, by God's grace, most of them will already be believers. In turn, this will mean that the parents treat these children as God's children, inheritors of salvation, called to faith, and held to a high standard of holiness. None of their salvation is "automatic," but always comes in the way of true faith. First the parents, then the children, must believe God's Word.

It seems to me that both Bullinger and De Brès have an operating assumption—sometimes more, sometimes less obvious—namely, that they (and we) are faced with a dilemma. On the one hand they are faced with the Reformed confession of original sin and the condemnation it entails for the little children, but on the other hand God promises to be present with the children and receive them into his presence just as he does for their parents. Thus the dilemma: either one must affirm that the children of believers remain under the condemnation of original sin and therefore cannot be pleasing to God or one must affirm that God has made them pleasing to himself in the same way that he has made their parents pleasing to himself—by imputing to them the satisfaction and righteousness of Christ and by regenerating their hearts to receive this gift. Indeed, we noticed that Bullinger even spoke of God imputing faith itself to the infant.[77]

---

76. See further in this volume the contribution of Vreugdenhil, "Sanctified in Christ."

77. The idea of God imputing faith to the children assumes that they do not have faith as such in themselves but have faith counted to them by God. Some words of Theodore Beza distinguish the possibility of the children having faith from us knowing whether they have such faith. He writes, "And it is not very likely that they have faith because they do not have the use of understanding

This operating assumption derives, in their minds, from John 3, Romans 8, and other passages. They reason: if no one can enter or even see the kingdom of God unless he is born again (John 3) from above of water and the Spirit, and yet Jesus says that the children are in the kingdom of heaven; if all who belong to Christ have the Spirit of Christ, and yet the children have the promises of the covenant and belong to Christ; then the infant children of believers must be born again and have the Spirit of Christ. There is no third alternative; neither Bullinger nor De Brès are willing to leave the children in a kind of no man's land. In their minds, if we do not agree with them about the work of the Son for the children and the work of the Spirit in the children, we leave the children under condemnation rather than saying that they are sanctified in Christ.

It may be that subsequent Reformed debate about the children has yielded categories of covenantal sanctification, covenantal holiness, positional sanctification, and so forth. But whoever uses these categories is still faced with the question: are the children under condemnation or not? If not, in what sense are they acceptable to God? Could one today, for instance, affirm that *every* baptized child, head for head, has indeed been dedicated to God and is called to respond—a state that one could describe as covenantal sanctification—while also affirming that it is true that the children *in general* are indeed washed in Christ's blood and possess the Spirit of Christ for the formation of an age-appropriate faith? I would affirm. This latter position is open to misunderstanding, as if we might be saying that all the church's children are elect. This we cannot say, but we can and should treat them as elect until their doctrine and life show otherwise. Stephens correctly summarized Zwingli's views: "He combined this argument [regarding election] with the covenant, affirming that we may be confident of the election of those born within the covenant until we have evidence to the contrary, as we have later with Esau."[78] According to Stephens, Bullinger in his later treatise (1560) was more reticent about mentioning election in this connection. One could add that even if the doctrine and life of believers' children show

---

(Deut 1:39; Rom 10:14, 17), except God works in the extraordinarily (which does not appear to us)." He adds, "Although they do not have faith in effect such as those do who are of age, yet they have the seed and spring [of faith] in virtue of the promise." See "Theodore Beza's Confession (1560)," ch. 48, in Dennison, *Reformed Confessions*, 2:293.

78. Stephens, "Bullinger's Defence," 188.

otherwise, God himself certainly did confirm and seal their entire dedication to him in baptism—that is never lost; indeed, it will testify against them if they do not repent.[79] Beza wrote that "they have the seed and the spring [of faith] in virtue of the promise which was received and apprehended by their elders .... Then by what right do they [Anabaptists, etc.] refuse to give them the mark and ratification of what they have and profess already?"[80]

Surely another point worthy of noting in conclusion is Bullinger's statement that the benefits of Christ's blood and Spirit do not flow to the children through their parents or by reason of their descent from their parents, but by the grace of God's promises. By emphasizing this, one would be more apt to equally emphasize the call to faith that comes with one's baptism. *Grace and promises, not birth and parentage, call forth faith.*[81]

Our two authors did not assume something about this or that particular child being among God's elect but they absolutely affirmed that the children of believers—in general, and unlike the children of unbelievers—belong to God and therefore have his Son and his Spirit as gifts of God's love. This general truth guided their practices.

Nor did they regard as sound the Anabaptist argument that the power of reason should be present in the children before regeneration is possible—rather, by distinguishing the efficient cause (the Holy Spirit) and the efficient instrumental cause (the Word preached), they could insist that the Holy Spirit was not unalterably bound to the chosen instrument.

It would not be correct to say that Bullinger or De Brès taught that a presumed regeneration was the basis for infant baptism. Both authors started with the promises of God to the children in Genesis 17, promises repeated in the New Testament. They then proceeded to make arguments about the children receiving washing in Christ's blood by the Spirit uniting them to Christ and making them share in his benefits. Regeneration was one of the parts of this salvation package, but it was not the fundamental basis for baptism. If one were to suggest that it

---

79. This was a helpful point emphasized by Klaas Schilder.
80. "Beza's Confession (1560)," in Dennison, *Reformed Confessions*, 2:293.
81. The essay of Nicolaas Gootjes, noted above, is very helpful on the point that the Form for Baptism has both the side of God's promises and his calling that the child respond in faith. Gootjes, "The Promises of Baptism."

was, our authors would surely point out that the *whole work of God* for the child was really the basis, as given by promise. And to say that our authors were *presuming* would not be right either; they were simply taking God at his Word. They would say this is a matter of *believing*, not presuming.

Of the various arguments that were used by Bullinger and De Brès, their insistence on the universality of the application of the benefits of Christ's death and resurrection should also be highlighted. In their minds, to leave out the children as a whole and in principle, is to destroy the force of the "all" that occurs in many places in the New Testament. Likewise, we should appreciate their understanding that salvation is a "package deal," so to speak, in which one receives the Father, Son, and Spirit and their benefits together.

Our two authors also did not use the examples of John the Baptist leaping in his mother's womb and of Jeremiah being set apart from the womb as grounds to baptize children. Their use of these examples had a more limited application. They only wanted to say that these examples showed that it is possible for the Holy Spirit to work in a child who cannot understand good and evil and, indeed, to regenerate the child if he so chooses. Interestingly, it was the Anabaptists who argued that these examples pertained only to these men being called to prophetic office. On this point the Anabaptists were correct; but the corollary that anyone dedicated to such an office has also been made fit for the office by personal regeneration also seems to be quite reasonable. And, even if the latter is not granted, the examples do demonstrate that the Holy Spirit *can* cause regeneration in an infant if he so chooses.

The position of Old, that the Reformers sifted through the biblical material and carefully considered the place of the children in the church, is surely correct. They did not continue infant baptism thoughtlessly at all, but with a new understanding of its grounds, of the relation of sign and thing signified, and of the relationship of baptism, divine promises, catechesis, and faith.

Bibliography

Book of Praise: Anglo-Genevan Psalter. Winnipeg: Premier, 2014.

Bullinger, Heinrich. *Adversus Anabaptistas Libri VI*. Translated by Josias Simler. Zurich: Froschouer, 1560.

———. *De testamento seu foedere dei unico & aeterno Heinrychi Bullingeri brevis expositio*. Zurich: Froschouer, 1534.

———. *Von dem unverschampten Fräfel, ergerlichem Verwyrren unnd unwarhafftem Leeren der selbsgesandten Widerrtöuffern: vier Gespräch Bücher*. Zurich: Froschouer, 1531.

———. Letters. https://www.irg.uzh.ch/en/hbbw/datenbank.html. Accessed September 20, 2018.

———. *A moste sure and strong defence of the baptisme of children, against the pestiferous secte of the Anabaptistes*. Translated by Jhon Veron Sononoys. Worcester: Jhon Oswen, 1551.

———. *Sermons on the Sacraments*. Cambridge: Cambridge University Press, 1811.

Clutton, George. "'Abel Clémence' of 'Rouen': A Sixteenth-Century Secret Press." *Transactions of the Bibliographic Society* 20, no. 2 (1939): 136–52.

De Brès, Guido. *La racine, source, et fondement des Anabaptistes ou Rebaptisez de nostre temps*. [Rouen]: Abel Clémence, 1565.

Dennison, James T., Jr., ed. *Reformed Confessions of the 16th and 17th Centuries in English Translation*. 4 vols. Grand Rapids: Reformation Heritage Books, 2008–2014.

Ella, George M. "Henry Bullinger: Shepherd of the Churches." https://www.contra-mundum.org/mbs/mbstexte009.pdf. Accessed September 20, 2018.

———. *Henry Bullinger: Shepherd of the Churches*. Eggleston: Go Publications, 2007.

Gootjes, Nicolaas H. *Teaching and Preaching the Word: Studies in Dogmatics and Homiletics*. Edited by C. Van Dam. Winnipeg: Premier, 2010.

Kreitzer, Beth, ed. *Luke*. Reformation Commentary on Scripture. Downers Grove, IL: IVP, 2015.

Old, Hughes Oliphant. *The Patristic Roots of Reformed Worship*. Zurich: Juris, 1975.

———. *The Shaping of the Reformed Baptismal Rite in the Sixteenth Century*. Grand Rapids: Eerdmans, 1992.

Philips, Dirk. *Enchiridion: Oft hant boecxken van de Christelijcke leere*. [s.l.]: Pieter Hendricksz., 1579.

———. *Enchiridion: oder Handbüchlein von der Christlichen Lehre*. Lancaster, PA: Ehrenfried, 1811.

———. *Vander doop onses Heeren Iesu Christi, bekentenisse*. Middelburg: Jerome Wullebrecht, 1589.

Rainbow, Jonathan H. "'Confessor Baptism': The Baptismal Doctrine of the Early Anabaptists." In *Believer's Baptism: Sign of the New Covenant in Christ*, edited by Thomas R. Schreiner and Shawn D. Wright, 189–206. Nashville, TN: B&H Academic, 2006.

Schaff, Philip. *Creeds of Christendom*. Vol. 3. Grand Rapids: Baker, 1993.

Steinmetz, David. "Scholasticism and Radical Reform: Nominalist Motifs in the Theology of Balthasar Hubmaier." *The Mennonite Quarterly Review* 45 (1971): 123–44.

Stephens, Peter. "Bullinger's Defence of Infant Baptism in Debate with the Anabaptists." *Reformation & Renaissance Review* 4, no. 2 (2002): 168–89.

Valkema Blouw, Paul. *Dutch Typography in the Sixteenth Century*. Leiden: Brill, 2013.

Verduin, Leonard. "Guido de Bres and the Anabaptists." *The Mennonite Quarterly Review* 35 (Oct 1961): 251–66.

Vonk, Cornelis. *De Voorzeide Leer IIIb: De Nederlandse Geloofsbelijdenis*. Barendrecht: Barendrecht, 1956.

Wielenga, Bastiaan. *The Reformed Baptismal Form: A Commentary*. Translated by Annemie Godbehere. Edited by David J. Engelsma. Jenison, MI: Reformed Free Publishing Association, 2016.

Zwingli, Ulrich. *In catabaptisarum strophas elenchus*. Zurich: Froschouer, 1527.

———. *Selected Works of Huldreich Zwingli (1484-1531), The Reformer of German Switzerland*. Translated by Lawrence A. McLouth. Edited by Samuel Macauley Jackson. Philadelphia: University of Pennsylvania, 1901.

"Sanctified in Christ"

Arjen Vreugdenhil

The traditional Reformed liturgical Form for infant baptism asks of the parents:

> Do you confess that our children, though conceived and born in sin, and therefore subject to all sorts of misery, even to condemnation, are *sanctified in Christ* and thus as members of his church ought to be baptized [emphasis added]?[1]

The expression "sanctified in Christ" has been subject to much controversy, in the past and even today among the Reformed churches. What is its proper interpretation? This question is clearly important: for centuries, parents have made this confession concerning their children as the ground for their baptism. Likewise, the Christian upbringing of these children takes its starting point in the conviction that they were sanctified in Christ from the very beginning of their lives. What does it mean?

In this paper I will first consider the origin of the expression "sanctified in Christ." Then I will present some of the history of the controversies surrounding it. Next, I will analyze the difficult question underlying these controversies and place it in the context of contemporary church life. Finally, I will give a brief evaluation in light of the Reformed confessions.

Origin of the Expression

The history of the baptismal Form and its questions can be summarized as follows:

> The first part was translated word for word from the Liturgy of Heidelberg—one half of it having come down from the Genevan Liturgy prepared and supervised by Calvin. The old form was somewhat longer than that now in use which was authorized by the Provincial Synod of Holland

---

1. *Book of Praise*, 598.

and Zealand held at Dort in the year 1574, but the present Form differs in no expression from the other, being only condensed.

The Prayer between the preface and the questions is word for word a translation from the Liturgy of Zurich, and was written by the learned and the martyred Lavater in the year 1559.

The questions as they stand in the form must in all probability be referred to Dathenus from whom we receive them and who again took them from à Lasco.[2]

The Heidelberg version of the Form did not yet use the words "sanctified in Christ."[3] Thus this expression must be dated to the version published by Petrus Dathenus in 1566; it was subsequently ratified by larger ecclesiastical bodies, such as the 1574 Provincial Synod, and in 1619 by the National Synod of Dort. As mentioned in the above quotation, Dathenus echoed the questions in the Form drawn up by John a Lasco:

1. Do you bear witness whether these children that you present are the seed of this our church, that they by our ministry may legitimately be baptized here?
2. Do you also acknowledge that our doctrine, which you have heard concerning baptism and its mystery, is true, and that our children, although like all of us by nature children of wrath and death, yet already included with us in the divine covenant for Christ's sake, ought certainly to be sealed with the seal, instituted by Christ, of their acceptance and righteousness, that is, baptism?[4]

Note that the word "sanctified" is not present in a Lasco's version; Dathenus appears to have chosen it as a summary of being "included with us in the divine covenant for Christ's sake."

The expression "sanctified in Christ" is an obvious reference to 1 Cor 7:14:

> For the unbelieving husband is sanctified in the wife, and the unbelieving wife is sanctified in the brother: else were your children are unclean; but now they are holy.[5]

---

2. A Digest of Constitutional and Synodical Legislation of the Reformed Church in America, 77–78.

3. In the Heidelberg version of the Form parents were asked to respond to one question: "Do you desire, in true faith in the promises of God in Jesus Christ, given to us and our children, that he will be not only our God, but also the God of our seed, unto the thousandth generation, [and do you desire] on this ground that this child be baptized *and receive the sealing of being God's child* [emphasis added]?" (cited in Woelderink, *Het doopsformulier*, 71).

4. Translated from Pieters and Kreulen, 1–2.

5. Quoted from the American Standard Version to show the correspondence between "in Christ" and "in the wife/brother."

Obviously there is no direct textual connection between the context of 1 Cor 7 and baptism, let alone infant baptism. For instance, what we conclude from this verse about the *children* of believers we cannot apply to the unbelieving *spouses* of believers. Nobody would advocate such an application! Thus the meaning of the phrase "sanctified in Christ" in the baptismal Form cannot be determined through exegesis of this verse on its own. While it may express that "the unbeliever has already become and continues to be a part of a family unit upon which God has his claim and which he will use for his service,"[6] this does not in itself justify the administration of baptism to a newborn infant in that family.

Bavinck in his *Gereformeerde Dogmatiek* draws a similar conclusion:

> The holiness of which Paul speaks here must not be regarded as subjective and internal, but as objective and theocratic, for otherwise the children and the husband would be holy not because of themselves but rather because of the believing mother and wife. Moreover, Paul *is not at all thinking* of the baptism of infants or a possible ground for it. His only point is to show that the Christian faith does not sever the natural ordinations of life but rather confirms and hallows them; cf. vv. 18–24. However, for infant baptism this passage is relevant, as it teaches that an entire family is reckoned according to the confession of the believing spouse; the believer is called to serve the Lord, not for himself, but for all that is his and together with his family [emphasis added].[7]

Thus the use of 1 Cor 7:14 in the first baptismal question is meant as a shorthand reference to a larger body of theological thought. In the confessions of the Reformed churches the only similar language is found in Canons of Dort:

> We must judge concerning the will of God from his Word, which declares that *the children of believers are holy*, not by nature but in virtue of the covenant of grace, in which they are included with their parents. Therefore, God-fearing parents ought not to doubt the election and salvation of their children whom God calls out of this life in their infancy [emphasis added].[8]

If we assume that the Canons and the Form for Baptism speak about the same theological principle, we may conclude the following about the status of children of believers as "sanctified in Christ":

---

6. Mare, 1 Corinthians, at 1 Cor 7:14.
7. Bavinck, Gereformeerde Dogmatiek, 4:506 (§ 537). The translation is mine.
8. Canons of Dort, I.17. Book of Praise, 569.

- This sanctification is by virtue of the covenant of grace.
- They are included in the covenant and are members of the church.
- They derive this status from that of their parents.
- This status is the basis for their baptism.
- This status is sufficient reason not to doubt their salvation if they die at an early age.

History of Controversy

Within the scope of this paper I cannot give more than a very broad history of the controversies surrounding the expression "sanctified in Christ" in the Form for Baptism.

16th and 17th Centuries

In the early use of the Form there was no public controversy about this matter. This does not mean that theologians agreed about the meaning of the phrase "sanctified in Christ." Woelderink explains:

> In the explanation of these words there may never have been unanimity among the theologians of the 16th and 17th century. At least, when they discuss the grounds of infant baptism they differ on the question whether the children should be viewed as already regenerated. But at first there was no controversy about these things, and they did not denounce each other as heretics because of this difference. . . . [T]hey did not consider it a point of great importance. Even when discussing this subject, they often do not even refer to the first question of the Form for Baptism.[9]

One reason for this lack of strife and the silence on the issue could be that the phrase "sanctified in Christ" was sufficiently unclear and flexible, so that theologians could reconcile this language with their different views. But in the course of time the word "sanctified" acquired a specific soteriological meaning. Moreover, especially with the development of Reformed scholasticism, theological positions were further developed and points of difference became sharper.

---

9. Woelderink, *Het doopsformulier*, 178.

18th Century

In this time the distinction "internal/external" had become commonplace in theology.[10] Some theologians, following Gomarus and Trigland, interpreted the first baptismal question as speaking of an *external* sanctification, connected to the external covenant.

Other theologians, such as Jodocus van Lodensteyn, denied this, and interpreted "sanctified in Christ" as referring to an internal holiness, that is, regeneration. Because not all children of believers are regenerated, they concluded that one ought not make this declaration at the baptism of any specific child. Many of them omitted or altered the first baptismal question.[11]

A third view is presented by Wilhelmus a Brakel in his book *De Redelijke Godsdienst*,[12] published in 1700. According to him, to be "sanctified in Christ" does not mean that *every* child to be baptized or any *particular* child is elect and will be saved; but rather, that in general the children of covenant members have the right to the covenant benefits. The children of believers must then be viewed as God's children unless and until they prove to be otherwise.

Various synods dealt with the issue on some level, but they did not develop specific doctrinal statements to resolve the matter.

Secession Theologians

The Secession of 1834 came with a renewed interest in Reformed orthodoxy.[13] The old debates flared up again, often leading to vehement disagreements.[14] The main line of division was between the northern ("Drenthe") Secessionists and the southern ("Gelderland") Secessionists.

---

10. Information about the controversies in the 18th century is taken from Woelderink, 178ff.

11. A popular alternative was: "Do you believe that our children . . . *being sanctified in Christ*, ought to be baptized [emphasis added]?" The participial clause was interpreted as a conditional clause: "insofar as they are sanctified."

12. Chapter 26, section 8 (as cited in Woelderink, 181).

13. Information about this period is taken from Veenhof, *Prediking en uitverkiezing*, especially 58ff.

14. Thus Pieters and Kreulen, 1: "Anyone who is no stranger in the history of the Dutch Reformed Church knows that there are widely divergent views of the *holiness of Christian children*, as mentioned in the first question of our Form for Baptism [emphasis theirs]."

A prominent northern Secessionist was H. Joffers. He believed that the covenant of grace was established from eternity with the elect only and that baptism seals this eternal covenant to the elect children, who are fully sanctified in Christ even though they are not yet converted; when administered to the non-elect, baptism is then "a bare ritual" (*een bloot teken*), no more than an indication of separation from the world, whatever that might entail. Joffers' main opponent was A. Brummelkamp. The Synod of Leiden in 1857 adopted the following statement, leaving the matter essentially unresolved:

> During the exposition of the doctrine of baptism it must be shown that the children of the congregation, as members, must be baptized; but as not all were Israel that were of Israel, so also there are among the children of believers those who are unconverted and reprobate.[15]

In a book about infant baptism published in 1861,[16] K. J. Pieters and J. R. Kreulen defended the view that baptism signifies and seals the promise of the covenant of grace to *all* children of believers:

> Every baptized person receives baptism in the name of the Triune God; therefore the promises are for *him*. If this promise were not signified and sealed to every legitimately baptized person, but perhaps only to one out of a thousand, then the entire baptism would be a vain ceremony and, in fact, a serious deception. Moreover, it could not be of comfort or benefit to anyone, unless and until he be assured of his election. . . . Such a system, or rather nonsense, never came up in the thoughts of the Reformed church; our fathers sounded a serious warning against this view.[17]

According to Pieters and Kreulen, baptism seals God's promises to all baptized children but does not in itself confer grace. With an appeal to Calvin, the authors emphasize that the sacraments, like the Word, offer and display Christ and his benefits, but that they only benefit us if they are received in faith. They explain the expression "sanctified in Christ" as a referring to *covenantal holiness*, a holiness that flows from

---

15. Veenhof, *Prediking en uitverkiezing*, 59.

16. Pieters and Kreulen, *De Kinderdoop volgens de beginselen der Gereformeerde Kerk in hare gronden, toedieningen, en praktijk* [Infant Baptism According to the Principles of the Reformed Church in Its Grounds, Administrations, and Practice].

17. Pieters and Kreulen, 46–47.

the inclusion in the covenant, from the reception of all the covenant promises.[18]

Simon van Velzen opposed their view. He also spoke of covenantal holiness. But he interpreted the baptismal Form as saying that the children of believers *in general* are sanctified in Christ but that only the elect actually share in this privilege. However, since we do not know who these elect are, we must therefore view our children as sanctified in Christ even though not all of them are sanctified in Christ. Here Van Velzen sees a parallel with the Lord's Supper, whose participants are viewed as those for whom Christ died even though some of them may not be elect.[19]

The matter was submitted to the Synod of Franeker in 1863 when charges were levelled against the book by Pieters and Kreulen. The synod declared that there was unity in the essentials but that there were different views concerning details. Pieters and Kreulen were found to be orthodox; however, the synod explicitly stated that this did *not* imply that they presented the most correct expression of the Reformed view.[20]

American Secession Theologians

The more "objective" approach of Pieters and Kreulen gained popularity among Secessionists. Among the Dutch Reformed immigrants in America in the late 19th century, it was the dominant view. Of the seven American theologians listed by Jelle Faber,[21] six stand in this broader tradition: L. J. Hulst, G. E. Boer, H. Beuker, G. K. Hemkes, F. M. Ten Hoor, and W. W. Heyns; they "emphasize that *all* children of believers are children of the covenant and sanctified in Christ. The covenant promise of salvation is given to *all* these children. For *all* these children baptism is a sign and seal of the covenant of grace or that promise of salvation."[22] Only Geerhardus Vos represents the more subjective view.

---

18. Veenhof, 64–65.
19. Ibid., 75.
20. Ibid., 80.
21. Faber, *American Secession Theologians on Covenant and Baptism*, 17. Faber characterizes them as "infralapsarian" vs. "supralapsarian"; these labels should be interpreted in the broader, popular sense of the word. Ibid., 26.
22. Ibid., 37.

Kuyper and Bavinck

Woelderink speaks of the late 19th century as a time in which "baptism degenerated to an external affirmation that one was no heathen and lived under the offer of grace."[23] In this milieu Abraham Kuyper attempted to return to an understanding of baptism in a fuller sense.

For Kuyper, baptism seals something internal to the baptized child; once again, "sanctified in Christ" was interpreted as referring to the regeneration of the child, typically before or around its birth. The church was to *presuppose* that this regeneration had taken place, or at least was present in potentiality; this presupposition was the ground for baptism.[24] If the assumption turned out to be false, one would have to conclude that no real baptism had taken place.[25]

Herman Bavinck opposed the Kuyperian view as follows: "Ground for baptism is not the supposition that someone is regenerated, nor even regeneration itself, but only the covenant of God."[26] The right to be baptized belongs only to the believer, but Scripture teaches us to treat children of believers as believers. In Bavinck's view, baptism is objectively the same for all, but only the elect enjoy the benefits signified in it.[27]

Bavinck thus seems to take a mediating position between the dominant Secessionist view and Kuyper's position. He played an important role in the drafting of the doctrinal statements of the Synod of Utrecht in 1905. This synod had to arbitrate in various old controversies that had flared up after the merger of Secessionists and Kuyper's followers in 1892. Concerning infant baptism the synod declared:

> [T]he seed of the covenant, by virtue of the promise of God, *must be held to be regenerated and sanctified in Christ*, until upon growing up they should manifest the contrary in their way of life or doctrine; it is, however, less correct to say that baptism is administered to the children of believers on the

---

23. Woelderink, 186. Note that Woelderink and his target audience were in the *Hervormde Kerk*, and therefore not part of the Secession tradition. In fact, Woelderink does not discuss the developments among the Secessionists. While the Seceded churches were zealously fighting over their newly recovered orthodoxy, the established State church degenerated further and couldn't care less.

24. For a brief summary of Kuyper's view and criticism it encountered, see Berkhof, *Systematic Theology*, 639.

25. Thus summary in Venema, *Wat is een christen nodig te geloven?* 51–52.

26. Bavinck, *Gereformeerde Dogmatiek*, 4:508 (§ 537, 8°).

27. Here Bavinck appeals to Augustine's adage, *In solis electis efficiunt quod figurant* [Only in the elect is realized that which is signified].

> ground of their presumed regeneration, since *the ground of baptism is found in the command and the promise of God*; furthermore, the judgment of charity, with which the church regards the seed of the covenant as regenerated, *does not at all imply that each child is actually born again*, seeing that God's Word teaches that they are not all Israel that are of Israel, and of Isaac it is said: "In him shall thy seed be called," so that it is imperative in the preaching constantly to urge earnest self-examination, since only he that believeth and is baptized shall be saved.[28]

The synod also stated that there is no ground to believe that an elect child is actually regenerated before his baptism.

It is not difficult to see that the 1905 statement favoured Bavinck's position over against Kuyper. But the broad formulation (with expressions such as "it is less correct") left room for the Kuyperian view. In the following decades the Kuyperian position gained dominance.

Schilder and Hoeksema

In the middle of the 20th century two theologians opposed the Kuyperian establishment and became the leaders of new denominations, which are still represented today. In 1924 Herman Hoeksema laid the foundation for the Protestant Reformed Churches in North America, and in 1944 Klaas Schilder became a dominant figure in the "liberated" Reformed Churches in the Netherlands, whose heritage is reflected in the Canadian Reformed Churches. Both theologians disagreed with Kuyper but pulled in opposite directions.

Hoeksema followed Kuyper in his emphasis on the internal. His axiom was that "God's covenant is essentially the relationship of friendship between God and his people," the latter understood as the elect only.[29] Rather than being an instrument of salvation in history, this covenant was seen as an eternal relationship. Hoeksema gave it the place of honour in his strongly supralapsarian schema.[30] In it the covenant is the basis (and *telos*) of God's grace, God's blessing, and every spiritual benefit. Acccording to Hoeksema the non-elect do not receive grace in

---

28. Quoted from Hoekema, *The Covenant Theology of Herman Bavinck*, 179-80.
29. Hoeksema, *De Geloovigen en Hun Zaad*, 44.
30. Hoeksema, *Reformed Dogmatics*, 165.

any way: the earthly "blessing" they receive expresses God's hatred and judgment.[31]

This view defines Hoeksema's reading of the Form for Baptism. His favourite opponent was William Heyns, who emphasized that all children of believers are included in the covenant and addressed by God's promises. Hoeksema disagreed: "How could one separate the work of the Father and the Son on the one hand, and the work of the Spirit on the other?"[32] But he also opposed the Kuyperian view of presupposed regeneration: "[We may not] presuppose that all the children that are baptized are regenerated, for we know . . . that the opposite is true."[33]

Hoeksema and his followers often say that "God saves the believers and their seed," but with the tacit understanding that this is only the elect seed. The children of believers are "sanctified in Christ" in a general, "organic" sense; but one may not apply it to the individual children, head for head, for not all of them are elect. Baptism is thus said to seal the objective truth of God's covenant with his elect.[34]

Schilder also emphasized that the covenant seals an objective truth, arguing that the ground for baptism is the covenant promise, which comes to all children of believers, whether they are elect or not. In this view, which is much in line with that of Pieters and Kreulen and later Secession theologians in North America, the expression "sanctified in Christ" simply summarizes that the children belong to the covenant. This places them under God's special rule, which includes promises as well as threats.[35] "Sanctified in Christ," while true for every baptized child, is then not taken to mean that God's promises will be realized in each of them. To quote Schilder, "God gives us promises but no predictions."[36]

The legacies of Schilder and Hoeksema are particularly interesting because they led to a direct confrontation in North America in 1953.

---

31. Virtually any Protestant Reformed writer will support this from Psalm 73: "You place them in slippery places."

32. De Geloovigen en Hun Zaad, 17.

33. Declaration of Principles, III.A.1. Quoted from Appendix F of Hanko, For Thy Truth's Sake, 451. This is a summary of Hoeksema's argument in De Geloovigen en Hun Zaad, 33.

34. This is in harmony with Hoeksema's view of preaching, i.e., that it "is not a gracious offer of salvation on the part of God to all men, nor a conditional offer . . . to all that are baptized, but an oath of God that he will infallibly lead all the elect unto salvation and eternal glory through faith." Declaration of Principles, I.D.2., quoted from Appendix F of Hanko, For Thy Truth's Sake, 451.

35. Schilder, Extra-Scriptural Binding, ch. 59.

36. Ibid., ch. 7.

The two traditions continue to exist, with very little change in views or language, in the Protestant Reformed Churches (mostly in the United States) and the Canadian Reformed Churches (mostly in Canada). Any attempt to work on unity between these two opposites in the spectrum would cause the old discussions to flare up again.

An Analysis of the Issue

It should be clear from the preceding overview that the issue surrounding the expression "sanctified in Christ" has been ever-present in the Reformed Churches. Even today there is no agreement on the matter. Among the American churches of Dutch descent, this is most obvious in the extremes of the Protestant Reformed Churches (who fiercely defend and sometimes radicalize the Hoeksema position) and the Canadian Reformed Churches (who canonize the Schilder view). Within other denominations, such as the Free Reformed Churches and United Reformed Churches, one can expect to find a wide range of views on this matter.

At its core the problem consists in the paradox that (1) we wish to maintain a very high view of infant baptism, while (2) in practice it is clearly impossible to say with *certainty* that *every* baptized child *has salvation* which he or she *cannot lose*. Because of the reality of unbelief among children of the covenant, one must deny at least one of the four italicized terms in the previous sentence. This generates the following views.

- *First view*: One could deny the certainty of the sacrament, and instead merely *presuppose* that every baptized child has salvation. In this view the confession of parents that their child is "sanctified in Christ" applies to the baptized child personally—except that it is always possible that this presupposition turns out to be false and that the baptism was no real baptism after all. This is the Kuyperian solution.
- *Second view*: One could deny that baptism refers to *every* baptized child, head for head, and rather regard it as a general statement that the elect children of believers possess full salvation in Christ. In this view it cannot be known what precisely the sacrament signifies and seals personally to the child that is being baptized. This approach is

found in Van Velzen and Hoeksema.
- *Third view*: One could deny that baptism affirms the actual salvation, the washing of Christ's blood, the regeneration of the baptized child. In this view baptism signifies instead a covenant blessing that comes to elect and non-elect children alike. This covenant blessing, summarized in being "sanctified in Christ," then includes covenant membership and the covenant promise that the child will receive salvation on the condition of faith. This is the solution of Pieters and Kreulen and of Schilder.
- *Fourth view*: One could deny that baptism affirms a salvation that cannot be lost. In this view baptism affirms that the baptized child possesses salvation in Christ. But if he or she fails to respond in faith, that salvation is lost. This seems to be the position of Peter Leithart and other Federal Vision theologians, who use expressions such as "union with Christ which does not last."[37]

I believe that this schema may be useful in further discussions of the question what is meant by "sanctified in Christ." We all want to do justice to infant baptism as a rich sacrament, and we all know that the reality of sin and apostasy must be accounted for. What we disagree on—and have disagreed on ever since the Reformation, it seems—is how this accounting should happen. What aspect of our doctrine of baptism should we "sacrifice" in order to account for children who are baptized, yet do not receive ultimate salvation?

The choice one makes here will be informed by one's view of God, of man, of revelation, of the covenant, of the church, and so on. For instance, theologians who choose the first or second view are more likely to emphasize God's decrees, while theologians who choose the third view are more likely to emphasize his revelation in history. One's view of baptism, and particularly one's view of the meaning of the expression "sanctified in Christ," reveals much about one's broader theological framework.

---

37. Leithart, *The Baptized Body*, 98. Because Leithart and other Federal Vision folks move off the field of Reformed orthodoxy (perhaps in doctrine, but certainly in theological categories), we will not consider this approach in the rest of this discussion.

Evaluation on the Basis of Reformed Confessions

A full evaluation of these positions (and their many variations) is not possible within the bounds of this paper; nor can we discuss all that the Scriptures have to say in this regard. This last section will merely focus on the question which of the first, second, and third views outlined above is most compatible with the language of the Reformed confessions. For this purpose we will consider the Heidelberg Catechism, Q&A 74; the Belgic Confession, Art. 34; the Canons of Dort, I.17; and the Form for the Baptism of Infants.

The Heidelberg Catechism, Q&A 74

> Should infants, too, be baptized? — Yes. Infants as well as adults belong to God's covenant and congregation. Through Christ's blood the redemption from sin and the Holy Spirit, who works faith, are promised to them no less than to adults. Therefore, by baptism, as sign of the covenant, they must be incorporated into the Christian church and distinguished from the children of unbelievers. This was done in the old covenant by circumcision, in place of which baptism was instituted in the new covenant.[38]

The affirmative tone of this answer leaves little room for the the first view, the Kuyperian view of presupposed regeneration. It is one thing to make this presupposition in order to justify baptizing a child; it is a very different thing to make this presupposition in a creedal statement, implicitly and silently. The Kuyperian must rewrite the answer as: "Infants are to be presupposed to belong to God's covenant and his church...."

Equally incompatible is the second view. Hoeksema made very clear what his view does to Q&A 74:

> That in this question and answer of the Heidelberger not all the children that are baptized, but only the spiritual children, that is, the elect, are meant is evident. For:
> a. Little infants surely cannot fulfill any conditions. And if the promise of God is for them, the promise is infallible and unconditional, and therefore only for the elect.
> b. According to Canons II.8, ... the saving efficacy of the death of Christ is for the elect alone.

---

38. *Book of Praise*, 541–42.

> c. According to this answer of the Heidelberg Catechism, the Holy Ghost, the author of faith, is promised to the little children no less than to the adult. And God surely fulfills His promise. Hence, that promise is surely only for the elect.[39]

The claim is that the Catechism really means to say: "insofar as the infants are elect." But it is unthinkable that such an important restriction should be omitted so consistently. From the *Commentary* by author Zacharias Ursinus it is clear that he did not intend any such restriction: "for all the children of those that believe are included in the covenant, and church of God, unless they exclude themselves. They are, therefore, also disciples of Christ, because they are born in the church, or school of Christ; and hence the Holy Spirit teaches them in a manner adapted to their capacity and age."[40]

The third view seems to be more compatible with the statement in the Catechism, for it freely speaks of covenant inclusion of all children that are baptized. Moreover, Q&A 74 do *not* state in any way that all infants are actually saved, washed, or recipients of the Holy Spirit; rather, they are given a *promise* of these spiritual goods.

The Belgic Confession, Art. 34

> We believe [that the children of believers] ought to be baptized and sealed with the sign of the covenant, as infants were circumcised in Israel on the basis of the same promises which are now made to our children. Indeed, Christ shed his blood to wash the children of believers just as much as he shed it for adults. Therefore they ought to receive the sign and sacrament of what Christ has done for them, as the Lord commanded in the law that a lamb was to be offered shortly after children were born. This was a sacrament of the suffering and death of Jesus Christ. . . . [B]aptism has the same significance for our children as circumcision had for the people of Israel.[41]

Again, the language of the article is rich and generous. Note the statement that "Christ shed his blood to wash the children of believers" and that the sacrament signifies "what Christ has done for them." Does this also apply to the non-elect children of believers? If not, we must adopt the hermeneutic of the first or second view and understand an

---

39. *Declaration of Principles*, II.B.
40. Ursinus, *Commentary on the Heidelberg Catechism*, sub Q 74 (366).
41. *Book of Praise*, 514.

implied presupposition or restriction regarding "the children" in this article. The question concerns the extent of Christ's atonement: may we say that he shed his blood for the washing of people who turn out to be unbelievers? Is the availability of Christ's atoning sacrifice broader than its efficacy? I see no objections here, but the Reformed tradition is divided over this matter.

The Canons of Dort, I.17

> We must judge concerning the will of God from his Word, which declares that the children of believers are holy, not by nature but in virtue of the covenant of grace, in which they are included with their parents. Therefore, God-fearing parents ought not to doubt the election and salvation of their children whom God calls out of this life in their infancy.[42]

This is the only place in the Reformed confessions (apart from the first baptismal question) with an overt reference to 1 Cor 7:14:[43] "the children of believers are holy." Children of believers are holy, "sanctified," on the basis of covenant inclusion. If these covenant children die before they can exhibit personal faith (or unbelief), they are saved and shown to be elect. *There may be no doubt*, according to the Canons.

It is very difficult to reconcile this statement with the first view, in which the words "sanctified in Christ" can only be said on the basis of a presupposition which is known not always to be true. How can parents *not* doubt the validity of this presupposition with regard to their own child if it dies? At least equally incongruent is the second view, which openly teaches that some of the children of believers are reprobate and lost. Hoeksema himself felt this incongruence, but he intimated that the Canons are at fault here:

> This article certainly leaves much to be desired in clarity and precision of definition. One cannot deny that in the current form it cannot really be regarded as a creedal article. In a creed the church expresses what she believes concerning God's truth revealed to us in Scripture. And it cannot be said that this is what the church is doing here. If the Synod of 1618–19 had really intended to present a definite view concerning the salvation of children who die in infancy, then this article of the Canons should have been formulated very differently. It should have stated decisively: "We believe that

---

42. *Book of Praise*, 569.
43. Ibid., 569, n. 2.

[etc.]." Then at least the church had something definite, something whose meaning cannot be subject to doubt.[44]

Thus he concludes: "It certainly would have been no loss if I.17 had never been included in the Canons."[45]

Hoeksema does not say that the article is entirely wrong; he denies that anything objective is stated about the children. It is merely a pastoral admonition. Godly parents must not *doubt*, not because they have assurance of the election of their child, but because they trust that the Lord's way is best.

But this interpretation does no justice to the article in the Canons. The reason why parents must not doubt is not that the sovereign God knows best, regardless of whether the child is saved or not; rather, the reason is *God's Word*, which declares that our children are holy. While this obviously cannot mean that they are all automatically saved, we may be assured that our children are in the covenant of grace. Again, this language is most compatible with the third view: that baptism seals an objective truth to every child of a believer and that the children of believers belong to God and are recipients of rich promises. Because of that, they will be saved unless they exclude themselves in unbelief. Not only must the parents not doubt; believing parents may be assured of this!

However, there is truth to Hoeksema's observation that the language of Canons I.17 is very circumspect. From the historical context it is clear that this was to appease those who, like Hoeksema, tended to emphasize God's sovereign self-glorification in saving people as well as in condemning them. It was of great importance to come to a clear, positive statement, even though there was a broad spectrum of views among the Reformed.[46] Certain "harsh sayings" (*phrases duriores*) along those lines had been the occasion for the Remonstrant accusations.[47] In

---

44. Hoeksema, *Geloovigen en Hun Zaad*, 91–92.

45. Ibid., 94.

46. See Venema, "The Election and Salvation of Children," 85.

47. See the epilogue of the Canons, which rejects the allegations of those who taught that "many innocent children of believers are torn from their mothers' breasts and tyrannically thrown into hell, so that neither the blood of Christ nor their baptism nor the prayers of the church at their baptism can be of any help to them." But the Canons also recognize that Reformed ministers had given occasion to such allegations. Hence this concluding admonition: "Therefore . . . this Synod exhorts all fellow ministers in the gospel of Christ . . . to refrain from all those expressions which exceed the prescribed limits of the true meaning of the Holy Scriptures." *Book of Praise*, 588.

I.17 the Canons do not develop a detailed view of the state of infants (because there was disagreement among Reformed theologians), but rather outline the minimum requirement of faithfulness to God's Word.

The Form for the Baptism of Infants

The baptismal Form connects our baptism directly and personally to promises of the Triune God. "When we are baptized into the name of the Father, God the Father testifies and seals to us . . . ."[48] Adherents of the first view will affirm this but will keep in mind that the assumption that was made may, after all, turn out to be false. Adherents of the second view can only agree with the Form insofar as the elect children are concerned.[49] From the perspective of the third view one can fully embrace the rich language of the form. The promises on God's part are real and sincere; but they will be fully realized by the baptized person only if they are received in faith.[50]

The defence of infant baptism in the Form is centred on the covenant of grace. From the inclusion of children in the covenant with Abraham to the Lord's embrace of children, the biblical testimony is that children belong to the covenant, in which they are "received into grace in Christ."[51] This is very strong language; to be received in Christ may easily be understood as the reception of full salvation. Again, those who adhere to the first and second views cannot say this of all children that are being baptized. But if they cannot say this of all children, they have, according to the Form, no ground for the baptism of all children either.

I propose that, in line with the third view, we understand "received into grace in Christ" as an incorporation in the covenant of grace, without declaring all children of believers to be automatically saved. The expression "received into grace in Christ" is then synonymous with

---

48. *Book of Praise*, 597

49. In personal discussions with Protestant Reformed ministers I have heard them complain that the Form is not sufficiently clear. They read it with the understanding that all that is said is conditioned on the election of the child, but this condition is not explicit in the text.

50. In this regard it is significant that the Form states concerning the Holy Spirit "that he *will* dwell in us." The verb "will" must be read in its older sense; that is, the Spirit *is willing* to dwell in us. It leaves open the fearful possibility that covenant people reject the promises and oppose the Holy Spirit in unbelief.

51. *Book of Praise*, 597. The statement that they are "received into grace in Christ" was not found in the original Form of Dathenus but was added later to oppose Anabaptist tendencies. See Woelderink, 326.

"sanctified in Christ" in the first question asked of the parents.[52] It means being "heirs of the kingdom of God and of his covenant" and being "members of his church."

Conclusion

In the long and ongoing controversy about the precise meaning of baptism, the Reformed creeds point in a clear direction. We may (and must) view our children as those who are "sanctified in Christ." All children of believers, not merely in general or by presupposition, but each and every one of them, are declared holy, are included in the gracious covenant, are called God's sons and daughters. That is the basis of their baptism. The Lord promises to them salvation in Christ.

The difficulties arise if we wish to account for the falling away of some, in spite of their baptism. For the Reformed confessions this is no reason to back off or to speak in less certain terms. Even the apostate children of believers were sanctified in Christ, and carry the sign of heirs of the kingdom. If they fall away, it is solely on the basis of their own unbelief.

This view gives comfort to parents. It should also make us serious about the training of our children. That is why the Form reminds us that a covenant has *two* parts: the promise, but also the obligation. That is why the first baptismal question is followed by a third question, in which parents promise to raise and instruct their children.

---

52. There is an obvious parallel between the wording of the Form proper ("Just as they share without their knowledge in the condemnation of Adam, so are they, without their knowledge, received into grace in Christ") and that of the first question ("Do you confess that our children, though conceived and born in sin, and therefore subject to all sorts of misery, even to condemnation, are sanctified in Christ?").

Bibliography

Bavinck, Herman. *Gereformeerde Dogmatiek*. 7th ed. Kampen: Kok, 1998.

Berkhof, Louis. *Systematic Theology*. Grand Rapids: Eerdmans, 1996.

Book of Praise: Anglo-Genevan Psalter. Winnipeg: Premier, 2014.

Corwin, Edward T. *A Digest of Constitutional and Synodical Legislation of the Reformed Church in America*. New York: Board of Publication of the RCA, 1906.

Faber, Jelle. *American Secession Theologians on Covenant and Baptism*. Neerlandia, AB: Inheritance, 1996.

Hanko. Herman. *We and Our Children: The Reformed Doctrine of Infant Baptism*. Grand Rapids: Reformed Free Publishing Association, 1981.

———. *For Thy Truth's Sake*. Grandville, MI: Reformed Free Publishing Association, 2000.

Hoekema, Anthony A. *The Covenant Theology of Herman Bavinck*. Clover, SC: Full Bible Publications, 2007.

Hoeksema, Herman. *De Geloovigen en Hun Zaad*. Grand Rapids: PRC Mission Committee, 1946.

———. *Reformed Dogmatics*. Grandville, MI: Reformed Free Publishing Association, 1966.

Leithart, Peter J. *The Baptized Body*. Moscow, ID: Canon, 2007.

Mare, W. Harold. *1 Corinthians*. *The Expositor's Bible Commentary*. Vol. 10. Grand Rapids: Zondervan, 1976.

Pieters, K. J., and J. R. Kreulen, *De Kinderdoop volgens de beginselen der Gereformeerde Kerk in hare gronden, toedieningen en praktijk*. Franeker, 1861.

Schilder, Klaas. *Extra-Scriptural Binding: A New Danger*. Neerlandia, AB: Inheritance, 1996.

Ursinus, Zacharias. *Commentary on the Heidelberg Catechism*. Translated by G. W. Williard. Cincinnati, 1851.

Van der Zwaag, K. *Afwachten of verwachten? De toe-eigening des heils in historisch en theologisch perspectief*. Heerenveen: Groen, 2003.

Veenhof, C. *Prediking en uitverkiezing*. Kampen: Kok, 1959.

Venema, Cornelis P. "The Election and Salvation of the Children of Believers Who Die in Infancy: A Study of Article I/17 of the Canons of Dort." *Mid-America Journal of Theology*, 17 (2006): 57-100.

Venema, F. F. *Wat is een christen nodig te geloven?* Barneveld: Vuurbaak, 1985.

Wielenga, B. *Ons doopsformulier*. 2nd ed. Kampen: Kok, 1920.

Woelderink, J. G. *Het doopsformulier*. The Hague: Uitgeverij Guido de Brès, 1938.

Mature in Christ: The Practice of Covenant Nurture in American Presbyterianism

Eric B. Watkins

Few things are dearer to the hearts of parents and pastors than our covenant children. We pray for them and instruct them with the goal "that we might present everyone mature in Christ" (Col 1:28). At the centre of the church's ministry is the preaching of the gospel, but our ministry to our covenant children also includes "warning and teaching everyone with all wisdom" (Col 1:28) in the context of covenant nurture. One of our greatest hopes and joys is to see them profess their own faith in Christ in the context of spiritual wisdom, maturity, and servanthood. The purpose of this essay will be to reflect on the way in which covenant kids are nurtured toward spiritual maturity in American Presbyterian churches (primarily the Orthodox Presbyterian Church and the Presbyterian Church in America). This will be done by first giving a brief description of both denominations and the communicant membership vows required by each. Second, these vows will be set against a historical backdrop that helps to explain their current form and nuances. Third, empirical research will be presented that surveys the varying approaches taken within these churches, based on seven survey questions asked of ten representative churches from each denomination. An interactive summary and analysis of the answers given will follow. In the final section, pastoral reflections upon the relative strengths and weaknesses of this process in the American Presbyterian churches under consideration will be presented, followed by a summary and conclusion of the entire study.

A Credible Profession of Faith: Historical Backdrop

What is required of covenant children in American Presbyterian churches in order to make a profession of faith and begin partaking of the Lord's Supper? Perhaps the easiest way to answer the question is to quote from the church order of our two primary churches under consideration, the Orthodox Presbyterian Church (OPC) and the Presbyterian Church in America (PCA). The two sister denominations have quite a bit in common and have almost joined to form a single denomination twice in their history.[1] The OPC is the older of the two churches and was formed in 1936. It was born in the midst of a strident battle against theological liberalism that was creeping into the mainline Presbyterian Church (PCUSA), the same influences that had also begun to inundate Princeton Theological Seminary as early as the 1920s. The OPC's inception was numerically modest and humble with regards to the comforts of church property and social influence. This humble beginning led to what many have referred to as a pervasive "pilgrim people" identity in the OPC.[2]

In a situation like that of the OPC, the PCA was formed in 1973 along defensive lines and in a similar context of theological controversy, as the poison of liberalism slowly dripped down into the southern Presbyterian churches. Though the southern Presbyterian church and northern Presbyterians would eventually reunite into one (the PCUSA), many of the dynamics that set the stage for the formation of the OPC would not come to a head in the southern Presbyterian churches until decades later. This explains why the PCA formed in the south almost four decades after the OPC.[3] When the PCA was formed, however, it embodied far more social concern and material privilege than that of its older sister up north.[4] Thus, though the two conservatively Reformed denominations have slightly different stories, their constitutional commitments to the Westminster Confession of Faith are identical, and their books of church order are strikingly similar. There are, to be sure, slight differences in polity, culture, and practice between the two churches, but for the most part they are remarkably similar—especially on paper—and in reality

---

1. For a brief summary of this venture from an OPC perspective, see "The OPC and Ecumenical Relations," in Hart and Muether, *Fighting the Good Fight: A Brief History of the Orthodox Presbyterian Church*, esp. 135–38.

2. "History for a Pilgrim People: An Interview with Charles G. Dennison," 233.

3. Morton H. Smith notes that this came to a head in a 1972 declaration by the PCUS General Assembly that the church "operates with a detailed Confession, the 'fundamentals' of which are interpreted with considerable latitude." Smith, "How Is the Gold Become Dim," 44, cited in Frank J. Smith, *The History of the Presbyterian Church in America*, 9. This sounds remarkably similar to the "Auburn Affirmation" declarations in the PCUSA in 1924 that in part set the stage for the formation of the OPC.

4. Lucas, *For a Continuing Church*, 326.

might be best described not so much as ecclesiastical siblings but as twins.

We begin our comparison of requirements for a profession of faith with the older of the two denominations, the OPC. The five vows taken upon the occasion when someone makes a profession of faith are as follows:

1. Do you believe the Bible, consisting of the Old and New Testaments, to be the Word of God, and its doctrine of salvation to be the perfect and only true doctrine of salvation?
2. Do you believe in one living and true God, in whom eternally there are three distinct persons—God the Father, God the Son, and God the Holy Spirit—who are the same in being and equal in power and glory, and that Jesus Christ is God the Son, come in the flesh?
3. Do you confess that because of your sinfulness you abhor and humble yourself before God, that you repent of your sin, and that you trust for salvation not in yourself but in Jesus Christ alone?
4. Do you acknowledge Jesus Christ as your sovereign Lord, and do you promise that, in reliance on the grace of God, you will serve him with all that is in you, forsake the world, resist the devil, put to death your sinful deeds and desires, and lead a godly life?
5. Do you promise to participate faithfully in this church's worship and service, to submit in the Lord to its government, and to heed its discipline, even in case you should be found delinquent in doctrine or life?[5]

The five vows in the PCA are similar:

1. Do you acknowledge yourselves to be sinners in the sight of God, justly deserving His displeasure, and without hope save in His sovereign mercy?
2. Do you believe in the Lord Jesus Christ as the Son of God, and Savior of sinners, and do you receive and rest upon Him alone for salvation as he is offered in the Gospel?
3. Do you now resolve and promise, in humble reliance upon the grace of the Holy Spirit, that you will endeavor to live as becomes the followers of Christ?

---

5. *The Book of Church Order of the Orthodox Presbyterian Church*, 158.

4. Do you promise to support the church in its worship and work to the best of your ability?
5. Do you submit yourselves to the government and discipline of the church, and promise to study its purity and peace?[6]

Several preliminary observations are worth making regarding the membership vows in both the OPC and the PCA. First, the vows taken upon the occasion of a public profession of faith, in both denominations, are the same for covenant children who have grown up in the church as they would be for someone coming from outside the church and being baptized. Second, a point of contrast between the two sets of vows would be that the OPC vows are slightly longer and include an affirmation regarding Scripture and the Trinity, whereas the PCA vows do not.[7] Third, it is important to note that both polities are very careful to guard the idea that the covenant child making a profession of faith is *already* a member of the church, but is now entering into "full communion" with the church.[8] Finally, both the OPC and PCA contain a provision in this section for persons making a profession of faith to give a brief personal testimony in their own words to their faith in Christ, though this is not a requirement.[9] This leads to a topic that is worthy of reflection; namely, how is it, historically speaking, that the OPC and PCA came to require a profession of faith by covenant children in the first place?

From a historical point of view, Presbyterian churches have not always required a profession of faith by covenant children. To be clear, the point of bringing this up is not to suggest there is anything improper with the current practice of requiring a profession of faith by covenant children, but simply to note that within the historical narrative of American Presbyterianism such a requirement has not always been the case. Peter Wallace, in a very helpful and insightful article, notes that while making a profession of faith before the congregation has been a practice in the continental Reformed churches for centuries, it is actually a fairly recent

---

6. *The Book of Church Order of the Presbyterian Church in America*, 57.
7. These vows, along with the books of church order of each denomination, are not static but have undergone periodic revisions. Quotations above are from their current form.
8. Smith, *Commentary on the Book of Church Order of the Presbyterian Church in America*, 435–36.
9. Ibid.

feature for American Presbyterians.[10] To quote Samuel Miller, a pillar of Presbyterian polity who taught at Princeton in the mid 1800s, "Our fathers of the Church of Scotland know nothing of the public parade in the middle aisle now so common."[11] This innovation, at least as it pertains to American Presbyterianism, owes more to the influence of the conversionist piety of the nineteenth century (including the influences of the Second Great Awakening) than it does to continental Reformed practices. Within the narrative of these developments among American Presbyterians, tensions ensued over how to maintain the rich covenantal theology that had been handed down by the reformers and then codified by Protestant orthodoxy, while at the same time attempting to adapt to the rapidly evolving cultural scene witnessed by American Presbyterians.

Following the Civil War (also known as the "War Between the States"), a period of spiritual decline rendered many in the church discouraged and depressed over the ecclesiastical fissure that was one of many sad consequences of the war. It is in this context, following the war, that many Christians resolved themselves to prayer and evangelism as the only hope for rebuilding the fractured church.[12] A rift developed among Presbyterians along the lines of not only how to revitalize the church, but also how to account for the quickly expanding western frontier and so-called revivalist influences that were sweeping through the land. A group within the American Presbyterian church, referred to as "New School Presbyterians,"[13] embraced and advocated practices that were in some ways unfamiliar to the church, yet clearly had Second Great Awakening tendencies. The theological-cultural identity struggle that ensued would last for centuries—down to the present day.

In spite of its post-war struggles for identity, American Presbyterianism had deep roots that could be traced back to its Scottish predecessors, including a parish model of church government that considered individuals born to a particular area (parish) as members of the church and thus entitled to baptism as well as the privileges

---

10. Wallace, "Covenant and Conversion."

11. Ibid.

12. Hays, *Presbyterians: A Popular Narrative of Their Origin, Progress, Doctrines and Achievements*, 145–49.

13. For a fuller definition, see Hart and Noll, *Dictionary of the Presbyterian and Reformed Tradition in America*, 174–75.

and responsibilities that belonged to church members.[14] However, new questions before the church led to newly attempted answers, and certain innovations were endorsed as a means of attempting to hold on to the past while embracing the future. Rightly or wrongly, many nineteenth-century American Presbyterians wrestled with the influence of the Second Great Awakening, including some of its revivalist leanings, and decided along varying lines. Wallace helpfully summarizes as follows:

> But as Presbyterians gradually adopted the New England practice of requiring a personal profession of conversion, they also began adopting the Congregationalist ritual of public profession as well. The Presbyterian Form of Government stated that the session had the power to receive members. Traditionally this had been done by examination. The only public ritual that accompanied the admission of a person to the Lord's Table was the Lord's Supper itself.[15]

Though an examination by the elders was historically precedented and time-tested, the idea of a public profession before the congregation was a relatively late feature in American Presbyterianism. Prior to that, covenant children were simply examined by their elders and then they came to the Supper.

Proviso: The Empirical Nature of This Study

Before we enter into the next section of this paper, it may be helpful to pause and reflect on some of the empirical research that was done in order to paint something of a picture as to the practices of both the OPC and PCA regarding their methods of preparing covenant children for making a profession of faith. First, regarding the empirical inquiry, twenty churches were contacted (ten in each denomination, from different parts of the country and with different demographic profiles). In addition, denominational employees from both the OPC and PCA who work in this area were consulted in order to attempt to ascertain the various courses of instruction used in order to lead covenant children to the point of being able to make a profession of faith. Responses were received from sixteen of the twenty churches contacted, from either the pastor or a staff member. In addition to the particular churches

---

14. Wallace, "Covenant and Conversion."
15. Ibid.

that responded, denominational staff members of agencies serving in the area of Christian Education proved to be particularly helpful. An interested reader wishing to pursue further inquiry should peruse the websites (particularly the Christian Education sections) of both the OPC and PCA, as each contains a deep well of resources, including related articles and books and, in some cases, information about annual conferences on the work of training and educating covenant youth.[16]

One very striking observation that needs to be stated early and clearly is that in the case of both denominations (the OPC and the PCA), there is no singular, homogenous practice of preparing covenant children for making a profession of faith. In both denominations it is quite clear that the exact path for preparing covenant children for making a profession of faith is left up to the discretion of local churches and sessions (boards of elders). Thus, while denominational agencies (i.e., Committees on Christian Education) exist to help serve the church, beyond that which is required by the binding documents—Scripture (primary), the Westminster Confession of Faith and the Larger and Shorter Catechisms (secondary), along with their respective Book of Church Order (tertiary)—there is no exact paradigm to which either denomination strictly adheres. This is arguably an outworking of a Presbyterian principle that local churches are free to order themselves according to the ways they believe are most fruitful and effective, as long as those practices are consistent with the standards of the church and do not explicitly violate them. Thus, in both denominations, practices vary—sometimes rather significantly.

Survey Questions:

1. At what age do you begin a communicants class for covenant kids?
Summary: This question is narrowly focused on when instruction intentionally leading toward a profession of faith *might begin*. Most respondents noted that this ultimately begins at a young age with family worship, sitting under the means of grace, etc. Particular instruction (a class for profession of faith) began for some churches for kids as young as seven years old; in other churches such instruction was reserved for

---

16. See https://opc.org and https://pcanet.org.

kids as old as fourteen.

Comment: This question partially anticipates question number 6 below, regarding the age at which a child might be considered old enough to actually make a profession of faith. Clearly the practice among American Presbyterians varies, with some churches beginning a formal process rather early, others beginning much later. In all cases, the means of grace, family worship, and catechetical instruction feature in the life of the child and the instructional ministries of the church. That said, it is noteworthy that a communicants class could begin for kids as young as seven in some churches and as old as fourteen in others.

2. What is the process for covenant kids to become communicant members?

Summary: The process for this also varied greatly among churches as some have full-blown classes, from as short as five weeks to as long as thirteen weeks. As the *Book of Church Order* in both the PCA and the OPC has membership vows for communicants, nearly every church had a class that culminated in a study of these vows. Interestingly, more than one church had no communicants class at all, but simply allowed children to come before the session when they or the parents felt a child was ready. For the churches that do offer classes, some offer them once a year, others twice. Several churches indicated that they viewed their entire Christian Education ministry as a propaedeutic ladder leading to the crescendo of a public profession of faith.

Comment: Of particular interest is that some churches seem to lean heavily on the perception of the parents regarding the child's readiness; other churches, by stark contrast, were careful to avoid this, wanting to make sure that the desire to become a communicant member was ultimately the child's desire, and not simply a capitulation to parental pressures to do so. Two churches actually had the practice of waiting until the child *requests* to take the class or make a profession of faith—clearly as an outworking of making sure the desire to become a communicant member is actually the child's desire and not just that of the parents or elders.

3. What role do parents, pastors, and youth ministries play in nurturing covenant children toward spiritual maturity?

Summary: Nearly every church indicated that preparing for a profession of faith begins with the parents. Parents are viewed as the first line of defence in raising up the next generation. After that, practices varied greatly—some churches having full-blown program ministries with Youth Pastors or Directors of Youth Ministry, other churches having no other staff but a pastor. Most churches were somewhere in the middle, and whether having volunteer or paid youth leadership, most of those who responded had some sort of ministry that focused on youth and saw part of their role as helping to prepare covenant children for making a profession of faith.

Comment: It is important to note that some churches indicated strong opposition to the youth ministry paradigm, while others seemed to wholeheartedly embrace it. It would be difficult to flesh out in a simple way the ideological differences that separate the two groups. Each would surely claim to adhere to the importance of covenant theology, though their outworking of it in practice might look remarkably different. While not wanting to unhelpfully accentuate distinctions between the OPC and the PCA, it may be helpful to note that the PCA, while having in general larger churches, seems to also have far more comfort with the staffed Youth Ministry paradigm. That said, there were PCAs that clearly resisted this paradigm, just as there were OPCs that embraced it. One consistent factor, however, is that the churches that embraced the paradigm were consistently larger churches. This seems to suggest that a practical exigency forces larger churches to staff something that smaller churches tend to do through parents or lay volunteers.

4. What subjects are covered in the class?

Summary: Of those surveyed, several churches actually wrote their own material for the communicant membership class. But they were the minority. For the most part, churches in both denominations leaned on pre-written materials that covered the same subjects. Nearly every church covered the membership vows of its denomination. Most covered additional theological subjects as well as key areas of the Christian life. Of note was that some churches—especially those with the longer communicants class—tended to focus on things like the Westminster Shorter Catechism, the Apostles' and Nicene Creeds, etc.

Comment: It is interesting to consider that some of the churches polled tended to focus on theology and that others tended to focus on piety. For whatever reason, the churches that were committed to one or the other of these trails did so for what appear to be sincere and well-intended pastoral reasons. That said, there were clearly distinct emphases in certain churches in contrast to others—arguably reflective of historical and pastoral narratives that shaped the particular identity of these churches.

5. What book(s) are used for the communicants class?

Summary: This was one of the more interesting discoveries of the empirical study. Churches in the OPC and PCA overlap one another here in striking ways. Of the churches polled, a nearly equal number of churches in the OPC and PCA used *Confessing Christ*[17] as the book for the communicant membership class. This was the predominant book, with *Understanding the Faith*[18] as the runner-up. Many, if not most, churches made reference to the Westminster Shorter Catechism.[19] Some churches actually made up their own curriculum for the communicants course.

Comment: What is striking is that while the first book (*Confessing Christ*) was written by an Orthodox Presbyterian and the second book (*Understanding the Faith*) was written by a member of the PCA, each book seemed to be equally used and embraced by churches in the other denomination. Thus, it became difficult to tell from a statistical point of view if either the OPC or the PCA tended to prefer one book over the other.[20]

Of note is that some churches, particularly those who treated this class as a multi-year-long part of an overarching pedagogical process, also tended to include other books, whether focusing on systematic theology, apologetics, or personal piety.[21] As noted above, several churches in both denominations used the Westminster Shorter Catechism as a study guide.

---

17. Cummings, *Confessing Christ: A Study of the Christian Faith from a Biblical, Reformed Perspective*.

18. Smallman, *Understanding the Faith: A Workbook for Communicants Classes and Others Preparing to Make a Public Confession of Faith*.

19. This seems appropriate, as the 1648 Preface to the Shorter Catechism says that it was written for those of "weaker capacity."

20. Again, it needs to be remembered that the OPC is a significantly smaller denomination, with about 36,000 members in 2017. The PCA, by contrast, currently is about ten times the same size with approximately 374,000 members at the end of 2017.

21. See, e.g., two pamphlets published by the OPC, *What Is the Reformed Faith?* and *What Is the OPC?* as well as Oliphint, *Know Why You Believe*.

6. At what age could a child become a communicant member in your church?

Summary: This question seemed to expose the greatest amount of disparity between the churches polled, as many churches seemed to favour a strikingly young age at which a child might make a profession of faith, while other churches seemed to favour the polar opposite approach and reserved the idea of making a profession of faith until covenant children were much older. On the first pole were kids as young as five years old; on the other end were churches that waited until covenant kids were in their late teenage years, if not into their early twenties. Most churches fell in between the two poles and would allow a profession of faith for kids in middle or high school.

Comment: It should be noted that the churches who waited until covenant kids were older before allowing them to make a profession of faith were, for the most part, in sections of the country that had a strong Dutch-Reformed influence. This certainly reflects a Dutch-Reformed understanding of the covenant, personal piety, profession of faith, etc. On the other hand, it seemed almost as though the further south the church was geographically located, the younger a covenant child might be allowed to make a profession of faith, clearly reflecting the influence of certain nuances of American Presbyterian ideas, southern Presbyterian ideas in particular, and the barely restrained influences of those sympathetic to the paedocommunion view (which has a modest influence in both the OPC and PCA).[22] While these two generalizations require subtle nuances, they are generally accurate and, again, reflect the multiple personalities of which American Presbyterianism consists.

Finally, many churches polled actually have no set rule (see number one above) as to at what age a child might make a profession of faith, and thus leave it to pastoral considerations. Notably, in connection with this, both the OPC and PCA *Book of Church Order* give no guidance or rule in this area, thus leaving the matter to the pastoral discretion of local elders.[23]

---

22. Note that neither the OPC nor the PCA permit paedocommunion, though there are clearly churches in each denomination that push the envelope.

23. This is arguably due to the matter discussed above in the historical backdrop section regarding the point in history when American Presbyterians began requiring a profession of faith not just before the session but also before the church.

7. What questions are asked during the interview process?

Summary: This question seemed to invoke an almost dizzying sense of variation, as nearly no two churches had exactly the same answer, in either the OPC or the PCA. Most, but not all, churches in both denominations use the membership vows in their *Book of Church Order*, either as the only questions asked or as questions asked in the context of other questions. Several churches submitted rather long and theologically intense questions that are used during the interview process, while, by contrast, a couple of churches defined the interview process as predominantly relational, focusing on the prospective communicant's relationship with Christ and the church. One church, whose preparation process appeared remarkably thorough—bordering on setting a very high theological bar—only asked very basic questions at the point of the communicant's interview by the session.

Comment: This variation of practice is significant, as it reflects the liberty of each local church, according to American Presbyterian polity, to order its affairs as its elders deem fit. Also, a principle that is not held to by all American Presbyterians, but has been argued by some, is that church membership ought not to be restricted to the theological elite, or, as some have put it, that the doors of the local church should not be narrower than the doors of heaven.[24]

Bonus question: Is there anything else related to this topic that should be considered?

This question proved to be helpful as it elicited some interesting feedback. More than one respondent commented, with a bit of angst, upon the fact that Presbyterian polity seems to almost require too much of children wishing to make a profession of faith by requiring them to have the intellectual maturity of an adult (or at least a teenager) before doing so. One respondent noted that there is "nothing magical about age thirteen," and another commented that the withholding of communion from younger covenant children may be withholding from them the very grace that might help them grow spiritually within the covenant. As noted above, numerous influences bear down upon Presbyterian polity—including Baptistic influences—and there are also those who

---

24. Hodge, "What Is Presbyterian Law?" 480. For a similar view, see Dabney, "The Westminster Confession and Creeds," 582.

ardently resist such influences, including those with leanings toward paedocommunion.

On a separate note, one pastor responded that after thirty-one years at the same church, he had seen only one covenant child born into the church who did not eventually make a profession of faith. That is remarkable. Another respondent rather helpfully suggested the importance of cultivating a sense among covenant children that following Christ will require sacrifice and suffering at times—as the world does its best to choke out the faith of covenant youth. This leads to the consideration of certain pastorally related matters before concluding this study.

Pastoral Reflections

As noted above, American Presbyterianism is a hodge-podge of varying influences. While the OPC and the PCA have much in common, especially on paper, they each have particular personalities and cultures that embody their distinctive character and commitments. The above survey reveals a propensity in the PCA to be more program-driven than the OPC. This may be due to its size, among other things, and should not be overstated. The OPC has many churches with well-developed program ministries, but on the whole there are far fewer of these churches in the OPC than in the PCA. For the majority of OPCs, ministry to covenant youth is more grass-roots (led by lay people, etc.) than staffed and funded. In both denominations the family is viewed as the epicentre of ministry to covenant youth, and concentric circles of supportive ministry are wrapped around the family.

One significant feature of American Presbyterianism that is worthy of attention is the emphasis on evangelism within the context of ministering to covenant children and preparing them for a profession of faith. Setting aside for a moment whatever long-lasting impact the Second Great Awakening had on American Presbyterianism via its influence on New School Presbyterians, it is worth noting that both the PCA and the more culturally (if not theologically) conservative OPC saw their ministries to covenant youth also as a means to minister to children who were *outside the covenant*. Edmund P. Clowney very helpfully articulates this in a 1946 article that is certainly indicative of the educational and evangelistic ethos that would mingle in both the

OPC and the PCA.[25] Historically speaking, the inception of Sunday School was an educational and evangelistic paradigm begun in England during a time in which many illiterate orphans wandered the streets of that country as tattered waifs. In this educationally depressed context, the Bible was used by churches Sunday morning, outside of worship, as a tool to teach illiterate children to read.[26] The evangelistic underpinning is clear. In time, however, Sunday School would be adapted by the church as a vehicle primarily used for educating covenant youth. Eventually, at least in many churches, it would focus almost exclusively on the children of Christian families.

This narrative appears somewhat similar to that of the afternoon (second) service in the continental tradition. What began as a pedagogical service for those who were unfamiliar with the truths of Scripture uncovered in the Reformation (making it a largely evangelistic effort) would in time become much more than simply a service for teaching the uninstructed.[27] Eventually it would become a full-blown worship service regularly offered on Lord's Day afternoons or evenings, with a focus on worship and preaching rather than on evangelistic instruction.

In this context it is arguable that American Presbyterians and those from the continental tradition have much in common and could learn from one another. For the former, evangelism is so important that much of the church's theological identity is often and too easily sacrificed on the altar of evangelistic church growth.[28] Of course, there are those in the American Presbyterian tradition who resist this trend (sometimes stridently, and sometimes at the expense of evangelistic fruitfulness). Yet even the most theologically conservative American Presbyterians view their Sunday School programs as a means of outreach to unchurched children. In addition, each of the books used for the communicants class contains chapters on personal evangelism or confessing Christ to others.

On the other hand, however, it is arguable that even the most family-

---

25. Clowney, "Sunday Schools for Evangelism." Clowney would later leave the OPC to join the PCA in the 1980s. Thus, as one who certainly had a prolific influence on both denominations, his article is rightly perceived as representing the commitments of each denomination.

26. Hart, *Between the Times:The Presbyterian Church in Transition*, 166.

27. Ibid.

28. By contrast, the OPC has insisted, "We must place before even the command to evangelize the lost this prior responsibility of bringing up the children of the church in the nurture and admonition of the Lord." Cited in Hart and Muether, *Fighting the Good Fight*, 158.

centric churches in American Presbyterianism pale in comparison to the trans-generational covenant faithfulness found in some of our Dutch-Reformed sister churches. In addition, American Presbyterians struggle greatly to maintain a high view of the Lord's Day and to sanctify it consistently. While this is likely born out of the fact that many American Presbyterians are relatively new to the church, it is still the case that there is much that American Presbyterians can learn from our Dutch-Reformed neighbours about how to develop well-ordered families, pass on the covenant from one generation to the next, and especially how to honour the Lord's Day. The lingering influence of the Second Great Awakening may have spurred many American Presbyterians to greater evangelistic fervour but may also have unintentionally undermined certain aspects of familial and ecclesiastical health. What ought to be a "both-and" approach often regrettably descends into an "either-or" approach—something that needs to be considered and reformed in every church.

In this context a word or two about covenant discipleship is in order. It has become a staggering concern that, especially in the American church (not speaking narrowly of Presbyterians), women outnumber men by two to one. Men are notably absent in the American church.[29] In the African-American church, this statistic is quadrupled; there women outnumber men in the church by four to one.[30] The American church is in grave danger of becoming feminized. Broken homes, once a way of describing unchurched families, have sadly become an earned caricature of the evangelical church in America as well. In this context the importance of discipleship and modelling, as well as evangelism, needs to be underscored. The American church is in a fragile place as the winds of secularization swirl all around it at hurricane speed and the church's root structure appears shallower than ever. The need for biblically Reformed, gospel-centred discipleship is of paramount importance. Programs may have their place in the church, but they can never replace the family, the means of grace, or the important role of one-on-one discipleship, i.e., modelling.[31]

---

29. Farley, *Gospel-Powered Parenting*, 125.
30. Ibid.
31. Modelling is arguably the "first principle of biblical leadership." Ibid., 107.

Summary and Conclusion

In this study we have considered the vows required in the OPC and PCA of covenant children desiring to make a profession of faith. Those vows were set against the historical background that shaped them, and in this context the nuances of those vows were seen as an outworking of the particular narrative of each denomination, its distinct culture, and its current identity. An empirical study followed, engaging seven questions that were asked of twenty churches (ten from each denomination, from varying areas of the country and with varying demographics). The point of the survey was to ascertain the particular practices of American Presbyterian churches, particularly the OPC and the PCA, as to the role of parents, pastors/elders, and programmatic ministries such as Youth Ministry and Sunday School as they relate to preparing covenant children for making a profession of faith. Answers were summarized and interacted with, and following this section, pastoral reflections were offered that considered the relative strengths and weaknesses of this process in the two denominations. A brief suggestion was offered regarding the way in which American Presbyterian churches and churches from the continental tradition might learn from one another.

Who could doubt that our covenant children are the future of the church? We love them. We pray for them. We labour for them in the workplace week after week and in the church every Lord's Day. And yet, in spite of our labours on their behalf, there is a constant battle for their souls. The world tirelessly vies for their attention, and the attrition rate of teenagers in the church is nothing to balk at.[32] Many of our covenant children feel under-challenged in church.[33] Youth groups and pizza parties will not keep them in the covenant. But the gospel will, by the grace of God. What our covenant children need most is gospel-centred parenting, gospel-centred churches, and gospel-centred discipleship. Young men need older men to speak truth to them and to model what it means to be a godly man; young women need older women to show them the glory of womanhood and what it means to follow Christ. As parents, we need not fear. God is a covenant-making, covenant-keeping God and, as he is pleased, he will be faithful to make

---

32. Graustein, *Growing Up Christian*, 22.
33. Crowe, *This Changes Everything*, 48–49.

what is true of our children at their baptism also be true of them when they profess faith in Christ—they belong to him. Having this steadfast hope regarding God's covenant promises in our hearts, whether in worship, family devotions, Sunday school, or youth group, let us strive to serve our covenant children well, and to present each and every one of them—by the grace of God—mature in Christ.

Bibliography

The Book of Church Order of the Presbyterian Church in America. 6th ed. Lawrenceville, GA: Office of the Stated Clerk of the PCA, 2006.

The Book of Church Order of the Orthodox Presbyterian Church. 2015 ed. Willow Grove, PA: Committee on Christian Education of the OPC, 2015.

Clowney, Edmund P. "Sunday Schools for Evangelism." *The Presbyterian Guardian* 15, no. 3 (1946): 35–36.

Cummings, Calvin Knox. *Confessing Christ: A Study of the Christian Faith from a Biblical, Reformed Perspective.* Suwanee, GA: Great Commissions Publications, 1992.

Crowe, Jaquelle. *This Changes Everything: How the Gospel Transforms the Teen Years.* Wheaton, IL: Crossway, 2017.

Dabney, Robert L. "The Westminster Confession and Creeds." In *Paradigms in Polity: Classic Readings in Reformed and Presbyterian Church Government*, edited by David W. Hall and Joseph H. Hall, 524–37. Grand Rapids: Eerdmans, 1994.

Dennison, Charles G. "Thoughts on the Covenant." In *Pressing Toward the Mark: Essays Commemorating Fifty Years of the Orthodox Presbyterian Church*, edited by Charles G. Dennison and Richard C. Gamble, 7–21. Philadelphia: The Committee for the Historian of the Orthodox Presbyterian Church, 1986.

Farley, William P. *Gospel-Powered Parenting: How the Gospel Shapes and Transforms Parenting.* Phillipsburg, NJ: P&R, 2009.

Foote, Ted V., Jr., and P. Alex Thornburg. *Being Presbyterian in the Bible Belt: A Theological Survival Guide for Youth, Parents, and Other Confused Presbyterians.* Louisville, KY: Geneva Press, 2000.

Graustein, Karl. *Growing Up Christian: Have You Taken Ownership of Your Relationship with God?* Phillipsburg, NJ: P&R, 2005.

Hart, D. G. *Between the Times: The Presbyterian Church in Transition, 1945–1990.* Willow Grove, PA: The Committee for the Historian of the Orthodox Presbyterian Church, 2011.

———, and John Muether. *Fighting the Good Fight: A Brief History of the Orthodox Presbyterian Church.* Philadelphia: The Committee on Christian Education and the Committee for the Historian of the Orthodox Presbyterian Church, 1995.

———, and Mark A. Noll. *Dictionary of the Presbyterian and Reformed Tradition in America.* Downers Grove, IL: IVP, 1999.

Hays, G. *Presbyterians: A Popular Narrative of Their Origin, Progress, Doctrines and Achievements.* New York: J. A. Hill & Co., 1892.

"History for a Pilgrim People: An Interview with Charles G. Dennison." In *History for a Pilgrim People: The Historical Writings of Charles G. Dennison*, edited by Danny E. Olinger and David K. Thompson, 213–34. Willow Grove, PA: The Committee for the Historian of the Orthodox Presbyterian Church, 2002.

Hodge, J. A. "What Is Presbyterian Law?" In *Paradigms in Polity: Classic Readings in Reformed and Presbyterian Church Government*, edited by David W. Hall and Joseph H. Hall, 477–93. Grand Rapids: Eerdmans, 1994.

Lucas, Sean Michael. *For a Continuing Church: The Roots of the Presbyterian Church in America.* Phillipsburg, NJ: P&R, 2015.

Oliphint, K. Scott. *Know Why You Believe.* Grand Rapids: Zondervan, 2017.

Smallman, Stephen. *Understanding the Faith: A Workbook for Communicants Classes and Others Preparing to Make a Public Confession of Faith.* Phillipsburg, NJ: P&R, 2001.

Smith, Frank J. *The History of the Presbyterian Church in America: Silver Anniversary Edition.* Lawrenceville, GA: Presbyterian Scholars Press, 1999.

Smith, Morton H. *"How Is the Gold Become Dim": The Decline of the Presbyterian Church, U.S., As Reflected in Its Assembly Actions.* Jackson, MS: The Steering Committee for a Continuing Presbyterian Church, 1973.

———. *Commentary on the Book of Church Order of the Presbyterian Church in America.* Taylors, SC: Presbyterian Press, 2007.

Wallace, Peter J. "Covenant and Conversion." *Ordained Servant: A Journal for Church Officers* 14, no. 2 (2005): 31–39.

www.ingramcontent.com/pod-product-compliance
Lightning Source LLC
Chambersburg PA
CBHW070545010526
44118CB00012B/1231